A History of Prince Edward County, Virginia, From its Formation in 1753, to the Present;

CHARLES EDWARD BURRELL, LL. B., D. D.,
Minister, First Baptist Church, Farmville, Va.

A History of

PRINCE EDWARD COUNTY VIRGINIA

———

FROM ITS FORMATION IN 1753, TO THE PRESENT

———

Compiled mainly from
ORIGINAL RECORDS AND PERSONALLY
CONTRIBUTED ARTICLES.

———

With a Brief Sketch of the Beginnings of Virginia,
A Summary of the History of the County Seat,
And a Special Chapter on the Churches of the County

———

By CHARLES EDWARD BURRELL, LL. B., D. D.

THE WILLIAMS PRINTING CO,
RICHMOND, VA.
1922

A755534

Printed and Bound in the United States of America, 1922.

To The

Good people of Prince Edward County, Virginia;

the noble offspring of a splendid ancestry;

this work is most humbly dedicated.

Historians ought to be precise, faithful, and unprejudiced; and neither interest nor fear, hatred nor affection, should make them swerve from the way of truth, whose mother is history, the rival of time, the depositary of great actions, witness of the past, example to the present, and monitor to the future.—Cervantes

——— praecipuum munus annalium reor, ne virtutes sileantur, utque pravis dictis factisque ex posteritate et infamia metus sit —Tactitus, Annales III. 65.

FOREWORD

Prince Edward county is not a large county. The possible constituency for such a work as this is, therefore, decidedly limited. Hence, in order that it shall have an adequate circulation; a circulation worthy of the county; it will be necessary that its natural appeal shall be supplemented by county pride. The urge of possible profit will not be sufficient to secure for it any large reading under the circumstances. The author entertains no expectation of monetary remuneration. The task has, with him, been a real work of love. Prince Edward county has never had a "History" published. It will be too bad if there is not discovered sufficient pride of county to secure for this belated effort a fitting response.

The author believes that such county pride does exist in such measure as will make welcome this effort to make permanent some of the splendid history of the county. Few counties of Virginia are richer in historical material than is Prince Edward. It ought to have been published long ere this. This is at least an honest effort to supply the deficiency It will provide a real starting point to some future more serious attempt to do justice to a great subject. This is the sincere desire of the present writer.

PREFACE

This unpretentious volume is put forth in the sincere hope that it may prove of some value to the student of history, as well as to the present life of the Old Dominion, as it is contributed to by Prince Edward county.

Of necessity, the record must be fragmentary and faulty in many respects, but in the more vital things, the author ventures the hope that reasonable accuracy has been attained. He is a pioneer in-so-far as this county is concerned.

An effort has been made to link up the present with the past in a real way, hence the work is something more than a mere recital of past events. Much of present events and conditions, together with the life story of many now living, contributors to the sturdy progress of affairs in this part of the State, is included. The encyclopaedic method has been deliberately and purposely adopted. The orthodox historian will doubtless be shocked at this The net result will doubtless be, however, that the lay reader will find it all the more readable and interesting. That is one objective aimed at A serious attempt has been made to bring the study down to even date, and this could be the more easily accomplished by the adoption of this method. "Ancient" history usually finds but the "faithful few" really interested.

No history of the county having been previously published, the present worker found himself beset by a bewildering mass of material. Out of this he was forced to make selection in a most arbitrary fashion. A previously mapped out course has been more or less rigidly adhered to, in spite of the many resulting inequalities. Doubtless much that is worthy of inclusion will be found to have been sacrificed, and much about which a question might very legitimately be raised will be found included. This is, perhaps, inevitable. All could not be used.

Particular attention is directed to the chapter on "The Churches of Prince Edward." A fine history of the county might very easily be erected out of the story of her Churches. This is, perhaps, the first time in Virginia that a serious attempt has been made, in a county history, to give due credit to the Churches as history-making mediums

And the attention of the reader is also directed to the chapter on "Prince Edward county in the World War," where the most complete roster and record of all Prince Edward county soldiers and sailors who served in that terrible conflict, ever compiled by any county, after any war, is to be found. It is extremely desirable that such a record shall be preserved and we have ventured to include it here.

That so much space has been given to the affairs of war requires, perhaps, some word of explanation. The late World War cost, in terms of human life, 10,000,000 soldiers and sailors: and 30,000,000 civilians, who but for that sanguinary event might be living today, were sacrificed. In terms of money, as related directly to the objects of the war, it cost one hundred and eighty-six billions of dollars!

What "War" means to the United States will, perhaps, best be understood, if we can apprehend what it is claiming as its proportion of our national revenues It is perhaps but little realized by the average layman, that ninety per cent. of our revenues go to pay our bills to "War" Of this alarming proportion, sixty-eight per cent goes for past wars, and twenty-two per cent. for the maintenance of our present Army and Navy. Of the small balance remaining, education receives one per cent. and labor, commerce, and the general public are expected to divide the balance amongst them!

And all this, in this good day of Our Lord, the Prince

of Peace! From these considerations it will readily be seen
that "War" has not been given undue notice in this volume,
for Prince Edward county has shared in due proportion in
all that pertains to that phase of national life. Humanity
is mortgaged to the hilt that "War" may be fed

America simply *must* lead the war-weary nations of the
earth to a better day. The author breathes a fervent prayer
that a future historian may have the happy privilege to
record the death of "War" The responsibility of leadership in that direction is upon·us We must not falter in
leading the way to universal disarmament, and to ultimate
peace.

I submit the book to the public in the satisfying conviction that I have not been remiss in the effort to ascertain
and to record the truth as it pertains to the history of this
part of the Old Dominion: the bare and simple truth, without fear or favor. That there has been much of diligent
research will be made manifest by a reading of the chapter
on "Bibliography." And I have done my best to make the
record easily readable It is enough for the servant that he
be found faithful and, in this my humble effort, I have
striven to merit that commendation

1922.   C. EDWARD BURRELL.

EXPLANATORY

Perhaps a brief note respecting some archaic terms, unavoidably employed, is here in order, so that the reader may readily possess the definitions necessary to a proper understanding of some passages in this work.

"TITHES." "TITHABLE." For many years, from the beginning of the Colony, taxes were levied, not on property, but on persons as such, so that a "Tithable," generally speaking, was such a person thus subject to taxation; usually all males above sixteen years of age and servants of both sexes above that age. The "Tithe," therefore, was the tax thus imposed upon such taxable persons.

"POUNDS, SHILLINGS, ETC." It must be borne in mind that the pound was not the pound sterling. The pound here spoken of, amounted to but twenty shillings, i. e., the equivalent to $3 33½. The shilling, too, was not the modern shilling; it was the equivalent to 16 2-3 cents.

"THE TEST." In Colonial times an Oath was administered in which the affiant declared it to be his belief that there is not the "real presence" in the elements of the Communion of the Lord's Supper; an echo of Old World conflicts. This was the "Test" so-called.

"PRISON BOUNDS" This was an area, which was not in any case to exceed ten acres, about the jail, or place of confinement, where prisoners, not committed for treason or felony, had liberty, on giving proper security that they would not break "bounds" but would continue therein until discharged. This provision was, for the most part, for the benefit of persons imprisoned for debt. This privilege was to last for only one year.

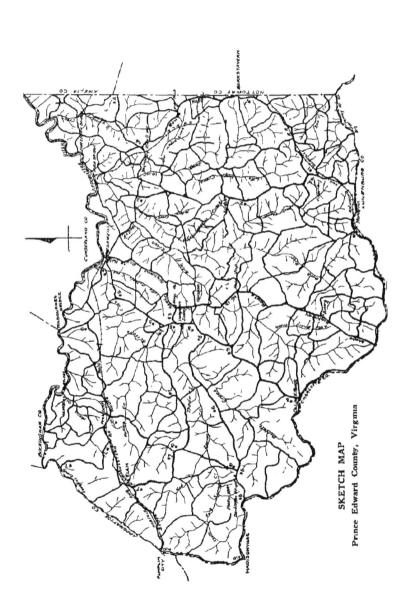

SKETCH MAP

Prince Edward County, Virginia

CONTENTS

Chapter One

A Short Account of the State

A SHORT ACCOUNT OF THE STATE

A proper history of Prince Edward County requires that there shall precede it, a brief sketch of the beginnings of the State of which it forms an honorable part. For it ought always to be remembered that Prince Edward County is a part of what was once a mighty Principality of vast dimensions.

All of North America between Nova Scotia, or New Scotland, on the north; and Florida, Land of Flowers, on the south; was once known as "Virginia." Queen Elizabeth of England, to which crown the country then belonged, was so charmed by the accounts given by the sea captains under Sir Walter Raleigh, of the wonders of the coasts of the Carolinas in 1585, that she named the whole country "Virginia," in honor of herself, the "Virgin Queen," of which designation she was particularly proud.

All of Raleigh's efforts to found a colony on those shores were doomed to failure. The fate of one attempted colony on Roanoke Island, North Carolina, remains a pathetic mystery to this day.

However, in the reign of James I, a successful settlement was made in what is now Virginia proper. A Royal Charter, granted to the "Virginia Company of London," in 1606, gave to that body the right to found a colony one hundred miles square, anywhere between the thirty-fourth and the forty-first degrees of north latitude; that would be between the mouth of Cape Fear river in North Carolina, and the mouth of the Hudson river in New York; and to the "Virginia Company of Plymouth," a similar right between the thirty-eighth and forty-fifth degrees, which would be between the Potomac river and Nova Scotia; both of course, in "Virginia" as then constituted Either Company might occupy in the overlapping territory, but were proscribed from making a settlement within one hundred miles of each other.

Operating under this charter, the "Virginia Company of London" founded the settlement of Jamestown, named for James I, under which monarch the Charter was granted, on May 13, 1607. This Settlement thus ante-dated the Plymouth Colony, founded under the Mayflower Compact by 13 years, though what glory may attach to being the first American Colony, is most frequently ascribed to the "Pilgrim Fathers," who made their landing at Plymouth Rock, from the Mayflower, in 1620 This mistake has arisen from a confused interpretation of the records, and that in turn, from a failure to appreciate the fact that the Virginia of that period extended far north of the New England states of the present day and, of course, embraced Massachusetts and Plymouth Rock.   Both the Jamestown Settlement. and the Plymouth Settlement were therefore, in 'Virginia', the Jamestown Settlement being prior to that at Plymouth Rock, as we have seen, and in what is today, Virginia proper. The Jamestown Colony was conveyed from England in three small vessels, the combined tonnage of which. was less than that of the "Mayflower." Indeed the Mayflower herself was partly owned by men then living at Jamestown ! These three were the Sarah Constant, 100 tons; the Goodspeed, 40 tons; the Discovery, 20 tons

The "Virginia Company of London" was granted a second Charter in 1609, under the terms of which the boundaries of the Jamestown colony were extended along the coast for some two hundred miles, north and south, from Point Comfort, and further, "up into the land throughout from sea to sea, west and north-west, and also, all the land lying within one hundred miles along the coasts of both seas." Naturally, these bounds were never attained The term "from sea to sea" could have had but one construction and meant from the Atlantic to the Pacific ocean, and, with the line projected "west and north-west." embraced practically all the states of Ohio, Indiana, Illinois, Michigan, Wisconsin, with a part of Minnesota, as well as nearly all the Great Lakes. This territory, with that already granted under the former Charter, meant that this Company was given control of an immense Principality. As things then were, with the primitive methods of travel, etc., it was a practical impossibility for them to cover such vast territories or to come into actual possession of them. As a simple matter of fact, they did not succeed in doing so.

To the latter part of this territory, subsequently known as the "Northwest Territory," Virginia did actually claim title under the Charter granted the "Virginia Company of London." Moreover, she later got actual title by conquest of her own soldiers under George Rogers Clark, who operated under orders from the famous Patrick Henry, the then Governor of the State, during the Revolutionary War. However, in order to quiet dissension, she, in 1784 ceded it to the Federal Government, reserving only so much land therein as was necessary to enable her to fulfill her promise of land grants, made to her own soldiers who served in the Revolutionary and Indian Wars.

The Settlement at Jamestown languished, and made little or no progress, till about 1620, but soon after that time it began to grow and had some prosperity. In 1622 the population is said to have numbered about 4,000 persons. Previous to this time there had been a period known as the "Starving Time," when there was much suffering through the failure of agriculture, so that many of the people were forced to eke out a precarious existence on roots, acorns, berries, nuts, herbs, and even on skins and snakes In 1620 however, and from then on, a change took place. There was a great abundance of fruits, vegetables, and grains. Wine and silk were made in considerable quantities. Some 60.000 pounds of tobacco were produced each year. Cattle increased greatly in numbers The Settlement was now, at last, in a prosperous condition.

At about this time, women were imported, white women of course, and were sold to the colonists! By reason of competition, the price of a wife rose from one hundred and twenty pounds of tobacco, to one hundred and fifty pounds!

Thus far the settlers had succeeded in living in some measure of amity with the Indians, some religious work being done amongst them. Pocahontas, daughter of King Powhatan, whose real name was Matoax, rescuer of Captain John Smith, was the first convert gained from amongst these savage peoples In 1613 she was married to John Rolph, an Englishman. Her baptismal name was Rebecca. In 1616 she went with her husband to England, where her eldest son was born, and where, at Gravesend, she died.

But on Friday, March 22, 1622, occurred the great and terrible massacre incited by Opeckankanough, in which three hundred and fifty men, women, and children were ruthlessly slain, and the cattle driven off, so that the remnant of the Settlement were left sorely distressed. The wily and savage Opeckankanough, pretending a desire to become a Christian, so beguiled the pious head of the College, Mr Thorpe, that he took much pains in instructing him and was led to place considerable confidence in his sincerity, but on that fatal Friday, that good man, with the rest, was cruelly massacred according to the secret plans of the treacherous savage, who, under the mask of religion, had plotted the sudden and entire overthrow of the English. He was the implacable enemy of the white man, harboring no illusions as to the ultimate fate of the Indian if the white man were suffered to gain a firm foothold on what he considered to be his soil He died as he lived, a brave, implacable savage.

The progress of the Settlement was seriously retarded by this awful event, so that the extension of the frontiers was very greatly delayed. The general and continued hostility of the Indians, which succeeded the massacre, and which seriously threatened the very life of the Settlement, also hindered development and growth. However, with true Anglo-Saxon courage, the colonists ultimately recovered themselves and development began in real earnest, never again to be seriously threatened.

Shortly before the massacre of 1622 (1619), a Dutch vessel, probably a camouflage for the "Treasurer," brought into Jamestown, the first cargo of negro slaves that were ever introduced into America, and here was sown the seed that resulted in the horrors of the War Between the States, of 1861-1865.

Chapter Two

The Genesis of Prince Edward County

THE GENESIS OF PRINCE EDWARD COUNTY

The original division of the Old Dominion into "Shires," after the English fashion; as performed by the Assembly of 1624, at which time the State was divided into eight such "Shires," as follows· James City; Henrico; Charles City; Elizabeth City; Warrick River; Warrosquyoake; Charles River; and Accawmack, and the later, and more intensive divisions of the same territory, give much aid in tracing the development of the various counties of the State as at present constituted.

Prince Edward county, named for Edward Augustus, a son of Frederick, Prince of Wales, followed the division of the old "Shire" called Charles City.

In 1703 Prince George was erected out of Charles City, and from Prince George was later carved, Brunswick in 1732; Amelia in 1735; and Dinwiddie in 1754.

In 1753 an Act was introduced to separate the present Prince Edward county from Amelia and the separation took place accordingly in 1754. Nottoway was a further division of Amelia county by an Act of 1789.

A further division of the ancient "Shire" of Charles City, produced Lunenburg county from Brunswick. in 1746; Halifax, in 1752; Bedford, in 1754; Charlotte, in 1765; Mecklenburg, in 1765; Greenville, 1781. Pittsylvania was separated from Halifax in 1767; and Henry in 1777. In 1791 Patrick was taken from Henry. In 1782 Campbell county was separated from Bedford and, in 1786, a part of the present Franklin county was erected out of Campbell county

A general pedigree sheet of Charles City Shire would look something like the chart on the following page:

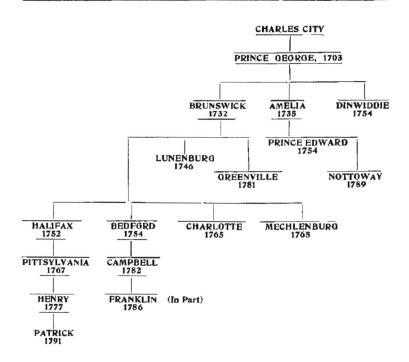

This COUNTY is situated in the south-central part of Virginia, its nearest border-line being some sixty miles southeast from the City of Richmond.

It is about twenty-five miles long and about twelve miles wide   It contains an area of 345 square miles, over one-third of which is in a state of cultivation   The population of the county is (1921), 14,767.

The Appomattox River runs on the northern border of the county, and, with its many branches, waters the surrounding lands   Farmville is the head of the old Batteau navigation, now discontinued, although the stream is navigable much higher up. Small fish are found in some abundance in the stream

The Appomattox River is capable of furnishing considerable water power at this point, which is, as yet, practically unutilized.

Transportation within the county, and with the outside world, is furnished by the Norfolk & Western; the Southern; and Virginian railways, in addition to the fine system of public roads.

Road building within the county is in a state of great activity, several stretches of State and National highways being either already completed, or under construction. For the most part, the roads of the county compare very favorably with those in other parts of the State. Farmville is the "hub" of the system of roads being built under the direction of the State Highway Commission in this part of the State.

With her splendid schools, fine churches, clear water, rich soil, equable climate, good roads, and central location, Prince Edward county is one of the 'very best counties' in the Commonwealth in which to make happy and prosperous homes.

Chapter Three
The Organization of Prince Edward County

THE ORGANIZATION OF PRINCE EDWARD COUNTY

As stated elsewhere, Prince Edward county was formed in 1753, from a part of Amelia county. The first minutes of the new county, recorded in the "County Court Orders, 1754-1758," says: "The Commission of Peace being first read, and the Commission of Dedimus Potestatom, David Flournoy and John Nash, Jr., administered the Oath of Chancery to John Nash the elder, George Walker, Joseph Morton and James Wimbish, Gentlemen, who also read and subscribed the Test; whereupon John Nash the elder administered in like manner, the aforesaid Oaths, to David Flournoy and John Nash, Jr., Gentlemen, who also read and subscribed the Test.

The Court being thus Constituted."

And thus Prince Edward county came into active being. These, and many succeeding minutes, were laboriously transcribed in quaint old English characters, by John Nash, the elder, Clerk of the Court.

At a succeeding Court, held February 12, of the same year, John Nash, Jr, duly appointed Sheriff of the County, and John Nash, Sr, were appointed a Commission to solicit the Court of Amelia to appoint a Commission to act with them in running the county lines

At the same Court, George Walker, James Wimbish, and David Flournoy were "appointed to review the proposals of the people for building a Court House, and to report the several proposals to the next Court." One Charles Cuppler, was at this time recognized as an Attorney at Law; the first in the new county. At the June Court of the same year, 'Arthur Neal was appointed Constable and took the Oath

The findings of the Committee appointed to ascertain the

proposals for the building of the Court House and report, and the results following therefrom, will be found set out in Chapter Four of this work.

The county was divided into Six Magisterial Districts, as follows   Buffalo District; Farmville District: Hampden District; Leigh District; Lockett District; and Prospect District.

The county is in the Fourth Congressional District, and in the Fifth Judicial District. For further matter respecting the Judiciary of the county, see Chapter Fifteen of this work

The Honorable E T Bondurant is the present representative of the county in the House of Delegates.

The Honorable Louis E Epes is the present representative of the county in the State Senate.

The present Board of Supervisors of the county are

Buffalo District.   W. W. Swan

Farmville District ·   J Ashby Armistead

Hampden District   W. A. McCraw.

Leigh District ·   F. H. Kauffman

Lockett District.   W B Bruce.

Prospect District ·   R W. Fuqua

Samuel W. Watkins is the Treasurer of the county: E. L. Dupuy, Commissioner of Revenue; and Judge Asa D. Watkins, Commonwealth's Attorney

REPRESENTATIVES IN THE HOUSE OF DELEGATES AND SENATE

Allen, James, 1782.

Anderson, Samuel C , 1828-29, 1842-43, 1843-44, 1844-45, 1846-47

Bibb, Richard, 1783, 1784-85, 1785-86, 1786-87.

Bibb, William, 1779, 1780-81, 1784-85.

Booker, Edward, 1813-14, 1814-15, 1815-16, 1816-17, 1819-20.

Booker, John, 1803-04, 1804-05

Booker, Richard A., 1861 (Jan.).

Booker, William, Convention 1776; House 1776-77.

Branch, Tazewell, 1874 (Jan.), 1874-75, 1875-76, 1876-77.

Burke, Samuel D., 1840-41.

Burton, R. M., 1891-92.

Carter, Samuel, 1805-06.

Champlin, N. H., 1881-82.

Clarke, John, 1784-85, 1785-86, 1786-87.

Clarke, John, 1817-18, 1818-19, 1821-22.

Dickinson, Asa D., 1857-58, 1859-60.

Dillon, James, 1829-30

Dupuy, Asa, 1820-21, 1821-22, 1822-23, 1823-24, 1824-25, 1825-26, 1826-27, 1827-28, 1828-29, 1829-30, 1831-32. 1833-34, 1834-35.

Dupuy, W. P., 1885-86, 1887 (March), 1887-88, 1889-90.

Evans, W. D., 1877-78, 1879-80.

Ewing, W. H , 1910, 1912.

Farrar, Stephen C., 1827-28.

Flournoy, John J., 1817-18, 1818-19.

Flournoy, Thomas, 1777, 1779, 1781-82.

Flournoy, William C., 1850-51, 1852 (Jan.).

Griggs, N. M., 1883-84, 1884 (Aug.).

Henry, Patrick, Convention 1788; House 1787-88, 1788, 1789, 1790.

Holcombe, John, 1782.

Jackson, Thomas P , 1869-70, 1870-71.

Johnston. Peter, 1792, 1793, 1798-99, 1799-1800. 1800-01. 1801-02, 1802-03, 1803-04, 1804-05, 1805-06, 1806-07, 1807-08, 1810-11.

Jorgenson, Joseph, 1871-72, 1872-73.

Lawson, Robert, Convention 1788; House 1778, 1780-81, 1782, 1783, 1787-88.

Lindsay, William, 1813-14, 1814-15, 1815-16, 1816-17.

M'Dearmon, Samuel D., 1845-46.

McIlwaine, Richard. Convention 1901-02.

Madison, James, 1835-36.

Molloy, Thomas. 1795.

Moore, Joseph, 1781-82.

Morton, John, 1777.

Nash, John, 1778

Owen, John, J., 1899-1900, 1901-02, 1904, 1906, 1908.

Purnall, (Purnell), John, 1791, 1792, 1793, 1794, 1795, 1796, 1798-99, 1806-07, 1807-08, 1808-09, 1809-10, 1810-11, 1811-12, 1812-13.

Scott, Charles, 1797-98, 1799-1800.

Southall, Stephen, O., 1852, 1853-54

Stokes, Colin, 1893-94, 1895-96.

Thornton, John T., Convention 1861.

Tredway, Thomas T., 1855-56, 1861-62, 1862, (April), 1862, (Sept.), 1863 (Jan.), 1863-64, 1864-65.

Venable, Abraham, B., 1800-01, 1801-02, 1802-03, 1803-04.

Venable, Nathaniel E., 1836-37, 1838 (Jan), 1839 (Jan.), 1839-40.

Venable, Richard N., Convention, 1829-30; House 1797-98, 1820-21, 1830-31.

Wade, James, 1795, 1796.

Watkins, Asa D., 1897-98.

Watkins, Henry E., 1812-13, 1819-20, 1820-21, 1822-23, 1823-24, 1824-25, 1825-26, 1826-27, 1832-33.

Watts, William, Convention 1775; House 1776.

Wilson, James H., 1841-42, 1852 (Jan.).

Winston, Peter, 1914, 1916, 1918.

Womack, Archer, 1809-10.

Womack, Benjamin W., 1847-48.

Woodson, Charles, 1811-12.

Woodson, Tarlton, 1788, 1789, 1790, 1791, 1794, 1808-09.

Wootton, William T., 1848-49, 1849-50

Bondurant, E. T., 1920.

PRINCE EDWARD AND APPOMATTOX

Watkins, F. N., 1865-66, 1866-67.

SENATE

Paul Carrington, 1776, 1777-78, 1791, 1792, 1793, 1794.

Walter Coles, 1778, 1779, 1780-81.

Nathaniel Venable, 1781, 1781-82, 1782.

William Hubard, 1783, 1784-85, 1785-86, 1786-87.

John Coleman, 1787-88, 1788-89, 1789, 1790.

David Clarke, 1795, 1796, 1797-98.

George Carrington, 1798-99.

Gideon Spencer, 1799-00, 1800-01, 1801-02, 1802-03.

Isaac H Coles, 1803-04, 1804-05, 1805-06, 1806-07, 1807-08, 1808-09. 1809-10, 1810-11.

Joseph Wiatt (Wyatt), 1811-12, 1812-13, 1813-14, 1823-24, 1824-25, 1825-26, 1826-27, 1827-28, 1828-29, 1829-30, 1830-31, 1831-32, 1832-33.

William Rice, 1813-14, 1814-15

John Hill, 1815-16, 1816-17, 1817-18, 1818-19.

Howson Clark, 1819-20, 1820-21, 1821-22, 1822-23.

Henry E Watkins, 1833-34, 1834-35.

Archibald A. Campbell, 1835-36, 1836-37

Louis C. Bouldin, 1838, 1839, 1839-40, 1840-41, 1841-42, 1842-43.

William H. Dennis, 1843-44, 1844-45, 1845-46, 1846-47. 1847-48, 1848-49, 1849-50, 1850-51

Thomas H. Campbell, 1852-53, 1853-54, 1855-56, 1857-58.

William C. Knight, 1859-61.

Asa D Dickinson, 1859-61, 1861-63, 1863-65

Christopher C McRae, 1865-67

James D. Bland, 1869-71 (Negro).

John T Hamlett, 1869-71.

John Robinson, 1871-73 (Negro).

Edgar Allan, 1874-75, 1875-77.

Calvin H Bliss, 1877-79, 1879-80, 1881-82, 1883-84, 1885-87.

N. M. Griggs, 1887-88, 1889-90 (Negro).

Joseph W Southall, 1891-92, 1893-94, 1895-96, 1897-98

Asa D. Watkins, 1899-00, 1901-04.

William Hodges Mann, 1904, 1906, 1908, 1910.

Robert K. Brock, 1912, 1914-15.

George E Allen, 1916, 1918.

Louis E. Eppes, 1920.

Prince Edward County Senatorial representatives have served two or more counties, changing with various re-distributions.

Chapter Four

The Court House

THE COURT HOUSE

The site of the first Court House of Prince Edward county, was at the village of Worsham, near to the location of Hampden-Sidney College. The first courts were held in private residences in that immediate vicinity. A Public Square was purchased and suitable buildings erected thereon in due course. This place was named for the Worsham family, the most conspicuous of them, in the affairs of the county being Branch G. Worsham, who became County Clerk in 1825 and continued till after the Civil War.

At the February Court, February 12, 1754, Charles Anderson offered the use of his kitchen as a temporary lockup until such time as a suitable prison could be erected, which offer was declined, doubtless with thanks

At the next court, the same Anderson was awarded the contract for the building of a Court House, Stocks, Pillory, and Whipping Post, at or near his house in the county, the jail building to be of logs, twelve feet by sixteen feet in the clear, and to bring in his account at the laying of the next levy. He was later, at the May Court, 1755, paid fifty-two pounds and fifteen shillings for the same.

At the October Court of the same year, arrangements were made for the painting of the Court House, the tarring of the roof, and for changing the character and the place of the windows.

Many entries are to be found in the minute books of the Court respecting the Court buildings, providing for their upkeep, renewal, etc., in the century and a quarter, or thereabouts that the Court House remained at Worsham. High hopes had been entertained as to the prospective growth of the little village, but they remained unfulfilled; the place did not grow.

A persistent agitation had grown up for the removal of the county seat to the larger and more convenient neighboring town of Farmville, which would not down. This agitation culminated in a decision of the people in favor of such a removal. The following order apears in "County Court Orders," under date of April 18, 1871: "The Council of the Town of Farmville having represented to the Court that the Corporation had contracted with James B. Eley, for the purchase of a lot of land containing not less than one-half acre, situated in the Town of Farmville, on the East side of the Main Street of said Town, between the Baptist and the African Baptist Churches, and desiring the Court to enter on record, its approval of said land as a location for a Court House, Clerk's Office, and Jail, it is ordered that the said location be hereby approved," etc.

This order was signed by the Hon. F. N. Watkins, then serving as County Judge.

The following entry of the 'County Court Orders,' on page 282, under date of February 12, 1872, shows progress:

"It being suggested to the Court that the Council of the Town of Farmville will, in a short time, tender to the Court a Court House, Jail, and Clerk's Office, built in Farmville in pursuance of the provisions of the Act of General Assembly, Approved 4th November 1870, and of March 4th, 1871, in relation thereto, it is ordered that R B. Berkeley, H. R. Hooper, and E. Wiltse be Commissioners on the part of the Court to confer with the Corporation of Farmville, and report to the Court whether said buildings are suitable for the use of the county, what stoves and other furniture will be necessary therefor, and the probable cost thereof, together with any other matter concerning the same, deemed pertinent thereto."

The final consummation of all these plans for removal to Farmville are attested in an Order of the Court, under date of March 19, 1872, and appearing on Page 287, 'County Court Orders' as follows

"A Deed, bearing date of February 1872, from the Town of Farmville to the County of Prince Edward, with certificate of acknowledgment annexed, was presented in Court and ordered to be recorded And, it appearing to the Court that the deed conveyed according to law, the lot in Farmville on which the Court House, and other Public Buildings are erected, it is ordered that the said Deed be accepted and approved

Commissioners Berkeley, Wiltse, and Hooper, appointed at the February Term to examine the new Court House, made a report, which was Ordered Filed.

The Court doth Order that it be certified on the records of the Court as follows, to wit ·

That the General Assembly of Virginia did (by an Act entitled, 'An Act to Authorize the Qualified Voters of the County of Prince Edward to vote on the Question of removing the County Court House to the Town of Farmville' Approved, 2nd November, 1870, and by an Act Amending the third section thereof, Approved 4th March, 1871) provide for the vote indicated in the Tables of said Acts. That said vote has been taken; that from the returns and abstracts of the votes so cast upon the Question of the removal of the Court House of Prince Edward, it appeared that a majority of the Votes were "For the Town of Farmville." That the Council of the Town of Farmville have caused to be erected a Court House, Jail, and Clerk's Office, in the corporate limits of said Town, on a lot of land not less than one-half or more than two, acres, and have tendered the same this day to the Court by an Order of the Council of the Town of Farmville, and have agreed to complete unfinished parts of buildings by Orders of the Council, herewith filed That the fee simple title thereto has been made to the County of

Prince Edward by a conveyance of General Warranty, which conveyance has been this day approved by this Court, and entered of record (See sep Acts, 69, 70 pa 550, and of 70, 71 pa 150) it is thereupon Ordered :—

FIRST   That the conveyance and Buildings herein mentioned be accepted and approved

SECOND: That as soon as practicable the Clerk of this Court remove the Books, Papers, and Furniture in the Clerk's Office, and in the existing Court House, and Jail, to the Clerk's Office, and Court House, and Jail, in Farmville, and thereafter the Court shall be held in Farmville.

THIRD   That the real estate and other corporate property of the County of Prince Edward, be, and the same is hereby delivered to the Supervisors of Prince Edward, to be used for public purposes, and managed and controlled by them according to law. This Court neither abandoning or compromising any right of, or title to the said property, or any part thereof, at any time held by the County.
That R. S. Hines. the present keeper of the old Court House and Jail, hold and take care of, according to law, the Public Property at, or near the old Court House, subject to the Orders of the Court or Supervisors; that he receive, hold, and deliver the keys of the Court House, Jail, and Clerk's Office to said Supervisors, and that the Clerk, without delay. certify this Third Section to the Supervisors.

FOURTH·   That a 'Superintendent of Public Buildings and Grounds' be appointed, who shall, till otherwise Ordered, keep the keys and take care of the Public Buildings and Grounds under the Orders of the Court, who shall cause fires to be made, and other conveniences provided for the Courts, who shall cause the Court and Jury rooms to be swept and kept clean. He shall prevent all pasting of advertisements on the walls of the buildings and enclosures, and shall give information of all violations of "The Act to Prevent Certain Offenses Against Public Property" passed 21st January, 1867. Provided, however, that this Order shall not apply to that portion of the Court House in which is situated the Clerk's Office and public room adjoining thereto, which rooms shall be under the care of the Clerk of the Courts

FIFTH: In-as-much as the Council of Farmville having, without expense to the County, erected the Public Buildings and conveyed the lot to this County, and have added a large room adjoining the Clerk's Office, for the use of the County, the Corporate Authorities of Farmville may, till further orders, use the said room for meetings of the Council, and for the Mayor's Court free of charge for rent, provided, however, that the cost of furnishing and keeping said room and supplying it with fires and attending the same, shall be supplied by the Town of Farmville.

SIXTH: That Henry J Crute be appointed Superintendent of Public Grounds and Buildings

SEVENTH: That the Clerk cause brief notice of the change in the County Seat to be printed, and that he deliver 50 copies to the Sheriff, who is directed

> to post not less than 4 copies thereof in each Township, and that he append thereto, notice of the Post Office addresses of the Officers of the County, and that a copy of the same be published weekly for four weeks in the "New Commonwealth"

The Hon. F. N. Watkins, was Judge, and F. H Armistead Deputy Clerk, at the time of this change of the County Seat.

The first sitting of the Court at the new County Seat was held on "Tuesday, the 26 day of March, 1872, in the 96th year of the Commonwealth," the Hon F. N. Watkins, Judge, presiding.

Wiltshire Cardwell qualified as the first jailor of the new Jail, March 26, 1872, and the following served as the Grand Jury at that first term: R. H. Carter, foreman; N. H. Champlin; J. B. Dupuy; C. C. Taliaferro; R H. Walker; and Richard Burton

And the Court House has remained at Farmville to the present day.

Chapter Five

Farmville: The County Seat

FARMVILLE: THE COUNTY SEAT

FARMVILLE, the principal town of Prince Edward County, and the County seat, is a thriving place of some 5,000 population, inclusive of suburbs It occupies a position of considerable importance as a tobacco manufacturing center, being the fifth largest in the State.

The State Female Normal School, with an average enrollment of over six hundred students, is located here. A splendid Training School, and an excellent High School are also located within the corporate limits of the municipality, while a good colored school is situated just outside the town on the Hampden-Sidney Road. Hampden-Sidney College, a Presbyterian institution, founded in 1775, is about seven miles distant, and is reached by a fine cement and macadam road.

The famous Farmville Lithia Springs are situated just outside the corporate limits, on the Cumberland County side of the Appomattox river. This water is noted for its curative properties, and is shipped to all points of this, and other countries. "The analysis of these waters is essentially the same as that of the celebrated Carlsbad Springs of Germany, but the Farmville Lithia contains more different kinds of salts, and is superior in consequence. The Farmville Lithia Springs, strictly speaking, is only a part of a straggling cluster of mineral springs which constitute one of Nature's greatest phenomena, some explored and some unexplored." Those springs explored outside of the Lithia are: Magnesia, for dyspepsia; Iodine, for blood troubles, Sulphur and Iron, for bony formations between the joints; Iodine, Iron and Sulphur, for complicated blood troubles; Alum, for chronic intestinal troubles, and internal piles; and Arsenous Chalybeate, for the nervous system. These wonderful Springs were known to the Red Man, as is evidenced by unearthing relics of the Stone-age and charcoal from their fires, in the work of excavation, also, living land-marks of the Indian Trail in the shape of large trees arranged to form an arrow pointing to a ford across the Appomattox river. To the White Man they have only been known for about half a century. Unfortunately, these wonderful Springs have never been intelligently and energetically developed and exploited. In their financial, as well as in their curative properties, they present a most alluring prospect

To the south of the municipality, on the Hampden-Sidney Road, is to be found the almost equally celebrated Pickett Springs of almost pure water, used as a specific for various form of Kidney Disease This water possesses radio-activity to approximately the following amount 240 x 10-11 grams Radium per U. S. gallon. It is sodic and calcic bicarbonated alkaline (silicious) water of value, according to an analysis made by Mr O. E Sheppard of the University of Missouri.

In Farmville, where a majority of the homes are supplied with these waters, not a single case of Typhoid has occurred for years, except by foreign contraction

Farmville is situated about seventy miles south-westerly from the City of Richmond It was established in 1798, on the property of Judith Randolph Charles Scott, Peter Johnston, John Randolph, Jr , Philip Holcomb, Jr., Martin Smith, Blake B. W. Woodson and Creed Taylor, were appointed Trustees to lay off the town in half-acre lots, on which the purchaser was required to build within seven years. The new town prospered from the very beginning and, in 1872, became the County-seat

The community boasts two newspaper printing offices; the "Herald" and the "Leader"; three banks, one Baptist, one Episcopal, one Methodist Episcopal, and one Presbyterian Church, for white people, and two Baptist, and one Methodist Episcopal Church, for colored people; one Conservatory of Music: a fine Motion Picture Treatre, and the educational institutions above noted. It possesses two fine grist mills. The "Farmville Mill," established in 1838, is the oldest in the county. It has a fine re-inforced cement elevator, with a capacity of 50,000 bushels, erected in 1921 at a cost of $30,-000, which compares most favorably with any of its kind in the State.

The "Prince Edward Mill," operated by the Prince Edward Milling Company, composed of Thomas Asbury Gray, William S. Gray, and Leland H Green, began operations in 1914. This mill has a capacity of 50 barrels of flour, 500 bushels of meal, 5,000 pounds of chop, and 2,000 pounds of mill feed, per day. In connection with the mill, the same company, operating under the name of the Prince Edward Ice Company, conducts an up-to-date ice plant and cold storage warehouse, with a capacity of 15 tons of ice per day, and separate storage facilities for eggs, poultry, apples, ice cream, and ice This entire plant has a valuation of $60,000.

The Farmville Ice Plant, owned and managed by William C Newman, was opened for business in 1909. The plant has a capacity of forty tons of ice per day, but specializes in ice cream, and, besides enjoying a large local patronage, ships its product to many outside points. The plant, with its equipment, represents an investment of about $50,000.

Four automobile concerns minister to the automotive necessities of the people

In the matter of hotel accommodation, the traveling public is well cared for The historic "Prince Edward Hotel" is owned and managed by Mr Charles T. Chick. The "Continental Hotel," managed by Mr. J. O. Hardaway, is also owned by Mr. Chick The third hotel, the "Ingersoll," is presided over by the Ingersoll Brothers.

Two large lumber concerns are located here; the Taylor Manufacturing Company, organized to succeed the Buffalo Mills Company, in 1919, and specializing in building materials; and the Farmville Manufacturing Company, organized in 1878 in succession to a concern originally located in Amelia county, and specializing in plow handles and building materials. The officers of the Farmville Manufacturing Company are, George M Robeson, President; Floyd B. Gilbert, Vice-President, and Erna L. Perrow, Secy.-Treas. The officers of the Taylor Manufacturing Company are, Bennett T. Taylor, Prospect, Va., President; Edward S. Taylor, Prospect, Va , Vice-President, and H. Carl Holesapple, Farmville, Secty.-Treas.

The Post Office, completed in 1920, is modern in all its appointment and is an adornment to the town.

Farmville is the center of the tobacco business for the county. Four tobacco factories are in regular operation, while five other factories are used for the hanging of tobacco. There are in addition, three warehouses and four storage houses. The property investment is well over the quarter million mark. An average of over 7,000,000 pounds of the weed are handled annually, for which approximately $1,000,-000 is paid out every year.

A strong and flourishing Chamber of Commerce, of which Mr. W. Clyde Duvall is President; Mr. E. Waller Sanford, Secretary, and Mr. J. Barrye Wall, Treasurer, is in operation, and doing good work.

The officers of the municipality are.

James A. Davidson, Mayor.

N. B. Davidson; Dr. R. L. Hudgins; E Lee Morris; E. Scott Martin; W. Clyde Duvall; W. C. Newman; H. A. Barrow; R B. Cralle; E. Southall Shields, Councilors.

C. Booker Cunningham, Clerk.

Horace B. Warriner, Treasurer.

Leslie Fogus, Supt. of Public Utilities.

E. D. Lipscomb, Chief of Police.

J. W. Crute: T. S. Whitlock, and J L. Sublett. police officers

Dr. William E Anderson, Public Health Officer.

AN OLD PICTURE OF A PART OF MAIN STREET, FARMVILLE, VIRGINIA.
See Page 17.

Dr. William F. Anderson; Dr. J H. Cocks, and Mrs. Roberta Large are the members of the Public School Board.

On March 1, 1912, an election of qualified voters was held in order to ascertain their will respecting the issue of school bonds for $25,000 to be used for the erection and furnishing of a new school house. The proposed issue was approved and, in process of time the present splendid school building was erected and put in use. The grounds cost $3,300 The present valuation of the entire property and equipment is in the neighborhood of $60,000.

The present teaching staff is as follows·

M. Blair Dickinson, A. B., M. A., Principal.

Herman Levy, A B., B S., Assistant Principal.

Miss Hannah Crawley, Danville College and University of Virginia

Mrs. L. P. Davidson, L. I , Peabody College.

Miss Grace Beard, B. S., Farmville.

Mrs. Brazeal Hobson, State Normal, Farmville

Mrs. John Lancaster, State Normal, Farmville.

Miss Ruth Woodruff, Averett College, Danville, Va.

Miss Virgie Bugg, State Normal, Farmville; Cornell and Columbia.

Chapter Six

Prince Edward County in the Revolutionary Period

PRINCE EDWARD COUNTY IN THE
REVOLUTIONARY PERIOD

Owing to the rather remarkable absence of data relative to this period as affecting the part that Prince Edward county had in that stormy controversy, but little by way of connected narrative can be given.

The Royalist Governor, Lord Dunmore, because of the antagonistic spirit shown by them against the Crown, often dissolved the Council of the Burgesses of Virginia, during the period from 1773 to 1776. After these successive dissolutions, instead of going to their homes as directed by the Governor, the Burgesses began, in 1774 to assemble at the Raleigh Tavern, at Williamsburg, the then Capital of the Colony, and resolved themselves into Revolutionary Conventions. One of these Conventions was convened in 1774, two in 1775, and finally into the famous Convention of 1776 Thus the very end that he strove to avert was really hastened by the ill-starred course of the Governor.

So odious indeed, did the name of Dunmore become, that a county that had been named in his honor, was re-christened "Shenandoah."

While these Conventions were being held the people generally bcame greatly aroused, and began to organize for the conflict that was more or less generally expected. They chose Committees of Safety, and put the militia on a war footing. Prince Edward county was quite as active as any in the Commonwealth in pressing forward these precautionary measures.

By an ordinance of one of the Conventions of 1775, the Colony was divided into eighteen districts for convenience in organizing.

The Committees of Safety in these various districts were very great factors in the war, being in reality a sort of military executive in each county. That of Prince Edward county was not less active than others. Membership in any of these Committees was a distinct badge of honor, so that descent from a Committeeman constitutes a clear title to membership in those later societies called, "The Sons" and "The Daughters of the Revolution."

Virginia declared her independence of the British Crown on the 29th of June, 1776, five days before the general declaration of Independence, on the 4th of July in that year

In all these activities Prince Edward county took a foremost and honorable part.

The great Patrick Henry, who was subsequently a resident of Prince Edward county, was the first Governor of the new "Commonwealth." To him the county, on the 19th of June, 1775, voted resolutions of gratitude and confidence on the occasion of the "rape of the gunpowder," which was actually the first active stroke in the Revolutionary War, for it stirred the Colonists to such unbounded enthusiasm that the success of the Revolution was practically assured.

VIRGINIA MILITIA IN THE REVOLUTION· PRINCE EDWARD
COUNTY

The list herein given is from a list which was contributed by Alfred J. Morrison, in the "Virginia Magazine of History," April, 1913, taken by him from the records
Officers appointed and commissioned in May, June, and July, 1777

CAPTAINS

Josiah Chambers.	David Walker.
John Bibb.	Andrew Baker.

LIEUTENANTS

Charles Allen.	John Dabney.
Jacob Woodson.	Sharpe Spencer.

ENSIGNS

Benjamin Allen	Richard Holland.
James Carter.	William Rice.

SECOND LIEUTENANTS

Robert Goode.	William Wooton.
	Henry Young.

It appeared from an order made July, 1777, that the following were then Captains of Militia Companies.

——— Clarke.
——— Owen.
——— Ligon.
——— Bigger.
Thomas Flournoy.
——— Chambers.
William Bibb.

In 1778 the following Captains were appointed: John Bibb; George Carrington.

In the same year the following Lieutenants were appointed. John Dupuy; Thomas Lawson

Also in the same year the following two Ensigns were appointed. Yancey Bailey, —— Bigger, Jr.

In 1779 the following Captains were appointed: Williamson Bird (in place of Charles Venable, resigned); Richard Holland; Sharpe Spencer; Thomas Moore.

And reference is made to the following as being. or as having been Captains of Companies· George Booker; Samuel Venable; Henry Walker; David Walker.

In 1779 the following Lieutenants were appointed: Nicolas Davis; Robert Venable; George Booker; Jesse Watson; William McGehee; Ambrose Nelson; John Langhorn.

In the same year the following Ensigns were appointed: James Parks; Drury Watson: Thomas Watkins.

In 1779 Thomas Haskins was recommended as Colonel of the Militia of the county, and George Walker as Lieutenant-Colonel

In 1780 the following were recommended, or appointed as Captains: Thomas Lawton; Dick Holland; Jacob Woodson.

And the following as Lieutenants: Jesse Watson; Drury Watson; William Price, Jr ; James Clark; James Wright; Joseph Parks

And the following as Ensigns. Stephen Pettus; William Booker; John Bell

In 1781 the following nominations were made and ratified· John Nash, County Lieutenant; George Walker, Colonel, Thomas Flournoy, Lieutenant-Colonel, John Clark. Major.

In the same year the following were appointed as Captains· Stephen Neal; James Clark; Ambrose Nelson (in the stead of John Bibb).

The following were appointed Lieutenants in the same year: Nathaniel Allen; John Richards; George Foster; George Pulliam; William Wooten; James Parks; John Clarke, Jr.; John Bell.

And the following were appointed as Ensigns. William Galespie; Peyton Glenn; Robert Walton; Philip Mathew.

MUSTER ROLL OF CAPTAIN JOHN MORTON'S COMPANY, OF PRINCE EDWARD MILITIA, JUNE 28, 1781:

OFFICERS

Captain, John Morton, (Morton had eight sons in the service).

First Lieutenant, John Holcomb.
Second Lieutenant, Obadiah Woodson
Ensign, Edward Wood.
Sergeant, James Morton.
Sergeant, Samuel Anderson
Sergeant, Charles Stogg
Sergeant, Charles Anderson.
Corporal, Robert Lawton.
Corporal, Thomas Hastie.
Corporal, William Wright.
Corporal, William Chambers.

PRIVATES

Anderson, Parsons; Ascul, William; Baldwin, Thoma·· Bigger, William, Boas, Meshack; Bird, William; Boas Michael; Brown, Isham; Byrk, Thomas; Casey, William:

Chaffin, Isham; Chaffin. Christopher; Cocke, Anderson; Cunningham, Nathaniel; Cunningham, John; Daniel, George; Davidson, Edward, Davidson, William, Davidson, David; Davis, Charles; Durham, Nathaniel; Edmunds, Jacob; Fore. Francis; Foster, Joshua; Fraser, John; Fraser, Thomas; Fugue, William; Garratt, Alexander; Gillespie, William; Hales, Peter; Hampton, Nathan; Holman, Alexander; Hord, William; Howerton, James; Jennings, Isham; Jennings. James; Johnson, William; King, Thomas; Lee, John, Lee, Archibald; Leigh, Charles; Martin, Samuel; McGehee, William; Morton, Thomas; Newcomb, Julius; Parker, Glover; Peak, Aaron; Pierce, Thomas; Pillon, Jasper; Rain, Nathaniel, Robertson, David; Rutledge, Dudley; Sharp, Moses; Smith, Robert. P , Smith, John; Smith, Alexander; Spaulding, John; Sutherland, Philemon, Southerland, William; Taylor, George; Thompson, John; Tuggle, Benjamin; Tuggle, Thomas; Walker, Thomas; Walker, William, 1; Walker, William, 2; Watkins, Abner, Webster, John; Whitlock, Josiah; Wilburn, Thomas; Woodson, Anderson; Woodson, John; Wright, Archibald.

Much further interesting information regarding Prince Edward county soldiers, serving in the Virginia Militia during the Revolutionary War may be found in McAllister's "Virginia Militia in the Revolutionary War "

Chapter Seven

Prince Edward County in the War of 1812-1814

PRINCE EDWARD COUNTY IN THE WAR OF
1812-1814

The Manifesto of John Randolph, of Roanoke

The following copy of the pamphlet, issued by John Raldoph of Roanoke, on May 30th, 1812, is given in full, with introduction, and adenda, because it expresses, as perhaps nothing can so well do, the actual predilection of the people of Prince Edward county, respecting that unfortunate struggle between the government of the United States and the British crown. The people had no "stomach" for that war and Randolph rightly gauged public opinion. as found in this county, at any rate.

"To the freeholders of Charlotte, Buckingham, Prince Edward and Cumberland.

Fellow Citizens:

I dedicate you the following fragment. That it appears in its present mutilated shape is to be ascribed to the successful usurpation which has reduced freedom of speech in one branch of the American Congress to an empty name. It is now established *for the first time, and in the person of your representative*, that the House may, and will, refuse to hear a member in his place, or even to receive a motion from him, upon the most momentous subject that can be presented for legislative decision.—A similar motion was brought forward by the Republican minority in the year 1798, (this motion was drawn, it is believed, by Mr. Gallatin, but moved by Mr. Sprigg, declaring it to be inexpedient at that time to resort to war against the French Republic) before these modern inventions for stifling freedom of debate had been discovered. It was discussed as a matter of *right* until it was abandoned by the mover in consequence of additional information (by the correspondence of our Envoys at Paris) laid before Congress by the President. In "the reign of terror" the father of the sedition law had not the hardihood to proscribe liberty of speech, much less the right of free debate on the floor of Congress. This invasion of the public liberties was reserved for self-styled Republicans, who hold your understandings in such contempt as to flatter themselves that you will overlook their every outrage upon the first great principles of free government, in consideration of their profession of tender regard for the privileges of the people. It is for you to decide whether they have under-valued your intelligence and spirit, or whether they have formed a just estimate of your character   You do not require to be told that the violation of the rights of him whom you have deputed to represent you, is an invasion of the rights of every man among you, of every individual in society —If this abuse be suffered to pass unredressed; — and the people alone are competent to apply the remedy; — we must bid adieu to a free form of government, forever.

Having learned from various sources that a declaration of war would be attempted on Monday next, *with closed doors*, I deemed it my duty to endeavour, by any exercise of my constitutional functions, to arrest this heaviest of all possible calamities, and avert it from our happy country, I accordingly made the effort of which I now give you the result, and of the success of which you will have already been informed, before these pages can reach you. I pretend only to give you the substance of my unfinished argument. The glowing words; — the language of the heart; — have passed away with the occasion that called them forth. They are no longer under my control. My design is simply to submit to you the views which have induced me to consider a war with England, under existing circumstances, as comporting neither with the INTEREST nor with the HONOUR of the American people, but as an IDOLATROUS sacrifice *of both*, on the altar of French rapacity, perfidy, and ambition.

France has for years past offered us terms of undefined commercial arrangement, at the price of a war with England, which hitherto we have not wanted firmness and virtue to reject. The price is now to be paid. We are tired of holding out;—and, following the example of the nations of continental Europe; entangled in the artifices, or awed by the power of the destroyer of mankind; we are prepared to become instrumental to his projects of universal dominion. Before these pages meet your eye, the last Republick of the earth will have enlisted under the banners of the tyrant and become a party to his cause. The blood of American freemen must flow to cement his power, to aid in stifling the last struggles of afflicted and persecuted man; to deliver into his hands the patriots of Spain and Portugal, to establish his Empire over the ocean and over the land that gave our fathers birth; to forge our own chains! — And yet, my friends, we were told in the days of the mad ambition of Mr. Adams, "THAT THE FINGER HEAVEN POINTS TO WAR." Yes, the finger of Heaven *does* point to war. It points to war, it points to the mansions of eternal misery and torture; as to a flaming beacon warning us of that vortex which we may not approach but with certain destruction. It points to desolated Europe and warns us of the chastisement of those nations who have offended against the justice and almost beyond the mercy of Heaven. It announces the wrath to come, upon those who, ungrateful for the bounty of providence, not satisfied with peace, liberty, security, plenty at home, fly, as it were, into the face of the Most High and tempt His forbearance.

To you, *in this place*, I can speak with freedom, and it becomes me to do so; nor shall I be deterred by the cavils and the sneers of those who hold as "Foolishness" all that savours not of worldly wisdom, from expressing fully and freely those sentiments which it has pleased God, in His Mercy, to engrave upon my heart.

These are no ordinary times   The state of the world is unexampled.   The war of the present day is not like that of our revolution, or any which preceded it, at least in modern t'mes.   It is a war against the liberty and happiness of mankind   It is war of which the whole human race are the victims, to gratify the pride and lust of power, of a single individual   I beseech you, put it to your own bosoms, how far it becomes you as freemen, as Christians, to give your aid and sanction to this impious and bloody warfare against your brethren of the human family   To such among you, if any there be, who are insensible to motives not more dignified and manly than they are intrinsically wise, I would make a different appeal   I adjure you by the regard which you have for your own security and property, for the liberties and inheritance of your children, by all that you hold dear and sacred, to interpose your constitutional powers to save your country and yourselves from a calamity, the issues of which, it is not given to human foresight to divine

Ask yourselves if you are willing to become the virtual allies of Bonaparte?   Are you willing, for the sake of annexing Canada to the northern States, to submit to the ever-growing system of taxation, which sends the European laborer supperless to bed?   To maintain by the sweat of your brow, armies at whose hands you are to receive a future master?   Suppose Canada ours.   Is there any one among you who would ever be the better for it? — the richer—the freer—the happier—the more secure?   And is it for a boon like this, that you would join in a warfare against the liberties of man in the other hemisphere, and put your own in jeopardy? or is it for the *nominal* privilege of a licensed trade with France, that you would abandon your lucrative commerce with Great Britain, Spain, Portugal, and their Asiatic African, and American dependencies—in a word, with every region of those vast continents?   That commerce which gives a vent to tobacco, grain, flour, cotton; in short to all your native products; which are denied a market in France.

There are not wanting men so weak, as to suppose that their approbation of war-like measures is a proof of personal gallantry, and that opposition to them indicates a want of that spirit which becomes a friend to his country; as if it requires more courage and patriotism to join the acclamation of the day, than steadily to oppose one's self to the mad infatuation to which every pepole and all governments have, at some time or other, given way. Let the history of Phocion, of Agis, and of the DeWitts, answer this question My friends, do you expect to find those who are *now* loudest in the clamour for war, foremost in the ranks of battle? or is the honour of this nation indissolubly connected with the political reputation of a few individuals, who tell you *they* have gone too far to recede, and that you must pay, with *your ruin* the price of *their consistency.* My friends, I have discharged my duty towards you lamely and inadequately I know, but to the best of my poor ability. — The destiny of the American people is in their hands. The net is spread for their destruction. You are enveloped in the toils of French duplicity; and if, which may heaven in its mercy forbid, you and your posterity are to become hewers of wood and drawers of water to the modern Pharaoh, it shall not be for the want of my best exertions to rescue you from the cruel and abject bondage. This sin, at least, shall not rest upon my soul.

JOHN RANDOLPH, of Roanoke.

May 30th, 1812

House of Representatives of the United States.

May 30th, 1812.

Soon after the House met, Mr. Fisk moved that "when the House adjourn, it adjourn to meet on Monday next." Which having been carried, he then immediately moved that the House do now adjourn. Negatived by a small majority.

Mr. Randolph said that rumors to which he could not shut his ears (of an intended declaration of war on Monday next, with closed doors) and the circumstances which had just passed under the eye of the House (alluding to the motion to adjourn) impelled him to make a last effort to rescue the country from the calamities, which, he feared, were impending over it. He had a proposition to submit, the decision of which would affect vitally, the best interests of the nation. He conceived himself bound to bring it forward He did not feel himself a free agent in the transaction. He would endeavour to state as succinctly as he could, the grounds of his motion, and he humbly asked the attention of every man whose mind was at all open to conviction; of every man devoted to the cause of his country; not only in that House, but in every rank and condition of life throughout the state.

The motion which he was about to offer grew out of certain propositions, which he pledged himself to prove; nay, without an abuse of the term, to demonstrate.

The first of these propositions was, that the Berlin and Milan Decrees were, not only, *not repealed*, but that our government had furnished to the House and to the world, unequivocal evidence of the fact. The difficulty in demonstrating this proposition arose rather from his embarrassment in selecting from the vast mass of evidence before him, than in any deficiency of proof; for if he were to use all the testimony that might be adduced, he feared his discourse would grow to a bulk not inferior to the volume which he held in his hand. He would refer the House to the correspondence, generally, of Mr Russell, our agent at Paris, accompanying the President's message of the present session,— He referred to the schedule of American vessels taken by French privateers since the first of November 1810. (the period of the alleged repeal of the French Decrees) · of these, it was worthy of remark, that "the Robinsonova, from

Norfolk to London, with tobacco, cotton and staves; the Mary Ann from Charleston to London, with cotton and rice; the General Eaton, from London to Charleston, in ballast; the Clio from London to Philadelphia, with English manufactures; the Zebra from Boston to Tarragona, (*then in possession of the Spaniards*) with staves; all coming under the operation of the French Decrees and *seized since the 2nd of November*, 1810, had *not* been restored, on the 14th of July last;" and that the only two vessels named in that schedule, which had been restored; viz, the Two Brothers from Boston to St. Malo, and the Star, from Salem to Naples (the one a port in France, the other virtually a French port) did *not* come within the scope of the Berlin and Milan Decrees. Indeed, the only cases relied upon by Mr. Monroe to prove the repeal of the French Decrees are those of the Grace Ann Green of the New Orleans Packet. On the first of these no great stress is laid because, having been captured by an English cruizer, she was retaken by her own crew and carried into Marseilles, where consequently her captors became French prisoners of war (See note A.) —— (mutilation) it was to be expected, that in the case of war between the United States and England, our privateers carrying their prizes into French ports should be proceeded against under those decrees. It was, therefore, on the case of the New Orleans Packet that the principal reliance was placed, to show the repeal of the obnoxious decrees. But even this case established, beyond the possibility of doubt, that the Milan Decrees of the 23rd November and 17th December, 1807, were in force subsequently to the period of their alleged repeal. This vessel hearing at Gibraltar, where she had disposed of part of her cargo, of the letter of the Duke of Cadore of the 5th of August, 1810, suspended her sales, and the supercargo, after having consulted with Mr. Hackley, the American consul at Cadiz, determined on the faith of that insidious letter, to proceed with the remainder of his cargo to Bordeaux. He took the precaution however, to delay his voyage, so that he might not arrive in France before the 1st of November; the day on which the Berlin and Milan Decrees were to cease to operate.

(Here Mr. Randolph was called to order by Mr Wright, who said there was no motion before the House. The Speaker overruled Mr. Wright's objection, as the gentleman from Virginia had declared his intention to make a motion and it had been usual to admit prefatory remarks).

Mr. Randolph said he would proceed in his argument without deviating to the right or to the left, and he would endeavour to suppress every feeling which the question was so well calculated to excite. "The vessel accordingly arrived in the Garonne on the 14th of November, but did not reach Bordeaux until the 3rd of December 1807, *expressly set forth,* for having come from an English port and having been visited by a British vessel of war " Thus this vessel having *voluntarily* entered a French port on the faith of the repeal of the decrees, was seized under them. "These facts, continues Mr. Russell, having been stated to me by the supercargo, or the American vice-consul at Bordeaux, and the principal one, that of the *seizure under the Milan Decrees* being established by the *process-verbal,* put into my hands by one of the consignees of the cargo, I conceived it to be my duty not to suffer the transaction to pass unnoticed." This *process-verbal* is neither more nor less than the *libel* of the Admiralty court drawn by the law officer of the French Government, agreeably to the laws of the Empire. What should we say to the libel of a vessel by the District Attorney of the United States, or her seizure by the custom house officers, under an act of Congress which had been repealed? The whole of this correspondence proves unequivocally that neither the Custom House Officers, the Courts of Law, nor the French cruizers, not even the *publick* ships of war had ever received notice from their government of

the repeal of the Berlin and Milan Decrees. This last fact
is further substantiated by the remonstrance of Mr. Barlow
to the Duke of Bassano of the 12th of March, 1812, in the
case of the "vessels *captured* and *burnt* by his Imperial and
Royal Majesty's ships Medusa and Nymph." It should be
recollected that all the decrees of the French Emperor are
given strictly in charge to certain public functionaries, who
are directed to put them in force. The only authorities to
whom the repeal of these decrees was to be a rule of action;
the Cruizers, Courts and Officers of the Customs; remained
profoundly ignorant of the fact. It is to be found no where
but in the proclamation of the President of the United States,
of the 2nd of November, 1810. "To have waited for the re-
ceipt of this proclamation (says Mr. Russell) in order to
make use of it for the liberation of the New Orleans Packet,
appeared to me a preposterous and unworthy course of pro
ceeding, and to be nothing better than absurdly and *basely*
employing the declaration of the President, that the Berlin
and Milan Decrees had been revoked, as the means of obtaining their revocation " They were then not revoked, or
surely our minister would not stand in need of *any means
for obtaining their revocation.* Proofs multiplying on proofs!

"The Custom House Officers of Bordeaux commenced un-
lading the New Orleans Packet on the 10th December and
completed that work on the 20th, as appears by their *process-
verbal* of those dates That of the 20th expressly declares that
the property was to be pursued before the Imperial Council
of Prizes, (the Court of Admiralty,) at Paris, according to
the decrees of the 23rd November, and 17th December, 1806,
or in other words, *under the decrees of Milan* " Mr. Russell's
remonstrance was submitted to the Council of *commerce*, and
further proceedings against the New Orleans Packet suspended. "*The papers were not transmitted to the Council
of Prizes*, nor a prosecution instituted before that tribunal;
which proves only that the prosecution at law was suspended,

not that the laws were repealed — "and the vessel and cargo on the 9th of January were placed at the disposition of the consignees, on giving *bond* to pay the estimated amount, should it be definitely decided that a confiscation should take place."

Recollect that this vessel voluntarily entered a French port on the faith of the repeal of those decrees. She is seized and libelled under them, but after great exertion on the part of the American minister, he obtains from the French government—What? Proof of the bona fide revocation of the decrees? Nothing like it A discharge of the vessel? Not at all,—the bond represents her—she stands pledged in her full value in case she should be found to come within the scope of the law; and yet we must believe the law to be repealed! What sort of a release is this? Mr. Russell makes a merit of having "rescued this property from the seizures with which it had been visited"—that is *rescued it from a court of justice;* and of "having placed it in a situation more favorable than that of *many other vessels and cargoes* which continued in a kind of *mortemain,* by the suspension of all proceedings in regard to them." And *this letter* and *this case* is adduced as a proof of the repeal of the Berlin and Milan Decrees, on the 1st of November, 1810!

It is true that in a postscript dated the fifth of July, (a month subsequent to the date of the letter to which it is appended, and seven months after his remonstrance to the French government) Mr. Russell states that orders had been given to cancel the bond in question. But surely this is no proof of the revocation of the decrees. Let us see what he says on the 15th of that month. "Although I was fully impressed with the importance of an early decision in favor of the captured vessels, *none* of which had been included in the list above mentioned"—("of the 16 vessels whose cargoes had been admitted by order of the Emperor"—probably under license) yet I deemed it proper to wait for a few days, before I made an application on the subject. On the 11th however, having learnt, at the council of prizes, that no new order had been received there"—(that on the 11th of July 1811, the French Admiralty Court had no notice of the repeal of the decrees) "adjudged it to be my duty no longer to remain silent. I therefore, on that day addressed to the Duke of Bassano, my note with a list of American Vessels *captured since the first of November.* On the 15th I learnt that he had laid this note, with a general report, before the Emperor, but that his majesty declined taking any decision with regard to it, *before it had been submitted to the council of commerce.*"

The House will take into consideration the distinction between the council of *prizes*, and admiralty court bound to decide according to the laws of the empire; and the council of commerce; which was of the nature of a board of trade; charged with the general superintendence of the concerns of commerce; occupied in *devising* regulations, not in *expounding* them; an institution altogether *political;* by no means *judicial.* His majesty then determined to consult his council of commerce, whether from motives of policy he should, or should not, grant a special exemption from the operation of his laws. In the same letter, learning from the Duke of Bassano that "the case of the brig Good Intent, must be carried before the Council of Prizes," Mr. Russell wishes to secure this case from this "*inauspicious* mode of proceeding:" that is, from the operation of the law. Why? if the law, so dreaded, was repealed?

"I had from time to time (he continues) informed myself of the proceedings in regard to the captured vessels, and ascertained the fact that the Duke of Bassano had made a report in relation to them. The Emperor it appears, however, still wished for the decision of his *Council of Commerce.*" What! to know if his decrees of Berlin and Milan

were revoked? was his majesty ignorant of the fact? Can
stronger evidence be adduced that they were in force, or can
the release (not by courts of law, but by special executive
interference) under *peculiar circumstances*, and after a long
detention for violating those decrees, of a *single vessel*, establish the fact of their repeal On the contrary ought not
the solitary exception (granting it to be one) to fortify the
general rule?

In passing, it is worthy of remark that the French minister, being interrogated by Mr. Russell on the subject of our
future commercial intercourse with France, "replied that no
such communication would be made at Paris, but that Mr.
Serrurier would be fully instructed on this head." The
House would recollect how much had been expected of Mr
Serrurier on his arrival, and how much had been obtained
An ex-Secretary of the State even had the temerity to charge
the President with having compelled him to desist from putting any interrogatories to the French minister on his arrival. But, be that as it may, one thing is certain, that application having been made to the minister, at the requisition of
the Senate during the present session, he had declared an entire ignorance of everything relating to the subject.

To dissipate the last shadow of doubt on the question of
the repeal of the French Decrees, Mr. Serrurier, in his letter
of July 23, 1811, to the Secretary of State, expressly declares,
that "the *new dispositions* of our government, expressed in
the supplementary act of the *2nd of March last*, having been
officially communicated to his Court, his imperial majesty,
as soon as he was made acquainted with them, directed that
the American vessels sequestered in the ports of France
since the 2nd of November, should be released, orders were at
the same time given to *admit American vessels*, laden with
American produce !"

Under these circustances, whatever difference of opinion
might exist as to the propriety of the President's Proclama-

tion in the first instance, there could be none as to its revocation. As soon as it was ascertained, not only from the proceedings of her cruizers on the high seas, but of her courts of law, and of her government, that France had acted, *mala fide*, towards this country, it surely became the duty of the President to recall that proclamation. He could have no doubt of his constitutional powers over the subject, having already exercised in a case not dissimilar. (Erskine's arrangement). That proclamation was the dividing line of our policy, the root of our present evil. From that fatal proclamation we are to date our departure from that neutral position to which we had so long and so tenaciously adhered, and the accomplishment of the designs of France upon us. In issuing it the President had yielded to the deceitful overtures of France, and it was worthy of observation how different a construction had already been put upon the act of non-intercourse (as it was commonly called) from that of May, 1810—although the words of the two acts were the same. In the first case, a modification of the decrees and orders of the belligerents, so that they should cease to violate our neutral rights was alone required. In the second, other matter was blended with them, although the words of the two acts were identically the same. This grew out of the insidious letter of the Duke of Cadore, the terms of which were accepted, with the conditions annexed, by the President of the United States. These conditions presented two alternatives: "That England should revoke her orders in council and abolish those principles of blockade which France alleged to be new, or that the United States should cause their flag to be respected by the English"—in other words, should become parties to the war on the side of France. In order to know what these principles were, the renunciation of which we were to require at the instigation of France, it would be necessary to attend to the language of the French decrees. By these it would not be denied that principles, heretofore unheard of, were attempted to be *"interpolated into the laws of nations."* —Principles diametrically adverse to those which the government of the United States had repeatedly recognized in their correspondence with foreign powers as well as in their publick treaties, to be legitimate and incentestible. The French doctrine of blockade behind the only branch of the subject embraced in the Duke of Cadore's letter of the 5th of August, 1810, would alone be noticed. These required that the right of blockade be restricted "to *fortified* ports, invested by sea and by land.—That it should not extend to the mouths of rivers, harbours or places not fortified."

Under such definition the blockade of May 1806. otherwise called Mr. Fox's blockade, stood condemned—but Mr. Randolph had no hesitation in affirming that blockade to have been legal, agreeably to the long · established principles of national law, sanctioned by the United States. In Mr. Foster's letter of the 3rd of July last to Mr. Monroe, he says—"the blockade of May 1806 was notified by Mr. Secretary Fox on this principle ("that no blockade can be justifiable or valid unless it be supported by an adequate force destined to maintain it and to expose to hazard all vessels attempting to evade its operation") nor was the blockade announced, until he had satisfied himself by a communication with the board of Admiralty, that the Admiralty possessed the means, and would employ them, of watching the whole coast from Brest to Elbe and of effectually enforcing the blockade.

"The blockade of May 1806, according to the doctrine maintained by Great Britain, was just and lawful in its origin because it was supported both in intention and in fact, by an adequate naval force." In a subsequent part of the same letter it is distinctly averred that "that blockade was maintained by a sufficient naval force:" and the doctrine of *paper blockade* is every where disclaimed in the correspondence, here as well as at London. "If (says Mr. Foster)) the orders in council should be abrogated, the *blockade of May* 1806 *could not continue under our construction of the law of nations, unless that blockade should be maintained by a due application of an adequate naval force."* The same admission will be found in Marquis Wellesley's correspondence with Mr. Pinkney.

The coast of France from Brest to Calais is what seamen call an iron-bound coast. It had been blockaded in every war during the last century, that short period of the American War excepted, when England lost the mastery of the channel. No British minister would be suffered to hold his place, who should fail strictly to watch the opposite coast of France Brest, her principal naval arsenal, protruded out into the Atlantic Ocean, confessed the want of suitable harbours for ships of war in the channels, while from Plymouth, Portsmouth, and the mouth of the Thames, the opposite coast is easily watched and overawed. From Calais to the Elbe the coast is low, flat and shelving, difficult of access, affording few good inlets, indeed none except the Scheldt. The blockade of this coast is as easy as that of Carolina. But it must not pass unnoticed that the blockade was in point of fact, (as appears from Mr Monroe's letters to Mr. Madison of the 17th and 20th of May 1806) limited to a small extent of the coast between Havre and Ostend; neutrals being permitted to trade, freely, eastward of Ostend, and westward of the mouth of the Seine "except in articles contrabrand of war and enemies' property which are seizible without blockade." And Mr. Monroe, in announcing this very blockade of May 16, 1806, to his own government, speaks of it as a measure highly satisfactory to the commercial interests. And yet the removal of this blockade, against which Mr. Monroe did not remonstrate, of which there was no mention in the subsequent arrangement of Mr. Erskine, which did not stand in the way of that arrangement of which no notice was taken in our proposition to England for a mutual abandonment of our embargo and her orders in council, is *now* by French device and contrivance to be made a *sine qua non,* an indispensable preliminary to all accommodation with Great Britain '

Mr Randolph had heard with sincere satisfaction many respectable gentlemen in the House and out of it, express a wish, that, by a revocation of the orders in council, the British ministry would put it in the power of our government to come to some adjustment of our differences with England. The position which he was about to lay down, and the proof of which the course of his argument had compelled him in some degree to anticipate, however it might startle persons of this description, was nevertheless susceptible of the most direct and positive evidence Little did these gentlemen dream, but such was the indisputable fact, that their removal at this moment would not satisfy our administration   In Lord Wellesley's letter to Mr. Pinkney of Dec. 29, 1810, he says: "If nothing more had been required of G. Britain, for the purpose of securing the continuation of the repeal of the French decrees, than the repeal of our orders in council I should not have hesitated to declare the perfect readiness of this government to fulfill that condition. On these terms the British government has always been seriously disposed to repeal the orders in council. It appears however, not only by the letter of the French minister, but by your explanation, that the repeal of the orders in council will not satisfy either the French or the American governments. The British government is further required by the letter of the French minister to renounce those principles of blockade which the French government alleges to be new."

This fact is placed beyond a doubt, by Mr. Pinkney's answer of the 14th January, 1811. "If I comprehend the other parts of your Lordship's letter," says he, "they declare in effect that the British Government *will repeal nothing out of the Orders in Council,*"—and again, "It is certainly true that the American Government has required as indispensable in the view of its acts of intercourse and non-intercourse, the annulment of the British blockade of May 1806."

Thus when the British Government stood pledged to repeal its Orders in Council, a question entirely distinct, has been dexterously mingled with it in our discussions with England; the renunciation of the right of blockade in the face of Mr. Madison's construction of the non-intercourse law, and of Mr. Smith's instructions to General Armstrong of July 5, and 2nd November, 1810, has been declared indispensable in the view of that act, and there is the fullest admission that *more* than the repeal of the Orders in Council was required; viz, of that blockade, against which we had not lifted our voice, until required to do so by France, which Mr Monroe (so far from remonstrating against it, which would have been his duty to have done if illegal) consider it *"as highly satisfactory to the commercial interests."* A blockade easy as would be that of the ports of Chesapeake, with a sufficient force stationed in Lynn Haven Bay. What is a legal blockade? A blockade with such force as renders the approach of merchant vessels dangerous.

Mark the wonderful facility with which Mr Pinkney, not only blends the question of the blockade of May 1806, with the repeal of the Orders in Council; but his disposition to go, *if he could*, the whole length of the French doctrine of blockade; a doctrine unheard of before the reign of Bonaparte. "It is by no means clear that it may not fairly be contended on principle and early usage that a maritime blockade is incomplete with regard to states at peace, unless the place which it affects, *is invested by land as well as by sea.*" And yet in the same letter he says, "You will imagine that the repeal is not to remain in force, unless the British government, in addition to the revocation of its Orders in Council, abandon its system of blockade. I am not conscious of having stated, as your Lordship seems to think, that this is so, and I believe in fact that it is otherwise. Even if it were admitted however, the Orders in Council ought nevertheless to be revoked."

The American doctrine of blockade is expressly laid down in Mr. Smith's letter to Commodore Preble of the 4th of February, 1804 "Whenever therefore you shall have formed a blockade of the port of Tripoli ('so as to create an evident danger on entering it') you will have a right to capture for adjudication, any vessel that shall attempt to enter with a knowledge of the blockade." The very same doctrine against which, at the instigation of France, we are now about to plunge into war!

Mr. Randolph said he was compelled to omit many striking proofs of his positions, from absolute weakness and inability, to read the voluminous extracts from the documents before him. If the offer should be made of a repeal of the Orders of Council which our people at home, good easy souls, supposed to be the only obstacle, the wound, as after the accommodation of the affair of the Chesapeake, would still remain incurable He had not touched upon the subject of impressment, because, notwithstanding the use which had been made of it in that House and in the publick prints, it did not constitute, according to the showing of our own government, an obstacle to accommodation; (the orders in council and question of blockade being the *avowed* impediments) and because it appears from Mr. Monroe's letter of the 28th February 1808 "that the ground on which that interest was placed by the paper of the British commissioners of Nov. 8, 1806, and the explanations which accompanied it, *was both honourable and advantageous to the United States*. That it contained a concession in their favor on the part of Great Britain, on the great principle in contestation, never before made, by a formal, obligatory act of the government, which was highly favorable to their interests "

In fact the rejection of Mr. Monroe's treaty had alone

prevented the settlement upon honourable terms, of *this*, as well as of every other topic of difference between the two governments.

He called the attention of the House to Mr. Smith's letter to Mr. Armstrong of July 5, 1810, requiring, in the name of the President, restitution of our plundered property as "a peliminary to accommodation between the two governments," —"As has been heretofore stated to you, a satisfactory provision for restoring the property lately surprised and seized by the order, or at the instance of the French government *must be combined with a repeal of the French edicts* with a view to non-intercourse with Great Britian; such a provision being an *indispensable* evidence of the just purpose of France towards the U. States!" Yet no restitution had been made: "that affair is settled by the law of reprisal." What had been the language held on this floor and by ministers of state in official communications to committees of Congress? "that the return of the Hornet should be conclusive as to our relations with France. That if Mr. Barlow should not succeed in attaining the most complete redress for the past and assurances for the future we would take the same stand against her as against Great Britain; that any *uncertainty* as to his success would be equivalent to the *certainty* of his failure." Such was the language held until the fact occurred, that NO satisfaction had been, or was likely to be obtained. Indeed, for some days after the arrival of the Hornet, these opinions had been maintained. They had however gradually died away and it was only within 48 hours past that a different language had been held. Was it necessary to remind the House of the shuffling conduct and policy of France toward us? Of the explanation attempted by DECREES, the minister of marine, in relation to the Berlin Decree and the subsequent annunciation of his government to Mr. Armstrong, with true French *sang froid*, that "as there was no excepting of the United States in the terms of the decrees, so there was

no reason foi excepting them from their operation." Have
we forgotten Champagny's declaration of war in our name,
"War exists then in fact between England and the United
States and his majesty considers it as declared."—In short,
for years past France has required us to make war with England as the price of undefined commercial concessions from
her. We have been told "that we ought to tear to pieces the
act of our independence—that we were more dependent than
Jamaica—that we were without just political views, without
energy, without honour, and that we must at last fight for
interest, after having refused to fight for honour "

France, whilst you required of her as a preliminary to
further accommodation, the restitution of her plunder, de-
coyed into her ports, required from you, as preliminary, a
war with England. Mr Barlow has now been ten months in
France, dancing attendance upon her Court, without being
able to obtain an answer to a few plain questions. Are your
Decrees repealed?—It is considered as improper to make the
enquiry,—Instead of the edict, rescript, the instrument of repeal, by whatsoever name it be called, he sends us the strict-
ures of the French Government upon the proceedings of
the American Congress, and a remonstrance to the Duke of
Bassano, that the repeal of the Decrees (in which he is compelled to feign a belief, because the President's proclamation
is the sole evidence of the fact) has not been given in charge
to the French cruizers, but that the publick ships of war
(Nymph and Medusa) continue to *burn* our vessels on the
high seas And what does the Duke of Bassano tell him in
reply? The same old story of Champagny to General Armstrong—"The United States will be entirely satisfied on the
pending questions, and there will be no obstacle to their obtaining the advantages they have in view, if they succeed
in making their flag safe!" In other words, make war with
England and you will be satisfied (and not until then) on
the pending questions. And what are they? On one of them

the required compensation for plunder,—your min'ster, after waiting for months for an *oral* answer, tells you, "This is *dull work, hard to begin and difficult to execute.*" This is the claim too, required by Mr. Secretary Smith, under the President's order, to be satisfied as a preliminary to the acceptance of the overture of August 5, 1810! It is possible the Wasp may bring out something, just to hush up complaints until we are fairly embarked in war; into which, if we enter, it will be a war of submission to the mandates of a foreign Despot—the basest, the most unqualified, the most abject submission   France for years past has offered us terms (without specifying what they were) at the price of a war with England, which, hitherto we have rejected   That price must now be paid. The Emperor deals only for ready money —and carrying his jealousy further than in the case of the President's Proclamation (which he would not believe until its terms were fulfilled) he requires to be paid in hand before he will make his equivalent.

In the celebrated case of insult by implication, or insinuation, offered by Mr. Jackson, there existed in the Archives of the country, a monument (such as it was) to the insensibility of this House to that insult.

If under such circumstances, without having received any shadow of indemnity for the past, or security for the future— if indeed security could be given by the French Emperor— the United States becomes virtually a party to the war in his behalf, it must confirm beyond the possibility of doubt, every surmise that has gone abroad, however gross, however injurious to the honour or the interests of this government— that there exists in our councils an undue, a fatal French bias. After the declarations of official men, after the language uttered on that floor, if the U. States become parties to the war with France against her rival, it must establish as clearly as the existence of the sun above us—this event has not happened, and God forbid it should—but if it does, the conclusion will be irresistible, and this government will stand branded to the latest posterity, (unless the press should perish in the general wreck of human liberty) as the pandars of French despotism—as the tools, the minions. sycophants, parasites of France. 'Twas to secure the country from this opprobrium that the proposition was about to be submitted.

This is not like a war for a Spanish succession or a Dutch barrier; for the right of cutting logwood on a desert coast, or fishing in the Polar sea. It is war unexampled in the history of mankind—a war.—separated as we are from the theatre of it by a wide ocean—from which it behooves us to stand aloof—to set our backs to the wall and await the coming of the enemy, instead of rushing out at midnight in search of the disturbers of our rest, when a thousand daggers are pointed at our bosoms But it is said we must fight for commerce—a war for commerce deprecated by all the commercial portion of our country, by New England and New York, the greatest holders of our navigation and capital!

(Mr. CALHOUN called to order; the question of war was not before the House. It was decided by Mr. Bibb, then in the chair, the Speaker having vacated a few minutes before that the objection was not valid, as the gentleman from Virginia had announced his intention to conclude with a motion, and it had been usual in such cases, to permit a wide range of debate)

Mr. Randolph thanked the gentleman from South Carolina for the respite which he had unintentionally given him, and which, in his exhausted situation, was highly grateful. This war for commercial rights is to be waged against the express wish (constitutionally pronounced, spoken in language which cannot be misunderstood) of the great commercial section of the United States—a war which must cut up commerce by the roots; which, in its operation, must necessarily drive population and capital beyond the mountains.

(Mr. CALHOUN said he would give the gentleman from Virginia another opportunity to rest himself. He repeated his call to order, and the Speaker decided that the motion must be submitted, reduced to writing, and seconded (thus reversing his own, and Dr. Bibb's previous decision). An appeal was taken from this decision, and it was affirmed; ayes 67; noes 42.

Mr. Randolph then said, that under the compulsion of the House, he would submit his motion.

"Resolved, that under existing circumstances, it is inexpedient to resort to war against Great Britain."

The motion was accordingly handed to the chair, and being seconded, Mr. Randolph was proceeding to argue in support of it, when Mr. Calhoun again interrupted him on the ground that a vote must be taken (without debate) "*to consider the motion.*" The Speaker decided that this was not necessary,—and Mr. Randolph, after thanking the Speaker for this decision, was re-commencing his observations, when the objection being repeated, the Speaker said he had given a hasty opinion, and reversed his decision. The vote to consider the motion was then put and negatived; ayes 37; noes 72. Which put a period to all further discussion "

The Manifestoe; the main body of which has thus been given; goes on for a full page to cite extracts from various letters and reports in support of the arguments used in the main body of the speech of Mr. Randolph, but are not necessary to our purpose here and will be omitted.

The war party succeeded and the war went on with but little glory to the United States, and with little advantage to France.

Chapter Eight

Prince Edward County in the War Between the States

1. Introduction.

2. Comparative Table, prepared by Mr. C. G. Lee.

3. Muster Rolls of Prince Edward Companies

4 Interesting Experiences. "Captain" Sam Paulett; "The Old Reb "

5 Local War History. Dr. James L. White; the "Beloved Physician "

PRINCE EDWARD COUNTY IN THE WAR BETWEEN THE STATES

INTRODUCTION

It is extremely unfortunate that even officials, specifically charged with responsibility in the premises, so often betray but little diligence in making and preserving important records and lists, and that the public are so slow in coming to realize the vast impotrance of such things to future generations.

This disposition is glaringly evident in the lackadaisical manner in which our war records are kept—or, rather, in the way in which they are not kept.

And all this is very evident in relation to the records of the War Between the States. Only such records of the part played by Prince Edward county in that colossal contest are available, as have been rescued from the rapidly disappearing mass, and compiled by private citizens. And they are pitiably meagre! Chief amongst those to whom the county owes a real debt of gratitude in this connection, is Captain Sam. W. Paulett, of Farmville.

At the risk of appearing to over-balance the records, we are printing all the materials thus collected, in the sincere hope that they may thus be preserved from complete and final disappearance, in which case Prince Edward county would be indeed a serious loser. Hence the peculiar structure of this chapter

TABLE PREPARED BY C. G LEE OF WASHINGTON, D. C. FROM RECORDS IN THE WAR DEPARTMENT

NORTHERN ARMY

Whites from the South	316,424
Whites from the North	2,272,333
Negroes	186,017
Indians	3,530
Total	2,778,304
Confederate Armies all told	600,000
Numerical Superiority of Northern Army	2,178,304

STRENGTH OF ARMIES AT CLOSE OF WAR

Aggregate Federal Army, May 1st, 1865	1,000,516
Aggregate Confederate Army, May 1st, 1865	133,433

Number of men in battles	Confederate	Federal
Seven Day's Fight	80,835	115,249
Antietem	35,255	87,164
Chancellorsville	57,212	131,661
Fredericksburg	78,110	110,000
Gettysburg	62,000	95,000
Chicamauga	44,000	65,000
Wilderness	141,160	

Federal prisoners in Confederate prisons	270,000
Confederate Prisoners in Federal prisons	220,000
Confederates died in Federal prisons	26,436
Federals died in Confederate prisons	22,570

The above table shows that the Federals let a little over twelve per cent of their prisoners die in captivity While the Confederates lost only eight and one-half per cent of their prisoners by death

The above statement is sworn to by C G Lee

CONFEDERATE MONUMENT
Farmville, Virginia.
See Page 89.

NOTICE!

The following petition will be heard before the county court of Prince Edward on Monday, the 19th day of December, 1898:

W. H. THACKSTON, Clerk.

To the Honorable J. M. Crute, Judge of the County Court of Prince Edward county:

The petition of S. W. Paulett; O T. Wicker; and R. D. Miller, respectfully represents:

That your petitioners served as soldiers in the defense of Virginia in the War Between the States of 1861 and 1865, inclusive; that they were members of a company of Infantry, enlisted for the most part in said county, in the commencement of said war. That said Company was raised for the defence of Virginia and did actually serve in one of the armies of the Confederate States of America, to wit: the Army of Northern Virginia, as Company F, 18th Virginia Infantry Regiment during the whole war.

They file herewith a muster roll of said Company of Infantry and pray that the same may be recorded among the records of said county. And to that end that your Honor will require the proper notice of this application to be published and render to your petitioners all such other and further aid in the premises as may be needed, and your petitioners, as in duty bound, will ever pray, etc.

S. W. PAULETT,
O. T. WICKER,
R. D. MILLER.

Virginia·—Prince Edward county, to wit:

I, Richard A Booker, formerly Captain of Co. F, 18th Virginia Infantry, do certify that S. W. Paulett, O. T.

Wicker, and R. D. Miller, whose names are signed to the within petition, were members of said Company of Infantry and were thoroughly reputable soldiers.

RICHARD A. BOOKER,
Formerly Captain Co. F, 18th Va. Infantry.

ROLL OF COMPANY F, FARMVILLE GUARD, 18th VA. REGIMENT, HUNTON'S BRIGADE, PICKETT'S DIVISION. LONGSTREET'S CORPS OF INFANTRY. C. S. A.

Captain—Richard A. Booker. Wounded at 2nd battle of Manassas; resigned and afterwards made Colonel of Reserves and served to the close of the war.

1st Lieutenant—Charles D. Anderson; left Company April, 1862; became an officer in the Richmond City Battalion and served during the war.

2nd Lieutenant—Charles H. Erambert. Resigned April, 1862; became an officer in the Richmond City Battalion, and served during the war.

3rd Lieutenant—Samuel B. McKinney. Health failed; resigned April, 1862; served during the war in the Q. M. G's office at Richmond.

1st Sergeant—Chesley Wood. Health failed; detailed in Hospital; served during the war.

2nd Sergeant—Wm. C. Priddy. Health failed; detailed in Hospital; served during the war.

3rd Sergeant—Wm H. Pettus. Transferred to Cavalry, 1862.

4th Sergeant—Wm. G. Venable. Discharged, May, 1861.

1st Corporal—James W Womack. Killed at Gaines' Mill, 1862.

2nd Corporal—Robert E. Warren. Health failed; put in a substitute; afterwards entered the Cavalry and served during the war.

3rd Coropral—C. D. Lindsey. Transferred to Co. K, 18th Va., Regiment, April, 1862, and served through the war.

4th Corporal—Samuel C. Price. Promoted to Sergeant-Major of the regiment, February, 1862; wounded at the 2nd battle of Manassass; promoted to Quarter Master of the regiment, fall of 1862, served during the war.

PRIVATES

Peyton B. Anderson, Killed at Gaines' Mill, 1862.

William F. Anderson, withdrew after 1st battle of Manassas; afterwards served in the Cavalry.

Z. A. Blanton, promoted to Sergeant; to Orderly Sergeant; to First Lieutenant; then to Captain; disabled by a terrible wound in the charge at Gettysburg.

George R. Boatwright, wounded at the battle of Drury's Bluff; killed at Hatcher's Run, March 31, 1865.

Chas. H. Brimmer, health failed; detailed in hospital, where he served during the war.

Thomas H Bryant, wounded at Frazier's Farm; killed at Gettysburg.

Robert M. Burton, made orderly with staff of Gen. G. T. Beauregard; there served most of the war.

Allison Brightwell, died in hospital.

L. C. Butler,—.

Joseph E. Chappell, wounded at Seven Pines; transferred to artillery.

Thos. A. Cliborne, wounded in several battles.

George W. Cliborne, died of disease, contracted in the army.

E. B. Coleman, transferred to Co. H, 18th Va.

Richard Crafton, transferred to artillery.

J. J. Chernault, detailed brigade butcher.

W. M. Davidson, served in the field, then detailed as Quarter Master's clerk.

C. H. Dowdy, killed at Frazier's Farm.

J. S. Davis, killed at Gettysburg.

W. C. Davis, put in substitute 1862.

E. P. Davis, put in substitute, December, 1861.

A. L. Deaton, died of typhoid fever, September, 1861.

James H. Dunnington. wounded and disabled at Gaines' Mill, 1862; afterwards served as Orderly for General Hunton.

Tom Dowdy, wounded at Bermuda Front, and died from its effects.

Pat Dougherty, killed at Hatcher's Run, 31st March, 1865.

J. T. East, died of typhoid fever, September, 1861.

Robert W. Elam, promoted to Orderly Sergeant; killed at Hatcher's Run, 31st March, 1865.

George W. Elam, promoted to 2nd Sergeant, then to Orderly Sergeant; killed at Gettysburg.

George W. Erambert, detailed in hospital, October, 1861.

J. T. Elam, detailed at General Hunton's headquarters.

Obediah East, wounded at Seven Pines and Gettysburg.

J. W. East, health failed; discharged.

John Eagles, wounded and disabled.

Peyton Enroughty,—.

A. L. Faris, wounded and disabled at the battle of Williamsburg, May 5th.

George R. Flippen, wounded at Gaines' Mill.

A. S. Foster, transferred to Co. K, 18th Va , killed at Seven Pines.

B. F. Foster, served faithfully through the war.

S. B. Foster, transferred to Co. C., 18th Va., Regiment, April, 1862; died about close of the war.

A. J. Fowlkes, wounded at Gaines' Mill; promoted to Orderly Sergeant; then to 1st Lieutenant.

John M. Foster, captured at Gettysburg; died at Point Lookout, Md.

James F. Foster,—.

Robert Gilliam, wounded at Gettysburg.

George Gills,—.

Henry G. Haines, transferred to Co K, 18th Va., April, 1862; supposed to have been killed in retreat from Petersburg.

B. J Harvey, detailed at Confederate shops at Farmville.

J. S. Harvey, served through the war.

B. A. Holt, transferred to Co. C, 18th Va., April, 1862; detailed at Richmond, June, 1862; became Captain of a local company of city guards.

T A. Holt, wounded at Sailor's Creek.

W. V. Holt, transferred to Co. K, 18th Va., April, 1862.

R. M. Hawkins, detailed as brigade blacksmith.

H H. Hooton, wounded at Gaines' Mill.

S. C. Hooton, wounded at Gaines' Mill, and killed at Gettysburg

A M Hughes, promoted to Sergeant, April, 1862; killed at Williamsburg, May 5th.

J. W. Hancock, health failed; discharged, February, 1862.

J. S. Hart, detailed at Confederate shops at Farmville.

Jeff Hawkins, transferred to 19th Va Regiment.

Jett Hawkins, wounded; transferred to 19th Va. Regiment

Henry Harvey, wounded

Elisha Hunt, killed at Gettysburg.

Tobe Hudgins, deserted at Gettysburg

Johnson Harvey, killed at Hatcher's Run, 31st March, 1865.

Jesse Harvey,—.

N. H. Jackson, promoted to 3rd Lieutenant; wounded at

2nd battle of Manassas; resigned, and afterwards served in the Cavalry.

Abram Jenkins, detailed as blacksmith in Richmond.

Jno. Jenkins, transferred to Cavalry

Henry Jenkins, detailed as blacksmith in Richmond.

Tom Jenkins. killed at Frazier's Farm.

Jno. Jackson, killed at Hatcher's Run, 31st March.

Archer Jennings,—

Elihu Morrissett, transferred to Co. C, 18th Va , April, 1862; wounded and disabled at Gaines' Mill.

T. L. Morton, detailed in hospital.

Nat. S. Morton, wounded at Drury's Bluff; promoted to 1st Corporal.

Wm. H. Morton, made Color Corporal, April, 1862; wounded at Gaines' Mill; transferred to Cavalry.

H. C. Middleton, detailed in hospital.

W. J. Morrissett, elected Lieutenant at Orange C. H.; promoted to Captain; slightly wounded once or twice

Eddie Miller, left marker.

R. D. Miller, captured at Gettysburg and kept in prison many months.

John Moss,—.

Rod Mayo,—.

William A. Miller, promoted to 1st Lieutenant; wounded at Gettysburg.

J. H. Minor, transferred to Co. E, April, 1862; health failed: detailed in hospital.

T. F. McKinney, wounded at Gaines' Mill; afterwards served in Cavalry.

W. J Nash, wounded at Frazier's Farm; promoted to Corporal.

Thos. J. Osborne, discharged,—ill-health.

V. C. Overton, died of typhoid fever, February, 1862.

Richard H. Page, killed at Frazier's Farm.

John H. Pearson, died of disease, contracted by exposure.

Samuel B. Partin,—.

John E. Paterson, detailed in hospital during 1861; made Commissary of 16th Va. Regiment, 1862.

T. J. Paulett, wounded at Gettysburg.

H. A. Paulett —

Samuel W. Paulett, right marker; wounded at 2nd Manassas; slightly wounded and captured at Gettysburg; severely wounded and captured at Sailor's Creek, 6th April, 1865.

Tom Price, killed at Bermuda Front.

E. T. Rice, detailed in hospital.

Chas. R. Richardson, detailed as clerk, October, 1861; afterwards returned to Company; killed at Bermuda Front.

Walter H. Richardson, discharged as farmer, Sept., 1861.

Jno. W Ransom, made Sergeant of Company.

Jesse Robertson, wounded terribly and died.

T. L Robertson,—.

J. J. Riggins, captured at Gettysburg.

George M Setzer, wounded at Frazier's Farm; promoted to Corporal; killed at Gettysburg.

W. G. Stratton, wounded at Hatcher's Run, 31st March, 1865.

W. F. Smith, transferred to Co. K, 18th Va., April, 1862.

Wm. Smith,—.

Joel W. Toney, discharged 1862: joined again in 1864.

Wm. A. Tuggle, killed at Frazier's Farm.

-- Tompkins, wounded at Hatcher's Run, 31st March, 1865.

Cicero A. Verser, transferred to Co. C, 18th Va., April, 1862; killed at Gaines' Mill.

Ed. Verser,—.

Paul C. Venable, transferred to Co D, 18th Va., Feb., 1862; promoted to Ordinance Sergeant of the regiment;

afterwards promoted to Captain of Ordinance, on Gen Wade Hampton's Staff.

C. M. Walker, transferred to Cavalry, and wounded at Spottsylvania C. H., Stevensburg, and Winchester.

L. A. Warren, promoted to Sergeant, and afterwards made Quarter-Master Sergeant.

W. H. H. Walthall, promoted to Color Corporal.

Thos. Weaver, killed at Bermuda Front.

B. C. Wells, served through the war.

T. A. Wells, served through the war.

W. C. Wells,—.

W. Archer Wilson, killed at 1st battle of Manassas; first man of the Company killed in battle.

Abram N. Womack, discharged for disease and over-age.

Nathan B. Womack, discharged; afterwards rejoined.

W. T. Worsham, wounded at Gaines' Mill; killed at Gettysburg.

Tom Walden, died at Point Lookout, Md.

Peter Wells,—.

J T. Wilkerson, discharged; afterwards put in 19th Va.

O. T. Wicker, wounded at Gaines' Mill; 2nd Manassas; Flint Hill; Gettysburg; and Bermuda Front.

Edgar Wicker,—.

Jno. D. Walthall, wounded at Gaines' Mill; and Gettysburg.

Conrad Zimmerman, wounded and disabled at Gaines' Mill; afterwards served as Conscript Officer.

NOTE: (The foregoing most excellent summary of Company F, was made under the personal supervision of "Captain" S. W. Paulett.)

NOTE: (R. D. Miller, one of the signers of this petition, died in October, 1921, and was buried in Farmville cemetery.)

ROLL OF CENTRAL GUARD OF COMPANY I, 23rd REGIMENT VIRGINIA VOLUNTEERS C. S. A.

NOTICE.

The following petition will be heard before the County Court of Prince Edward, on the 21st of April, 1899.

W. H. THACKSTON, Clerk.

To the Honorable Judge of the County Court of Prince Edward county:

The petition of N. H. Garland, C. C. Bass, and F. H. Davis respectfully represents:—

That your petitioners served as soldiers in defense of Virginia in the War Between the States of 1861 and 1865, inclusive; that they were members of a Company of Infantry enlisted for the most part in the said county, in the commencement of said war. That said Company was raised for the defense of Virginia, and did actually serve in one of the armies of the Confederate States, to wit: in the Army of Northern Virginia, as Company I, 23rd Virginia Regiment, during the whole war.

They file herewith a muster roll of said Company of Infantry and pray that the same may be recorded among the records of said county. And to that end that your Honor will require the proper notice of this application to be published, and to render to your Petitioners all such other and further aid in the premises as may be needed, and your Petitioners, as in duty bound, will ever pray, etc.

C. C. BASS,
F. H. DAVIS,
N. H. GARLAND.

Virginia.—Prince Edward county, to wit:

I, Branch Worsham, formerly Lieutenant of Co. I, 23rd Virginia Infantry, C. S A., do certify that C. C. Bass, N. H. Garland, and F. H. Davis, whose names are signed to the above petition, were members of said Company of Infantry, and were thoroughly reputable soldiers

B. WORSHAM,
Lieutenant Co. I, 23rd Va., Infantry.

ROLL OF CENTRAL GUARD OF COMPANY I, 23rd REGIMENT VIRGINIA VOLUNTEERS

This Company was organized at Prince Edward courthouse (now Worsham) and was the third to leave the county; was mustered into service May 22nd, 1861, at Richmond, and on Sunday, June 9th, 1861, left Richmond for Northwest Virginia, the Regiment being commanded by Colonel William B Taliaferro.

Captain, Moses T. Hughes; commanded until the battle of Carricksford, July 13th, 1861, when he resigned.

1st Lieutenant, J. P Fitzgerald; commissioned Captain of the Company from July 25th, 1861. Commissioned Major of the regiment from June 10th, 1863, and Lieutenant-Colonel from the 27th of November, 1863. Wounded at Sharpsburg; captured at Spottsylvania; carried to Fort Delaware, and from thence to the coast of South Carolina; exchanged at Charleston, July, 1864. Was with the Army of Northern Virginia at the surrender at Appomattox.

2nd Lieutenant, Branch Worsham; captured at the battle of Carricksford. Appointed clerk of the Circuit Court of Prince Edward.

3rd Lieutenant, William G. Trueheart; elected 1st Lieutenant, July 20th, 1861; subsequently resigned and joined the Prince Edward company of Cavalry.

1st Sergeant, Nathaniel G. Jones; served until discharged. Afterwards served in the 18th Virginia Regiment.

2nd Sergeant, Henry Venable; killed in the battle of Carricksford, July 13th, 1861.

3rd Sergeant, Christopher C Bass; wounded at McDowell, May 8th, 1862; served until July, 1862, when he was discharged for physical disability.

4th Sergeant, Gustavus A. Bass; elected 1st Lieutenant at the re-organization in May, 1862. He commanded the Company at the battle of Chancellorsville, 1863, where he was killed.

5th Sergeant, James H. Thackston; captured on the retreat from Northwest Virginia, and paroled, and when he was exchanged, joined some other company.

1st Corporal, Henry W. Edmunds; wounded at the battle of Carricksford, July 13th, 1861; captured and paroled, and when exchanged, joined the Cavalry, and was again severely wounded.

2nd Corporal, Thomas R. Farrar; killed at the battle of McDowell, May 8th, 1862; body sent home and buried in Prince Edward.

3rd Corporal, George W. Cliborne; exchanged into Company F, 18th regiment in 1863.

4th Corporal, William L. Gutherie; elected 3rd Lieutenant at the re-organization of the Company in May 1862, on the death of Lieutenant G. A. Bass, was made 1st Lieutenant. and became Captain of the Company in 1863; was captured at Spottsylvania Courthouse, May 12, 1864, and taken to Point Lookout, and thence to Morris Island, S. C, and, on being taken back to Lookout, died there from exposure and hardships endured while in prison.

5th Corporal, John M Booker; killed at the battle of Sharpsburg, September 17th, 1862.

PRIVATES

J. D. Allen, discharged for physical disability.

John J. Allen, discharged, January, 1862.

John R. Allen, captured July, 1861 on the retreat from Northwest Virginia, and paroled when exchanged, and did not rejoin the Company.

Robert P. Anderson, transferred in June, 1861, to Captain J. M. P. Atkinson's Company (Hampden-Sidney boys); captured at Rich Mountain, July, 1861, and, when exchanged, joined the Artillery.

Elisha S. Boatwright, served until late in the war, and discharged.

Richard F. Burke, served through the war.

Henry C Campbell, discharged, August 1st, 1861, on account of physical disability.

Wm. H. Campbell.

John A. Chappell, captured at Spottsylvania Courthouse. May 12th, 1864; imprisoned at Point Lookout until the close of the war.

John Carter, killed at Carricksford, July 13th, 1861.

Elijah F. Collins, killed at Carricksford, July 13th, 1861.

John W. Cave, wounded at Carricksford.

James A. Chrisp, served until late in the war, when discharged for physical disability.

Jeremiah G. Daub. wounded in the arm at McDowell, May 8th, 1862, and discharged.

Fayette H. Davis, captured at Spottsylvania Courthouse, May 12th, 1864, and kept a prisoner at Fort Delaware until the close of the war.

Richard A. Davis, captured on the retreat from Northwest Virginia, July, 1861, and paroled; when exchanged, joined another company.

Joshua Foster; killed at Carricksford, July 13th, 1861.

Nelson H. Garland, was made 1st Sergeant of the Company, and, at the re-organization in May 1862, was elected

2nd Lieutenant, and at the battle of McDowell, May 8th, 1862, was disabled by a wound through the arm, and after that was on detached service.

John R. Hughes, discharged July, 1861, for physical disability.

Shadrach H. Hines, discharged at the end of the first year's service as being over forty-five years old.

Thomas L. Hines, captured at Spottsylvania Courthouse and retained a prisoner at Fort Delaware until the war ended.

Samuel C. Hines, discharged for physical disability.

James H. Hailey

William Hamilton, died of disease, September, 1861.
Francis Hamilton, served through the war.

James Hamilton; served through the war.

Irby King, killed at Carricksford, July 13th, 1861.

Drury Lacy, wounded at Carricksford, July 13th, 1861; elected Lieutenant 1863; captured at Spottsylvania Courthouse, May 12th, 1864; carried to Point Lookout, and thence to the coast of South Carolina, and afterwards exchanged at Chambersburg.

Matthew L. Meadow, captured July, 1861, and never returned for duty.

Overton Meadow, served through the war.

Wm. J. Morris, wounded at Spottsylvania Courthouse. May 12th, 1864, captured and not released until the close of the war.

Elijah Morgan, captured at Spottsylvania Courthouse.
T. W. Price.
Joseph B. Price.
Albert G. Rogers, served through the war.

T. H Rogers, wounded in the leg at Sharpsburg, served to the end of the war.

R. T. Rice, discharged in March, 1862, for physical disability,

John F. Rice, Jr., captured at Spottsylvania Courthouse, May 12th, 1864, and not exchanged until after the war.

F. S. Scott, captured at Spottsylvania Courthouse.

Robert C. Thackston, wounded at Cedar Mountain, August 9th, 1862, and died of his wound in the hospital.

John S. Watson, captured at Spottsylvania Courthouse, May 12th, 1864, and taken to Fort Delaware; on his return, afterwards accidentally drowned by falling overboard the steamer at Baltimore.

John M. Williamson, captured July, 1861, and never returned to his Company.

Benjamin A. Womack, captured at Spottsylvania Courthouse.

RECRUITS WHO JOINED THE COMPANY IN THE FIELD

1861

N. E. Venable, served in 1861 in the Marine Corps, and, in September, 1864, resigned his commission and entered this Company as a private; was promoted to the Lieutenancy; was commander of the Company at Kernstown.

C. R. Venable, joined the Company September, 1861, and was made Sergeant.

1862

Wm. D. Allen, captured at Spottsylvania.

James J. Bigger, died of disease.

Archer L. Bagby, captured at Spottsylvania.

Robert Fitzgerald, died of disease.

John E. Campbell.

Richard Crafton, killed at the Wilderness.

Beverley Dupuy, killed at Chancellorsville.

George G Fowlkes, killed at Chancellorsville.

James T. Fowlkes.

Minford Fowlkes.

Darious Hash; died of disease.

John T. Hines.

Stephen Hines, died of disease.

George R Hughes, discharged and died.

John F. Jones, wounded at McDowell.

Wm. L. Meadow, died of disease.

James M. Morton, died of disease.

Nelson McGeehee, died of disease.

James Phelps, died of disease

Robert Reider.

Robert K. Thackston, wounded at Petersburg

John S. Thackston, captured at Spottsylvania.

Wm. A. Walton, became 1st Sergeant and was killed at Sharpsburg.

James L. Waddell.

(NOTE: Fayette H. Davis, one of the signers of this petition, died in 1920, and was buried in Farmville cemetery.)

PRINCE EDWARD COUNTY COURT
December Term 1898

On motion of the petitioners; W. H. Ewing, J. F. Walton, and H. W. Edmunds, and it appearing that the Muster Roll of Company K, 3rd Regiment, of Virginia Cavalry, Fitz Lee's Division, C. S. A., has been published for two successive weeks in the "Farmville Herald," and the Court being satisfied that the copy of said Muster Roll is as perfect as practicable to be made, doth order the same to be recorded as the law directs.   Teste: W. H. THACKSTON, Clerk.

———

Captain, John I. Thornton, elected Lieutenant-Colonel in 1862. Killed at the battle of Sharpsburg, 1862, while in command of the 3rd Regiment.

1st Lieutenant, Peyton R. Berkeley, elected to Captain in 1862. Resigned 1863.

2nd Lieutenant, H. I. Parrish. 2nd Lieutenant at organization; promoted to be "Aid De Camp," with rank of Captain; afterward Major, Lieutenant-Colonel, and Colonel of 16th Virginia Infantry.

2nd Lieutenant, F. D. Redd Retired at re-organizaion in 1862.

2nd Lieutenant, Richard Stokes. Retired in 1862.

1st Sergeant, E. N. Price, wounded at Five Forks in 1865.

2nd Sergeant, Jno. H. Knight, promoted to be 1st Lieutenant in 1863; Captain in 1864, wounded at the "White House."

3rd Sergeant, R B Berkeley. Transferred to Medical Department in 1863.

4th Sergeant, Frank H. Scott.

1st Corporal, L M. Penick.

2nd Corporal, R. W. Dalby.

3rd Corporal, A. B. Cralle.

4th Corporal, Daniel I. Allen.

Drury L. Armistead. Orderly for General Joseph E. Johnston.

Henry A. Allen.

Charles B. Anderson.

Frank C. Anderson.

H. Threat Anderson.

Charles I. Anderson.

Wesley W. Anderson.

M. L. Arvin, captured in the Valley.

James A. Baker.

John W. Baker, wounded at Front Royal in 1863, and Spottsylvania in 1864.

James A. Bell, elected Lieutenant in 1862; resigned in 1863.

Clifford A. Bondurant, wounded at Kelly's Ford in 1863.

Samuel J. Bondurant.

John J. Bondurant, discharged.

Samuel W Bondurant, put in substitute.

W. A. Binford.

George Booker.

J. Horace Booker.

William D. Booker.

A. A. Bragg, Quarter-Master Sergeant of the Company.

William Brooks.

Samuel A. Bruce.

William A. Bruce, orderly for Colonel Owen.

John Chaffin.

William T. Crafton.

John R. Cunningham, wounded at Kelly's Ford and disabled.

Charles E. Clark.

Charles W. Crawley.

John M. Daniel.

John P. Dickinson.

R. M. Dickinson, transferred to Infantry and promoted.

W. P. Dupuy, wounded at Buckland in 1863, and Tom's Brook in 1864.

Henry W. Edmunds, wounded and disabled at Kelly's Ford in 1863.

F. L. Elliott.

T. L. Elliott.

John W. Elliott.

R. C. Elliott, promoted to Sergeant and killed at Haws Shop in 1864.

William W. Evans, wounded at Front Royal in 1864.

W. H. Ewing, wounded at Front Royal in 1864.

John J. Ewing.

Charles Flournoy.

John J. Flournoy, wounded and discharged in 1863.

Thomas Flournoy, transferred.

Rolin Foster.

George W. Foster.

George Fowlkes.

James D. Fowlkes.

Lafayette Garrett, teamster.

J. H. Guthrie.

Johnson Harvey, killed at Sailor's Creek in 1865.

W. J. Harvey, transferred to Q. M Dept.

A. A. Haskins, promoted to Lieutenant in 1863.

Thomas E. Haskins, promoted to Orderly Sergeant in 1862.

John Z. Holladay.

George Hunt.

John C. Hunt, orderly to General Stuart and killed at Gettysburg.

Joby Hunt, wounded and lost a leg.

John Jenkins.

E. T. Jeffress, disabled and discharged.

Frank Jenkins.

John S. Kelley, a substitute. Captured in 1864.

E. S. Lockett.

Goodrich Ligon, died of camp fever in 1862.

R. V. Ligon.

George Nicholas, a substitute and deserted.

Charles Martin, professor at Hampden-Sidney. Promoted to Q. M. Dept.

H. I Meredith, captured at Boonsboro in 1862. Elected Lieutenant in 1863.

R. A. Miller.

B. M. Moseley.

W. H. Morton

Charles R. Moseley, transferred to Infantry.

F. J. Penick, wounded at Charles City in 1864.

Daniel Price.

B. H Ragsdall.

C. E. Redd, put in substitute.

John A. Redd.

John H. Redd.

Joseph T. Redd, discharged.

J Wesley Redd

R. L Redd

W. M. Richardson.

James C. Rowlett, wounded at Five Forks in 1865

John D. Richardson.

Junius C. Rowlett, lost a leg at Front Royal in 1864.

S S. Rowlett

Edwin Scott, killed on Picket near Newport News in 1861

Lafayette Scott, wounded at Kelley's Ford in 1863.

James C. Spencer, killed in Charles City county in 1864.

N. B Spencer.

J. D. Spencer.

L. A. Starling.

P. B. Sublett.

Charles B. Spencer.

Nat. Thackston, captured at Williamsport in 1863; wounded at Trevillians in 1864.

A. K. Todd.

W. C. Trueheart.

Charles Venable.

A. R. Venable, transferred to Q. M. Dept., and promoted to Captain.

John F. Walton.

L. D. Walton.

R. H. Walton.

R. H. Watkins, elected to Lieutenant in 1862; to Captain in 1863; wounded at Aldie in 1863; at Tom's Brook in 1864; disabled and retired.

Marcus West.

Oscar Wiley, transferred, 1861.

Jack C. Williams

James H. Wilson, killed at Haws Shop in 1864.

Ed Witt, captured the same day he enlisted.

A. C. Womack.

A. W. Womack, discharged.

D. G. Womack.

Eugene Womack, killed at Tom's Brook in 1864.

W. W. Womack, discharged.

Frank L. Womack.

Willie W. Wootton.

Samuel T. Wootten, wounded at Louisa Court House.

Thomas Watson.

Jimmy Womack, discharged.

Note: (The following series of articles regarding the experiences of Co. F, 18th Va. Regiment, in the war between the States, were written by "Captain" S. W. Paulett, of Farmville, Prince Edward county, known locally as the "Old Reb." who served throughout the war in that unit, and were published in the Farmville "Herald" during 1897. They form a most interesting, and at the same time a most valuable, history of that Company, and are well worth preserving.)

PLEASURES AROUND THE CAMP-FIRE— INTERESTING EXPERIENCES

Thinking it might be interesting to many of my old, as well as young friends, it has often occurred to me to write in my feeble way, an account of some of the scenes and incidents through which I passed, and was an actor, during my four years' service in the so-called "Rebel Army."

Today my mind seems ill at ease. I find it drifting back to the scenes of long ago; ever and anon I catch a faint glimpse of some little incident happening along our line of march, or while in camp. At this time one in particular looms up which I think will interest some of your many readers. Returning from North Carolina in May, 1863, my division, (Pickett's) was ordered to cross the Blackwater, surround, and make an effort to capture Suffolk, Va. We remained there a few days, when we were ordered to Petersburg, and thus began the long and weary march across the State of Virginia, and to Gettysburg, Pa. The incident recalled, and which I wish to portray, occurred while in camp near Hanover Junction. We had, on that day, made quite a long and weary march, and were glad indeed, to see the head of our column file left and enter a maple woods, where we would camp for the night. No one but those who participated in these stirring times have any idea how light-hearted the old Rebs were, both in camp and on the march. While many had their fun, yet Bob Miller, otherwise known as "Hootsy B," and the writer, alias, "Bonsy," were said to be the life of our company, being ready at all times, and in all places, to carry out some devilment to relieve the tedious hours as they passed.

Now, in our company, there was a well-known character by name of Obediah East, who was always ready for fun and frolic, and also one of our best soldiers. It was on this individual we had set our hearts on this occasion. I can recall him now, with his short-stem pipe, sitting quietly by himself near his shake-down, before retiring to obtain the much needed rest all old soldiers know so well how to enjoy. Sitting thus, and anticipating the good night's rest, he is startled by the approach of two striplings, namely, Bob and Sam. Obediah knows something is up. The two quietly take their seats just opposite him, and they too light their pipes and begin to smoke. Not a word has been spoken. Obediah becomes restless, uncomfortable; he is satisfied we are there for a purpose; he can stand it no longer; so he jumps up and says "Fetch take it all, what did you two little devils come here for?" "To give you a gentle army drag tonight, old boy," is the reply. "I am blamed if you do. I's gwine to set up all night." "All right, if you can stand it, we can." So silence once more falls on the three, while others are watching to see what the two little devils are up to. The striplings hold the fort. After many hours, Obediah falls back and draws his blanket closely about him.

The two little devils are now wide awake and all attention, awaiting the sound they knew was soon to follow. Soon the snore, deep and loud, is heard; the time has come; the little ones are up and ready for the fun. "Hoots," says Sam, "get him by the other leg." Hoots gets his hand under the blanket, when he is startled by Obediah saying, "Take your hand outen dar, I ain't sleep yet." So the boys fall back and bide their time, knowing full well the time will come, for Obediah is tired and sleepy.

Another hour has passed and Obediah begins to twitch, squirm, and cry out. We now know the time has come, and throwing the blanket off, we each take a leg and start on the run down the hill toward the river, Obediah following like greased lightning in our wake, and making every effort to break away, but the two little devils have him good and fast, and take him nearly to the river and drop him a hundred yards from the starting point. We then ran for our lives, fully expecting rock, stick, and oath; we are surprised to hear Obediah crying in a loud voice: "Fetch take it all, I am d—n glad you dragged me, I had one of them blamed things on me," meaning he had a night-mare, which he was subject to all during the war.

Mr. Editor, of such is army life, and it affords old soldiers much pleasure to review the many pleasant hours spent around the camp-fires. But as we review them, they all remind us of the solemn fact that the story of our lives will soon be finished. Since 1865 how rapidly have our comrades, who sat with us around those camp-fires, passed out into the shadowy night. 'Tis a sad thought, yet true. The ranks are thinning. Soon the last survivor of those times will be gone out; darkness will fall; and that scene of tremendous activity, and terrible reality to us, be only as a silent memory of the past.

Now my old comrades, you who may read this, penned by one of your kind, let it remind you as we linger on the border land, and as we assemble around our last camp-fire with the sunset in our faces, we may listen in silence and hear the ripple of the mystic river over which we soon must pass, and, as with our noble leader, Stonewall Jackson, and with the faith that ever shone brightly with him, we may say as he did, "Let us pass over the river and rest under the shade of the trees."　　Fraternally, the old Reb.

S. W. PAULETT,
Co. F, 18th Va. Regiment.

THE BATTLE OF GETTYSBURG AND OTHER THRILLING INCIDENTS INTERESTINGLY NARRATED

With your permission, and for the benefit of your many readers, I will continue to give some of my recollections of the war.

June, 1863, found us in camp near Hanover Junction. At this time the Federal Army under General Hooker, re-occupied the heights opposite Fredericksburg, where it could not be attacked except under very great disadvantage, so our great and notable leader determined not to await the pleasure of "Old Fighting Joe," but to draw him out from his impregnable position.

General Lee determined, if possible, to free Virginia, for a time at least, from the presence of the enemy, to trans-fer the theatre of war to the northen soil, and, by selecting a favorable time and place, to take the reasonable chances of defeating his adversary in a pitched battle. To that end. and in pursuance of that design, General Lee, early in the month of June, moved his army northward by way of Cul-pepper, and thence to, and down the valley of Virginia, to Winchester.

The army had now been reorganized, designated the first, second, and third corps, and commanded respectively by Lieut.-Gen'ls Longstreet, Ewell, and A. P. Hill. On the 12th of June, the second corps being in advance, crossed the branches of the Shenandoah, near Front Royal. Coming in contact with the enemy under General Milroy, he proceeded in his usual manner to attack, gave them a good thrashing, captured a great many, and the remnant sought safety be-hind the works at Harper's Ferry. General Ewell, with three divisions, crossed the Potomac in the latter part of June, and, in pursuance of General Lee's orders, traversed Mary-land, and advanced into Pennsylvania. General Hill, whose corps were the last to leave the line of the Rappahannock, followed with his three divisions in Ewell's rear. My division, (Pickett's) was attached to the first, or Longstreet's, corps, and it is of this particular division which I shall deal in this paper.

Breaking camp at Hanover Junction, the division was formed and headed for Culpeper C. H., from which point we moved by way of Ashby's and Snicker's Gaps into the Valley. By this move we covered the movements of the second and third corps which had preceded us. Here we left General Stuart the task of holding the Gaps of the Blue Ridge mountains with his corps of cavalry, and we passed down the Valley and into Williamsport, when we crossed the Potomac into Maryland. Here an incident, which I recall, occurred.

Just after the battle of Fredericksburg, a substitute belonging to Co. E, 18th Regiment, deserted. He was captured, brought back, court-marshalled, and ordered to be shot. This man's name was Rhiley. For some cause the sentence of the court had not been executed up to this time, but we knew Rhiley would be shot before sunset on this day. After crossing the river, the head of the division was turned to the right into an open field where it was formed into three sides of a square, and the orders given, parade, rest, and we waited the coming of the doomed man. Soon the band struck up the dead march, and from the right was seen approaching, 1st, the band; 2nd, the coffin borne by four men; 3rd, Rhiley: 4th, and last, the detail of twelve men who constituted the firing party. This procession, and in this order, marched around the three sides of the square until they reached the fourth, or open side; here they halted. Now was seen the stake to which the prisoner would be tied. The officer in command advanced and taking Rhiley by the hand, he conducted him to the stake, ordered him to kneel so that his back rested against the stake, he was then tied and blind-folded. The firing party now advanced to within ten paces and made ready to do their duty. Guns were loaded and capped, the officer gave the command, "ready"——. At this Rhiley raised his head and said, "Good-bye boys, aim at my heart." At the command "fire" the guns spoke out in no uncertain sound and Rhiley had passed in his checks. The grave had already been prepared, his body was placed therein and we camped for the night.

The next day we passed through Hagerstown and headed for Chambersburg, Pennsylvania, which place we reached on or about the 27th of June. Here we remained until the morning of the 2nd day of July. The battle of Gettysburg began on the 1st, but we knew nothing of this, as General Hill, with the 3rd corps, held our advance in that direction, and was concentrating his corps at Cashtown, with Heath's division thrown forward toward Gettysburg. Just about break of day on the morning of the 2nd, the long roll sounded in our camps, ranks were formed, rolls called, and we moved through Chambersburg and on to Gettysburg. It was a hard march, as we were moving rapidly forward to aid the 2nd and 3rd corps then engaged with our old enemy, the army of the Potomac, commanded by General George C. Meade; fighting Joe Hooker having been relieved and laid on the shelf. Owing to a wagon train belonging to the 3rd corps cutting in ahead of us and the pike being filled with beef cattle which had been captured and sent to the rear, our march was retarded. Thus delayed, we did not reach the field as quickly as we otherwise would have done. We camped near Gettysburg and cooked rations, but began the march again long before day on the morning of the 3rd. I would say between 6 and 8 o'clock we arrived at, and took up our position, along, Seminary Ridge. The division was placed in line of battle as follows: Kemper's brigade on the right; Garnett's (my brigade) on the left; Armistead's brigade just in rear of the two first, and in supporting distance. Our 4th brigade; Corse's; was left in Virginia.

After the boys had been lined up they were ordered to lie down. At this time, everything was so quiet none but those who would participate in this death grapple would have thought there was a hundred men within a mile. Yet along those lines there were, of the Yankee army, one hundred and five thousand men, and of General Lee's army, sixty-two thousand. Just think of it, the audacity of 62,-000 men making that glorious and daring attack on 105,000, and on ground of their own selection! Yet the charge was made and failed. General Meade was afraid to follow up his success. Notwithstanding our failure on the 3rd, General Lee held the field all day on the 4th in absolute quiet, and withdrew from their front without serious molestation. General Sickles testified before the committee on the conduct of the war, that the reason the Confederates were not followed up was on account of differences of opinion whether or not the Federals would retreat, as it was by no means clear in the judgment of the corps-commanders, or of the General in command, whether they had won or not. If we had had 75,000 men there would have been no doubt in General Meade's mind as to who had won.

But to resume my story, being always of an inquisitive turn of mind, and wishing to know all that was going on in sight, I took occasion during this lull, to view the ground and surroundings. I tell you the sight was not an encouraging one! In our immediate front, say distant three-fourths of a mile, was that strong position, known in history as Cemetery Heights. This position, though strong by nature, had been made doubly so by the erection of breast-works, behind which men of all arms, and in great numbers, were stationed to slap the life out of us gentle Rebs as we crossed that open field, without shelter to hide the size of a man's head. Now, look to our right, and there stands Little Round Top Mountain; a giant indeed, crowned with artillery and infantry, ready as we advanced, to pour death

and destruction into our ranks. After taking a general survey, and noting the difficult and dangerous path we must
travel in order to reach those Yanks, my heart almost failed
me, and my hair and hat began to rise as I thought, "Can
we win?" Then turning to the company, I said: "This is
going to be a heller, prepare for the worst." Oh, no; this
remark created no laugh! The boys had looked and seen for
themselves! They knew that many of us had answered our
last roll-call, and no doubt asked themselves, "Is it me?"
or "Is it I," but none can tell. Soon the signal gun is fired,
and never before or since, has such artillery thunder been
heard. This continued for about two hours, then came down
the line the simple word, "Attention"; the boys sprang to
their feet, reeling from the effects of the hot July sun, but
soon they became steady, and the line was ready to face and
charge the mighty host of men and guns on Cemetery
Heights. At this time Gen. Pickett rode in front of our brigade, (he having been our former commander) and raising
hmiself in his stirrups, he pointed to the Heights, and said:
"Boys, you see that battery; I want you to take those guns.
Remember you are Virginians." Forward! The line moved
out at quick step. Passing through our line of artillery, we
made for the Heights. Our line being in full view from
the start, the Yanks opened on us with round shot, then
shell. Nearing the Emmittsburg road Little Round Top on
our right, having enfilade fire, opened with shell, which
tore great gaps in our line; sometimes as much as 30 feet
of men would go down from the effect of one shell! Did the
boys falter? No; the order would come: "Close to the right,
boys," and, continuing the advance, the gap would be closed!
A few yards farther on, and the batteries in front opened
with grape and cannister, mowing the boys down by the
hundred. Does this stop the living? No; the advance continues, but the worst is yet to come. Their infantry had
reserved their fire until we were within 30 yards of their

works, then with round shot and shell, grape and cannister, pistol and musket; it seemed that heaven and earth had come together with a mighty crash; the earth trembled; men fell to rise no more; and in a few moments the pride of Virginia manhood had burned their last powder!

Official report puts our loss at 3,333 men! The Farmvill Guard had the following killed and wounded: Killed—Bryant; Elam; Davis; Hooton; Hunt; Setzer; and Worsham. Wounded—Captain Z. A. Blanton; East; Gilliam; Paulett, J. T.; Paulett.S W.; Wicker; and Walthall. Here I was captured with others of my company, and carried to the rear of the Yankee army, so, for the present, my connection with the army of northern Virginia had ceased.

A few days ago Bob Miller met me on the street and asked if I remembered what passed between us on the field just after being captured I told him no. He said he came up to me while we were under fire of our own guns, then shelling the Heights, and asked me what had become of the boys, and I replied: "Hootsy, damned if I know." This to shown how utterly unconscious of fear boys became in war. Here I will close this, and if you so desire at some future time, I will narrate some of my prison experiences.

LIFE IN THE YANKEE PRISONS—THE HARDSHIPS INTERESTINGLY RECALLED

FARMVILLE, VA., MAY 25, '97.

In compliance with my promise in my last communication, I will now take up the thread of my story, and relate some of my experiences while a prisoner of war.

In my last I stated that I was captured in Pickett's charge at Gettysburg, and that for the nonce my connection with the army of Northern Virginia had ceased in the field.

On the night of July 3rd, after the battle, I, with many others who had been captured, was taken to the rear of the Federal army and put in camp, now strongly guarded by both infantry and cavalry. General Kilpatrick, a Yankee cavalry officer, rode in our midst and proclaimed in a very excited manner, that we must keep quiet, and that any attempt to escape would be met with death on the spot Under the circumstances, this was hardly necessary, inasmuch as were tired and worn out by hard fighting and marching

On the morning of the 4th, we were formed in line and ordered to march, guarded by their cavalry. Some hours' march brought us to a small town some distance in the rear of the Yankee army. Here we found General Stuart had been the day before with some of his cavalry. Owing to this fact, the cavalry guarding us became very uneasy, for fear that General Stuart would make a sudden dash and recapture us. The Old Rebs were highly elated at the prospect and prayed as they marched that Stuart would come, but our hopes were vain; it was not to be.

The next point reached, as I remember, was Westminister, Maryland, at which place we arrived during the afternoon of the 4th. Here, for the first time, we were given something to eat. We were marched into an open field surrounded by a high fence, outside of which the guards were stationed. I made a raid and succeeded in stealing a large ham, which we enjoyed very much The rain was now coming down in torrents; no shelter; no blankets; no oil clothes; we were indeed in a pitiable condition as we stood in this weather, looking as best we could while the rations were issued. A worse looking set of men I never in all my life beheld. Tired and worn; ragged and dirty; wet and hungry; surrounded by our enemies, and gazed at by the curious town people who had left their comfortable homes in order to see what we Rebs looked like, was a sad sight and engendered feelings long to be remembered Here we remained during the night of the 4th, sleeping in the mud and mire like so many hogs.

On the morning of the 5th we were put in the cars and started for Baltimore. Reaching that point just about dark, we were taken off and marched through the streets of the city to Fort McHenry, when we were placed in the open ground around the fort without food or shelter. I thought it had rained at Westminister, but it was only a drop out of the bucket. Here the clouds seemed to reverse themselves, turning bottom-side up, spilling all the water from on high. In this condition, and in this weather, we remained during the night. No rations ever issued, and the poor old Rebs slept as best they could, being hungry and cold, with no shelter or bedding of any kind.

On the morning of the 6th, rations of coffee, hard tack, and meat were issued. This made us more comfortable and we began to feel like men once more. My recollection is that we remained at Fort McHenry during the day and night of the 6th. Here I will insert the names of my company who were with me at that time: R. D. Miller; S. B. Partin; J. J. Riggins; J. W. Foster. Richard Thackston joined us later.

On the morning of the 7th we were placed on board a steamer and taken to Fort Delaware, then under command of General Scheopf. Landed at the fort, another new experience had to be encountered. We were formed in double rank, open order, and ordered to remove our shoes from our feet! I thought, can this be holy ground? But I was soon to find out. Soon a detail of Yankees came down the line searching each Reb as they passed, confiscating all money, or other contrabrand of war, found in their possession. I did not have one cent and doubt if the clothes on my back would have sold for that sum. Here a roll of the prisoners was made up; names were listed and to what command we belonged, and from what State we came. We were then put in barracks and our prison life began in reality.

Miller, Partin, Riggins, Foster, and myself, were placed in the old barracks. To those barracks were attached a mess, or eating hall, where we obtained our GRUB. As the northern people have seen fit to cry down the way we fed the Yankee prisoners on this side, and to praise the manner in which we, the rebel prisoners, were looked after along this line on their side, I will here insert our daily bill of fare, for the benefit of the hungry: Our breakfast consisted of one cup of warm water called coffee, and made from the grounds used in the Yankee hospital, redried, barreled and sent to us; one and a half hard-tack or cracker, sometimes alive with little living worms; one-fourth of a pound of beef or pork Now for dinner! Remember we got only two meals a day! Same quantity hard-tack as for breakfast; and about one pint of what they called soup, made sometimes from potatoes, then cabbage, and again from carrots. A few of these were thrown into a large kettle of water in which beef or pork had been boiled, and was then served to us as first-class soup, fit for "the gods," but I have seen my hogs have better. I was in their hands for about six months, and to my recollection, this bill of fare never changed! Yet, I thank them for so much; it kept life in me and gave me strength to return to Dixie and feed back to them lead through my musket barrel!

To resume. There occurred many incidents at Fort Delaware prison which I recall; too many in fact, and for fear of tiring your readers, I will only state a few.

Rations being light, the first thing to look after was how to procure more. So I began to spy around in our mess hall. This hall contained eleven tables, at each of which one hundred men could stand. The mode of feeding was as follows: When breakfast or dinner was ready, a Yankee Sergeant would come out in front of the hall and announce the fact by crying out, "Fall in for Breakfast," or "Dinner," as the case might be. The Rebs would form in double rank, march to the door through which they passed in single file. This door was in the end of the building, and facing table No 1. As the Rebs marched in, the first man halted at the first tin plate, while the other passed to his rear, the second man halted at plate No 2, and so on until the eleven tables were filled. Noting this mode of procedure, Miller, Partin, and myself, always made it a point to fall in line on the outside so as to reach the middle of table No. 1. After getting to our plates we would exchange our coffee for a cracker, with some Reb, or else leave it This was done by crying out. "Here is your cup of coffee for a cracker." The exchange made, we looked out for the Yankee Sergeant, and when his head was turned, we would again enter the line as it was passing in our rear, and fetch up at the next table. Here the coffee was disposed of as before and we would again enter the line. We sometimes succeeded in getting to all the tables, thus getting the crackers intended for 33 men. Of course these men had to be fed! The Yanks knew that some Reb was stealing, but catching is before hanging, everything 'cept a fish. We had been here but a short while before we had hard-tack enough to stave off hunger.

Walking out on the levee one day I found my chum, Bob, in a bad fix. A Yankee guard had him on the double quick at the point of the bayonet, trotting up and down the levee I called out: "Hello, Hootsy B, what's up now?" He shook his head, said not a word, but as in the old song, he had to push along, keep moving. After about two hours of this work, the Yank turned him loose, and he told me the Yanks had caught him at one of our tricks and took him in charge. Well, I promised not to tell on him when we got home, so you must guess the trick.

One interesting place on the island was known as "Devil's Green." Here all manner of gambling was carried on. Some betting money, some crackers, and others tobacco. To illustrate, we will visit the Keno table. Here we found fifteen or twenty men sitting around the dealer, each having in front of him a card on which are three lines of figures, four figures on each line. Before the game begins each man puts up his chew of tobacco, the dealer draws a figure and crys out, the person having that figure would cover it with chip or button. The call continues, and figures covered, until one of the players has the four figures on the same line covered, when he tells the news by crying out "keno on top," "middle," or "bottom" line, as the case may be. He has won all the "chaws" in the pool, each puts up again, and the game continues as before. From early morn until late at night, the "Devil's Green" was full of men betting at some one of the games there displayed

Bob Miller and I had no money, so we were always pie-rooting around to see what we could pick up, owned by some other fellow. On one of these outings we each succeeded in hooking a hook and line. Call it stealing if you will, but remember soldiers don't steal, they only pick up what they need when it can be found and the other fellow ain't looking.

Having hard-tack in abundance, we proceeded to fish for meat. At one point in the bay all the slops from the mess hall were emptied. To this spot we went, and very soon had as many cat fish as we wanted. Ask any old Fort Delaware prisoner to tell you about the cat caught on Delaware Bay, his answer will interest you.

At this time we were not permitted to write to any northern friend for money. Going out to the water tank one night, I found a nice Yank on guard. I struck up a conversation with him, and unfolded my poor and penniless condition. After talking some time he agreed that I might write to some of father's friends in Baltimore asking for a little money, and he would forward it. You bet I wrote that letter without delay! Some days after this, a Yankee came in our barracks and hunted me up. He escorted me to Lieutenant Wolf, who was the meanest Yankee I ever saw. He questioned me very closely, trying to find out how I got my letter out, but he failed. Then he wished to know who I knew in Baltimore. I gave him the names of several parties, and among them, that of Messrs. Straus, Hartman, Hoflin & Co. Those were the gentlement who sent me the money. Finally, Lieut Wolf said: "Well I guess you are the man, or rather boy." I said: "Lieutenant, you can call me what you choose here, but I want you to know I can stand in a man's shoes when in Dixie." He then sent me under guard to the fort in which was Gen. Scheopf's office. The General was not in when I arrived, so I employed my time in looking at the pictures, of which there were many, hanging on the walls. His private secretary was writing at his desk and said to me· "Johnnie, you had better take off your hat." I informed him that "Johnnies" when at home did not take off their hats when in the General's office. He smiled, said no more, and continued his writing. I had almost forgotten where I was, so busy was I in looking at the pictures Pretty soon I heard the door open, and some one in a loud, hard voice said: "Take off your hat, sir." I turned and recognized the General. No talking back now; my hat came off in double quick time, and under my arm it went I knew the time had come, and hats off was in order. The General asked me many questions along the line in which Wolf had gone over, but he got no more information than Wolf did. He then ordered his secretary to give me an order on the Sutler for fifteen dollars. I was sent under guard to the Sutler's place of business. This man refused to give me money, but gave me the amount in 5, 10 and 25 cent Sutler tickets. On my return to barracks I placed myself near the Sutler's window and soon had my checks or tickets converted into Uncle Sam's green-backs. Chum and I were now in the swim. We bought of the Sutler baker's bread and golden syrups. Could you have seen us licking in that soft bread, and those lasses, after eating hard-tack, pork and carrots for so long, it would have done your heart good.

Among the Yankees here, there was one to whom the Rebs had given the name of "Hack Out." His duty was to look after and keep things straight in barracks. He obtained his name in the following manner: While making his rounds some old Reb would get in his way, when he would squall out: "Hack out of this" Some of us remember the many little acts of kindness done for us by this old man while we were prisoners at Fort Delaware. Come down, Hack Out, to see us; we will be delighted to repay you an hundred fold. Old Hack was a particular friend of mine, telling me often that I ought to be at home tied to my mother's apron strings I don't suppose at that time I weighed ninety pounds.

About this time they began to erect hospitals on the island. The lumber for this purpose had to be carried on men's shoulders from the wharf across the island for half a mile. The Rebs were detailed to do this work, for which they received three meals per day of soft bread, meat, coffee, and soup, in addition each man received a small piece of tobacco.

Old "Hack Out" made me a Sergeant, and gave me thirty men. My duty was very light; I remained at the wharf to see that each man carried his allotted number of turns before each meal. At this wharf the steamer Oseola landed every day, bringing the mail and passengers for the fort. Being here every day, and seeing the people aboard this steamer, it struck me that some money might be made. On my return to barracks I went among the Rebs who were making fans, rings, tooth picks, and many other articles. I succeeded in buying a nice lot for a very small sum. Next morning on the arrival of the steamer, I called attention to the wares made by the Johnnies, and to my surprise and delight, found no difficulty in selling out at a big profit Some of the ladies did not even ask the price. All they wanted was some article made by a rebel prisoner. I sold one lady a locomotive for the sum of twenty-five dollars. I carried on this business so long as I remained at the fort Chum and I lived on the fat of the land.

One very great drawback here was the vermin. Never before in the history of man, was there so many lice on the same number of men! They were in our clothes, on the blankets on the bunks, in every crack and crevice, on the roof, on the ground; in a word, they were everywhere! One of our boys seemed to be sweet meat for them. I'll not call his name, for he is now living. He had them to perfection. When "taps" was sounded at night for lights out, he could be seen taking off his shirt and turning it wrong side out. About twelve o'clock he would get up and go through the same performance. After a while our curiosity was aroused, and we asked why he did in this manner. He replied: "I am flanking these d—n lice; while they are going around, I am sleeping." You now see how smart he was; every time he turned his shirt he placed the lice on the outside, and, in order to get at his meat again, they had to perform the flanking act.

With my last communication I fully intended to discontinue my description of prison life and enter again the field where the army was doing actual work, but since its appearance, many of your readers, and among them many of our oldest citizens, have requested me to continue the narration   With your permission I will now continue to do so.

To describe to the uninitiated the lights and shadows of prison life is indeed a hard task and should only be attempted by one whose descriptive powers are far above mine. I shall do the best I can, hoping to please some of your readers. I learn that some of my lady friends object to some of my sayings; for instance they think the "Kuss words" and "Louse story" might have been left unsaid. They seem to forget that I am trying to give a truthful narration of incidents happening in a varied prison life, and, to record them properly it must be done in order, and just as they occurred.

During the month of August the heat at Fort Delaware was very oppressive, in fact almost unbearable. The barracks had but few windows, and these were placed on line with the first, or lower row of bunks. We who occupied the second, or upper row, received but little air from these. Miller and I determined to cut a small window just at the head of our bunk. We knew that the guard had orders to shoot any prisoner caught doing this sort of work, but this did not deter us The guard's beat was not twenty feet from where we would do the cutting; we had decided to have air from some point. The boys near us objected to our cutting saying, some of us would be killed. We paid no attention to them and began the work. We selected a plank about twelve inches wide, and with our pocket knives proceeded to cut an opening about ten by twelve inches.   While one was cutting the other would watch the guard, whose beat was nearly under where we were at work. Finally we cut nearly through and notified the boys to get out, which they did in double-quick time This left the ground clear for the guard to shoot. We procured a stout stick, and getting as far from the piece to be knocked out as possible, we gave it a quick, hard thrust, and ran for our lives. It was well we did, for the piece had scarcely touched the ground before the guard raised his rifle and fired at the hole in the wall. It is needless to tell you he did no damage, except to the barracks, as all the "Johnnies" had left, and gone where the Whang-doodle mourneth and the conscript officer cometh not. We had made all our preparations for this shot, and got out of the way. Knowing old Hack-out would be around trying to find out who did the cutting, we did not venture back for several hours. We had fresh air, and did not serve our time in a dungeon under the fort, as would have been the case had we been caught.

Fort Delaware is a large fort situated on an island in Delaware Bay, just opposite Delaware City, and about 1¾ miles from the Delaware, and 2½ miles from the New Jersey shore. Of course the water surrounding it is at all times very brackish and not at all drinkable. I remember that at one time we were forced to drink that or nothing. Drinking water used for prisoners, was hauled by a water boat from the Brandywine river to the Island and then pumped into large wooden tanks by forcing it with a small engine such as we use here for fire purposes The tanks were very large and placed outside the barracks Sometimes before the water could be consumed it became very hot, as there was no protection from the sun During this time, green slime, such as we see on our frog ponds, or stagnant pools of water, would often form two inches thick on the water in these tanks. Five or six faucets were placed at intervals around the bottom of these tanks from which we drew our drinking water. At one time some accident happened to the water boat, and before it could be remedied, we consumed all our drinking water, and General Scheopf, in the kindness of his heart, permitted us to use water from the reservoir under the fort. We drank this so low there would soon be none left for the garrison, and the General called a halt. Our only resort for water now was

that in the Bay, which we procured in the following manner:
We would take several canteens, and swim some distance out
in the Bay, uncork the canteens, dive down as near the bottom as we could and permit them to fill. Thus we obtained
water a little cooler than that at the surface, but just as salt.
This we drank for several days, and, from its effects there was
scarcely a well man among the seven thousand prisoners on
the Island! This was enough to kill us, but there was another enemy entering the fold. We had withstood the storms
of battle, the long march, and the hardships of prison life,
now we were to undergo another trial. Small-pox put in its
appearance, and the poor boys had to succumb to that dread
disease, and many there were who found their last resting
place in the State of New Jersey, far from home and kindred.
The place selected to bury these poor fellows was in New
Jersey, just opposite the fort. Many times have I been to
the wharf where the dead were placed to be taken over, and
found from eight to twenty-three dead men, all of whom had
died during the preceding twenty-four hours! This was not
the case only one or two days, but for many days. No doubt
a scene such as this would touch the hearts of many of my
youthful readers, but on us, whose hearts were hardened, it
made no impression. Dead men were no rarity to us, scarcely a day passed that we did not see one, often one hundred,
and sometimes thousands! What man could behold these
sights and not become callous where even the dead were concerned? So dead to fear had we become, I believe if dead
bodies had been piled as so many railroad sills to the height
of six feet, an old Reb would not hesitate, in order to get
off the damp ground, to spread his blanket and oil-cloth on
the pile and sleep as quietly and as peacefully as any of my
readers do now in their feather beds!

The barracks at the Fort were built in a hollow square
with a sally-port on two sides; leading to these was a plank
walk-way three feet wide. These were used by the prisoners

to keep out of the mud, which consisted of a black, slimy, salty substance, in which it would not do to walk barefooted. Remember, not one in a hundred of these seven thousand had shoes on their feet, and any who ventured in this mud without shoes lived to regret it. Their feet would turn blood-red, and after a few days, burst wide open, exposing the bone and sinew; intense suffering followed and many died from this cause alone.

While on the wharf one day, I purchased a water-melon and carried it in for Bob and I to enjoy. We took it out on the canal, a dirty pool of water, and then cut and ate it. We had nearly finished when a "tar heel" prisoner came along, and, eyeing the rind, he opened up as follows: "Say, mister, can't you give me that ar rind for a sick man?" We told him no, we did not wish to kill the sick man. For fear that he would eat it if left on the bank, we put our muddy feet all over it, and threw it in the canal. We went off a little way and watched him Soon he procured a stick, fished out the rind and ate the last bit of it.

Our stay at Fort Delaware was now fast drawing to its close. For several days the rumor had been afloat that we would soon be exchanged and sent back to Dixie. During the month of October the names of seventeen hundred prisoners were taken, as we thought for exchange. Among this number was Partin, Miller, Foster, Reggin, and myself. Early one morning we were placed aboard the transport steamer, "Philadelphia," weighed anchor, and steamed out of the bay. The men were packed like sardines in a box. When we struck old ocean many became deathly sick. I need not tell you what they did; if you have ever been sea-sick you know. The steamer was short of hands and, not knowing what else to do, I volunteered, and took a hand at hauling the lines. This gave me the privilege of the upper deck among the sailors. I had some green-backs and very soon bought from one of the sailors a quart of good old rye. You bet I was now in the swim in good earnest. I went below where Hootsy and Partin were, and offered them a smell out of the quart. They refused, saying they had more in their stomachs than they could contain. I thought so too after hearing them call "york" a few times. We had a very rough passage. The boys did not seem to mind it much as we were "gwine back to Dixie." Alas for our hopes, the Yanks had fooled us. They were merely transferring us from one prison to another! One morning about light, the old transport came to anchor, and we found ourselves in the Potomac river just off Point Lookout, Maryland. Here we disembarked, and, after being searched from head to foot, as at Fort Delaware, were placed in the bull pen and again took up prison life. The place selected for this prison is on a point of land between the Potomac river and Chesapeake Bay, known as Point Lookout, Maryland. This prison differed from Fort Delaware in many respects. There was no fort or barracks. The prison consisted of a number of acres of land between the river and the bay. These acres were enclosed by a straight up and down fence about sixteen feet high Near the top of this fence was a parapet on which the guards were stationed, say every twenty feet apart. Near the main gate was a battery of artillery so placed as to comb the entire camp with grape and cannister should it become necessary to do so The prison was laid off nicely by streets, along which tents were erected, in which from ten to twenty Rebs were placed for shelter. The boys were formed into companies and divisions. Ours was company B, division seven. Roll was called night and morning to see if any Johnnie had, by hook or crook, made his escape. At meal times each man fell in with his own company and marched to the mess hall where he got his cup of hot water and his hard-tack. We found to our sorrow that we could not flank rations here as at Fort Delaware. The Yanks had placed Rebs in charge of the cook-houses and, for fear of los-

ing so fat a job, they watched us closely, thus many times
we left the mess hall hungry. The drinking water here was
terrible. The wells were sunk in camp, and, being between
the river and bay, both of which at this point are salty, we
obtained water not fit for human beings to drink. It tasted
as if a quantity of Sulphate of Iron had been put in each
gallon. The effect of this water on our poor old Rebs can
be better imagined than described.

During November and the part of December while I
was at Point Lookout the cold was intense. The winds storms
coming across the bay loaded with fine snow and hail, found
us poorly provided against its attacks. The boys each had
but a single blanket with which to cover, and they would lie
down in huddles like so many hogs in a bed, draw the blanket
about them as best they could, shiver and cuss, groan and
pray, until morning, when the sun, in a measure, would warm
them up again. But, you ask, why didn't we keep our fires
going? Let me answer you by telling you how we obtained
the little fuel we had. One hundred men under guard, were
permitted to leave camp by the main gate, and were marched
about a mile up the point, where there was a lot of small
dead pine. This the boys would break up and take as much
as they could carry on their shoulders, and march back to
camp. This detail of one hundred men consisted of one man
from each tent, and the wood he brought back must last
that tent for twenty-four hours The Yanks may have done
better after I left them, but, remember, I am giving you
my personal experience. I remember being on this detail
one morning, and we had all assembled at the main gate on
the inside, thereby blocking the way out right much. Soon
a Yankee officer, "Capt. Sides," who was on the inside, and
wishing to go out, rode in among us. We being so crowded,
could not open up the way fast enough for him, angered
him. Without a word he drew his pistol and fired into the
crowd. The Rebs scattered as best they could, and ran for

their lives. However, before the way could be cleared, he succeeded in killing two, and wounded three of the boys. Every shot counted and found its mark, and yet the officer who did the shooting was never punished on earth that I knew of, but I do hope the devil got him at last and put him in the North-east corner at the bottom of the bottomless pit, there to remain. So mote it be.

Rations were very nearly as "scase" as wood Bob and I decided to pie-root and see what could be done along that line. We hunted the camp over but found nothing to lift. We now turned our attention to the bay. About one mile from shore there was an oyster bed, from which large quantities of oysters were gathered daily for market. The water over the beds was quite deep and the oystermen gathered them by using long handled tongs. While grappling with the tongs they would loosen a great many, which on account of the tide and restless motion of the water, would float shoreward. I determined to capture a few of these stray fellows and if possible secure a mess for chum and me. To think with me was to act. I wanted some of those bivalves badly. Mess pork and boiled carrots had about put me through, and a change of diet was about necessary Here was the chance and I took advantage of it. Calling Bob to book we proceeded to plan the battle. He was in, but not for going into the water. Said he was thin (and he is yet), and that his blood was poor, but that if I would go he would look after all that I caught and threw out. Darn his hide, he was no thinner than I, nor was my blood any richer than his, it was the cold water he was afraid of. But I agreed to lead the advance force, and proceeded to line up for a battle. Remember, this was the month of December, with the thermometer out o' sight. It was so cold that the water for ten feet from the shore was nothing but a perfect loblolly of powdered ice. This pack was about ten feet wide by about four feet thick. Nothing daunted, however, I stripped off my clothes and plunged in head foremost. If any man succeeds in reaching the North Pole, and becomes any colder than I for a few minutes after striking that ice, he will, I am sure, be converted into a solid block of northern ice. After getting through the ice, and reaching open water, I struck out swimming, and lay out about twenty yards from shore. I now stood erect and began to tread water, my whole body submerged up to my neck. When an oyster would float by me, I would go under, fetch it up, and throw it to Bob on shore. Thus for an hour or more I have remained in the water, sometimes catching more oysters than a half dozen hungry Rebs could eat When I came out I would again pass through this slush of ice. On reaching shore my poor little body would be blue and shriveled, my hands half closed and resembling hawk's claws After dressing I would get in the sunshine until Hootsey B. could boil the oysters, bringing me some with hot soup, as he called it, which was nothing but hot water flavored with the oyster. We had none of the ingredients with which to make a stew, so we boiled them. Permit me to say I have never since eaten any I thought half so good I made many trips in the bay after oysters. Although Bob was very much afraid of water, he was not so of the oysters. He would stick to the camp kettle so long as one remained at the bottom. I never begrudged anything I had to him, nor he to me We were chums indeed, always dividing what we had, yet he had the best of me, poor fellow, his legs were hollow and had to be filled first. Sometimes he would look like a grave-yard deserter, but fill him up with any kind of provender and he was ready to fight the whole Yankee nation, foreigners thrown in.

About the first of December my clothes had become very ragged and I had no shirt on my back. My little roundabout was so dilapidated it would scarcely hang on my shoulders. I was in a freezing condition. Many times have I walked about camp bareback, without shirt or coat, with a cold north-west wind blowing at the rate of fifty miles an hour, accompanied by snow, hail, or fine sleet. This, falling upon my naked back, caused a smart, tingling sensation, but, strange to say, I did not mind it. I was not very cold and never made an effort to shun the weather, no matter how cold or wet. I don't remember having a bad cold, or being sick in any way while in prison.

I wrote again to my good friends, Straus, Hartman, Hoflin & Co., of Baltimore requesting them to send me some clothes. They sent me a nice warm suit and other belongings, among which were two nice grey flannel shirts. I was very proud of the shirts and hastened to put one on. I soon found I could not wear it in any comfort, as my back had been so long without covering it seemed as if the shirt would burn it up. I felt as if a thousand sharp needles were sticking in me. I stood it for several hours then pulled it off and sold it to Davis, one of our tent mates, for the sum of five dollars Confederate money. I was afraid to try the other one, and laying it away, turned my back out to graze once more, and went about as before. Being out one cold, bitter night, between one and two o'clock, I ran across a hospital steward, who, seeing my back without coat or shirt, called and asked if I had a shirt. I told him no, which was a lie, but answered my purpose. I wanted two shirts. He invited me down to the hospital tent and gave me a beautiful percale shirt. I immediately put it on. Being of a different texture it did not worry me as did the flannel. By this means I again became accustomed to a shirt and continue to wear one to this date.

You can bet I was always on the lookout for some chance to make my escape and hoping the time would come. It did come, and, as usual, I was ready to try my luck. On about the 20th of December an order came to send out five hundred sick men for exchange, to City Point, Va. Finnigan, a Yankee sergeant, who had this business in hand, did not obey the

order as given. Being a Mason he went among the prisoners and selected Masons to be sent over. If a Reb with a good
roll of greenbacks was found, a bargain was made and the
fellow would go. Being too young to be a Mason, and not
sick, nor yet with sufficient funds to buy my way out, my only
chance was to flank. I determined to come over with that
five hundred if possible. I put my wits to work but found
it hard sailing, yet, not discouraged, I kept my left eye open.
For some cause the exchange boat did not come on time and
the men were put back in the pen to be called on the arrival
of the boat. As near as I can remember it was between one
and two on the night of the 21st. I had not given up, and
was out to see what would turn up. Soon I heard Finnigan
calling for the five hundred to report at mess house number
eleven. I worked my way to that point and awaited develop-
ments. Looking on for a while and hearing Capt. Patterson
calling the roll, I saw a very small opening for a flank movement and at once made my way very cautiously to the desired opening. Now was the trying time! Would I succeed? I decided then and there to make the effort, and
watching every point carefully, with every nerve strung, I
slowly edged my way toward the guard I must pass.　He
turned his head but for a moment; this was my time and
away I went into the darkness! Nearing the outer gate I
passed through with the others, and was safe for the present
on the outside. While waiting for the whole five hundred to
get on the outside, I approached a sentinel who was doing
parapet duty and asked him to call R. D Miller, company B,
seventh division. He did so and soon Chum put in his appearance I informed him in a whisper, through a crack in
the fence, that I had succeeded in flanking out, and he must
keep mum. We had quite a long talk before all were out of
the pen I gave him all my belongings in camp, and told
him to look out for some money I had written for, and when
it came to represent me and use it for himself, which he did,

and enjoyed, while I was in Dixie. I bade him good-bye, told him not to go in swimming for oysters, and if he didn't die, I thought at some time he might see Dixie again. Thanks to a strong constitution and a mean disposition, he did live to get home. I left him with a sad heart. If he could have come with me all would have been lovely; to leave the old chum was indeed hard to bear. We had become as it were more than brothers. In camp, on the march, or under fire, we were always together. Now, to leave him in prison and wend my way to home and friends, touched a soft place in my nature, and I almost regretted having made my escape. But such is life! Made up of sunshine and shadow, and each to be enjoyed or endured as the case may demand.

All the Rebs for exchange were now outside the pen and were formed in two ranks and marched to the wharf, put aboard the steamer "City of New York," which now weighed anchor and steamed away for Fort Monroe. Here we remained for an hour or two, then steamed for James river. Entering this beautiful stream we made our way up to City Point, where the exchange would take place. On our arrival we found the Confederate exchange boat had not yet put in its appearance. The "City of New York," now cast her anchor in mid-stream to await the Confederate boat. None of us were permitted to land. Maj. Mumford, the Federal agent of exchange, went ashore in a row boat to ascertain what detained our boat. He soon came aboard again and informed us, our boat, on its way down, had hung upon some obstructions placed in the river by our own government to prevent the Yankee gunboats from ascending. Owing to this it would not reach us until the next day. We did not relish this much and wanted him to land us at City Point so we might march to Richmond. This he said he could not do. The boys got mad and informed him we would consent to remain on board until ten o'clock next day, and if by that time our boat had not arrived, we would land by force if necessary. At this he threatened to weigh anchor and take us back to Fort Monroe. He was told we would not submit to that; we were now in old Dixie, and would die before we would go back to prison. We meant what we said. Fifty men were detailed to guard that anchor during the night, with orders to give the alarm should any attempt be made to lift it. Major Mumford did not expect to be delayed in making the exchange, consequently there were not rations enough on board to feed the men. Being hungry, and seeing no other way to get something to eat, the Rebs broke into the ladies' cabin where many good things were stored to be sent to the Yankee prisoners at Libby prison, and such a feast as we had you never saw. Ask Ned Erambert to tell you of what some of those things consisted. I understand he got some of our leavings after they were put aboard the Confederate boat. Nothing happened during the night to disturb us. Bright and early next morning we were up casting anxious eyes up the river for our boat. About nine o'clock we discovered a column of black smoke ascending far up the river. We were informed this was our boat. Sure enough, the smoke came nearer, until finally we saw the old boat, with a lighter either side of her, slowly approaching us. You hear us talk about the rebel yell! You ought to have heard the one given by those five hundred, as our boat came along-side the Yankee steamer! It fairly made the steamer, "City of New York," tremble. Our boat was very small, so all the Yankees were transfered to the "City of New York" before we could leave. As the last Yank stepped aboard the "New York," I jumped from the top deck, a distance of twelve or fifteen feet, to our boat. Thus, though a flanker, I was the first Reb on our boat!

All my fears were now at rest. I was safe at last! Here I found Ned and Jimmie Erambert, who had come down from Richmond as guards on our boat. We soon cast off and headed for Richmond, where we arrived after dark. After landing we were placed under guard and started for Camp Lee. The guard succeeded in getting very few to camp; the boys were making their escape all along the line. I did not reach Camp Lee until near day-break. I had right much money with me, flanked the guard early in the start and, taking a young fellow named Wilks with me, we proceeded to hunt up a bar-room, or restaurant. We soon found one, and after taking on several eye-openers at the price of five dollars a smell, I called for the best grub they had, and we proceeded to fill the vacuum in our rebel hides. After doing this we again went for the eye-openers, and succeeded in storing away several more, which began to make us feel good. We were now in good trim to see the town. You can bet your last cent we saw it all over before Camp Lee saw us.

I had now been from my home and people for more than nineteen months. I went to General Winder, who was in charge of us, and stated my case to him, telling him I had made my escape from Point Lookout, and had not seen my people for so long, and asking him to grant me a furlough to visit my home before again reporting to my command for duty in the field. He listened to my statement very patiently, and said he would look into my case, and if I had made my escape as stated, he would grant me a furlough for thirty days. I guess he found out my statement was true, as in a few days Captain Patterson, in charge of Camp Lee, handed me the furlough, and I left for home. I was not prepared for the change I found in old Farmville. It looked like a dead town. No business going on, nobody at home except the ladies, old men and boys, too old or too young to enter the army. The Yankees said we had robbed the cradle and the grave to fill our ranks. I must say it looked very much that way. Of course I was very glad to be at home with my dear mother, father, and the children, but the town was too dead for me. I remained several days, then putting on a "biled" shirt, and the best I had, I struck out for my company, now doing provost duty in the city of Petersburg. I remained with them to within a few days of the expiration of my furlough, then returned home to make my arrangements to rejoin the army for duty in the field, of which I shall, with your permission, have something to say later on in another communication in your paper.

Thanking you for placing before your readers all I have so far, in my feeble way, written, I remain, yours very truly

In the beginning of this article, permit me to say, I do not wish what I shall write to be misunderstood at any point. It will not be an attempt to blow my own horn, nor yet to silence that of another, but merely an honest effort to state facts and incidents as they occurred in my own varied experience in four years of war. In order to do this, of course the little "I" must necessarily show itself often at the front, but not in an egotistical way, and I trust my readers will not view my articles from that standpoint. Again, I say, remember I am not attempting to write a history of the war, but merely that part in which I was an humble participant. "Nuff sed." Now for the article!

In my last communication I stated that I remained in Petersburg with my company, to within a few days of the expiration of my furlough, then returned home to make arrangements to rejoin the army in the field, for duty. During by absence my dear mother had been hard at work making for me the very best clothes to be had, from the materials to be found at that time. To my surprise and delight, on my arrival at home, I found a nice new uniform, some underwear, and a pair of coarse shoes. The shoes I put on at once. Being new and very rough, they soon had all the skin off my heels. I paid very little attention to it at first, and the consequence was my heels became running sores: I could scarcely walk at all. Notwithstanding this, I determined to report to my command in time. So, at the expiration of my furlough, I reported to Dr Taliaferro, whose office was then on the second floor of the old two-story frame building standing on the ground now occupied by the new brick store-house owned by Mr. George Richardson. Here I asked for transportation, which was furnished by the government to all soldiers returning to their commands in the field While the clerk was preparing my papers, Dr. Walton, who was then stationed here, came in; he was the first surgeon of my regiment. Seeing me there he wanted to know my business. I told him I was on my way to rejoin my company. About this time my papers were ready, and I walked across to the clerk's desk to get them. The doctor now discovered the condition of my shoes. I could not bear to have them touch my heels so had "slip-shod" them and pushed my feet in. He made me take them off; examined my heels, and told me that I could not go back to the army in that condition, as I was not fit for duty. He said I could remain at my home, but to consider myself a hospital patient and to report every morning and he would report my case to the captain of my company. This was law, and I of course, had to obey. I remained under his treatment for twenty-one days, and again made application for transportation, which was granted

I knew my regiment had been ordered to North Carolina, but to what point I did not know until I reached Petersburg. Here I ascertained it was near Goldsboro. I then secured transportation to that point, via the Petersburg and Weldon railroad. On my arrival I found they were in camp about one mile north of the town On my way out to camp I passed the quarters of our head surgeon, Dr. Gaines; he too noticed my feet, which were now again in "slip-shod" shoes. He call to me to come by. I told him I was anxious to see the boys first, and to deliver letters and other articles, sent by me, to them. The boys were all glad to see me back in the ranks again. After chatting with them a while, I reported to Captain Morrissette for duty. He instructed Sergeant Elam to get my war harness. This consisted of musket, cartridge-box, cap-box, and about sixty rounds of ball cartridges. I now remembered my promise to Dr. Gaines, who had always been my good friend. I went up to see and shake hands with him. After some conversation, he, like Dr Walton, referred to my feet and examined them. He at once wanted to know if I had reported for duty. I told him yes. He said, return to camp, tell Sergeant Elam to put you on the sick list, get your belongings, and report to me here; you are unfit for duty; your heel is in very bad condition, and needs attention at once.

Law again and another rest in view! But this time I was with the boys and satisfied. The doctor had two very fine iron-gray horses, and one of which he turned over to me for my own use. This was a big thing for me; no duty, and when the boys marched in the mud and sand, I rode my iron-gray at their head! I also used the horse in my pie-rooting trips. The doctor's mess, of which 1 was one, lived high while my heel was sore, and I rather think he was mad when it was well. Sometimes I would be five miles from the marching column, and secured everything in reach that was good to eat.

My feet again in good condition, I reported to the company for duty. We had now reached Tarboro, and camped for several days. When orders came to march we formed column and head for Kinston and on arriving there, marched through its main street, which was knee deep in sand. We continued the march and crossed the Neuse river and went into camp about one mile from the bridge. Here we remained for some time, with nothing to do but camp duty, which was very light. Old Bow Harvey (who has since died in the Soldier's Home in Richmond), and I, had become chums, "Hootsey B" being still in prison. Bow and I, employed our time in fishing and in visiting some gunboats in course of construction at this point. I don't think they were ever completed, but blown up at the approach of some Yankee soldiers.

I will here state that the 8th, 19th, 28th, and 56th, Virginia Regiments of my brigade were still doing duty in Virginia, we, the 18th, having been detached and ordered to report to General Corse, otherwise known to the boys as "old puss in the boots." The old general was a heavy-set, short legged man, and wore boots reaching far above his knees, hence the pet name of "old puss in the boots." The old man was as brave as the bravest, and not only loved by the men of his own brigade, but by the whole of that grand division of Virginians.

General Pickett, who was now in command of this military department, was concentrating a small force in and around Kinston for the purpose of making an attack on Newberne. Everything being ready, on May the 3rd, orders came to break camp, and we commenced the march for Newberne. During the 3rd the roads were good, consisting mostly of soft sand, and very hard to march over. On the 4th we began to reach the lower country and here our troubles commenced. The whole country looked like one vast swamp; water standing all along the road from six inches to four feet deep where the creeks crossed our path. At first the boys began to coon the logs put up by the people to cross the deeper water. Our commander soon found this to be too slow, so he ordered the pioneers ahead to pull the logs down, which was done. Now the boys had to take it as it came, deep or shallow, in you go, out you come, clothes and all on! Our horses were very poor and could not get the wagon train along fast enough. A detail of men was made to help get the wagons ahead. Tucker Paulett, otherwise "Legs," and myself, were put with our ammunition wagon. Our duty was to assist the horses in getting through the swamps by shoving at the hind wheels. At first we would, on arriving at a swamp, pull off our clothes, jump in and get the wagon over, dress, and follow on again. We had two extra mules but no harness, so Legs and I rode them when we were not pushing the wagon.

Right here permit me to relate an incident that happened on this trip. The swamps had become so frequent, to undress and dress at each was too much trouble So I proposed to Legs that we strip, put our clothing in the wagon, and go it blind and stark naked, to which he agreed. The country was sparsely settled, so we ran little risk of being seen by many who wore the calico. At the next swamp we stripped off every rag and put them in the wagon. This proved to be a short one and we soon had the wagon over. We then mounted our mules and followed after the train. I admit it was a queer sight and created much fun for the boys, but Legs and I were as happy as a dead pig in the sunshine. The next was a very long swamp, something over a mile wide. We got down and tied our mules and helped to get the whole train over. To do this we did not go quite to the end, as the ground was firmer on that side. The last wagon out, we returned to deep water, washed the mud off ourselves, mounted our mules, and started across Just before reaching the opposite side we heard much talking and laughter. Not being able to make it out we halted and listened. It did not take long to discover, from the musical tones, and silvery laughter, that much calico was in that crowd. It seemed that all the women and children in that neighborhood had selected this point to see our army pass. How to get by them in our condition was the question. On either side of the road the bamboo briers were as thick as rabbit tracks in the snow, and no way to flank. So there was nothing to do but put on a brave front and charge straight up the road. I put my arms around the mule's neck, hung on, Indian fashion, on the off-side, gave him the stick, and shot past the crowd. They were astonished, failed to make me out, and no doubt thought me a strange compound, part mule and part man. But Legs was yet to come. He was afraid to do the Indian act, but with a yell he came charging up the road, sitting bolt upright on that mule! If the devil himself had come out of that swamp those people could not have gotten out of the way any faster. Legs did not even have time to say, "Just tell them that you saw me" before the last one was out of sight. I could not help but laugh when I thought of an old saying, heard many years ago: "Scatter, Sal: scatter, what the devil do you keep me now for." When Legs caught up with us he said, "Bones, we

will put on our clothes," and we did after passing the next
swamp. After going into camp that night, we were relieved,
and reported back to our company.

We were now near Newberne, and had captured several
stockade forts and many prisoners On the morning of the
2nd of May we continued to advance, and crossed the railroad leading out to Moorehead city, and rested our right flank
on the Neuse river just below Newberne. Here I saw the
first locomotive converted into an iron-clad battery. The
Yanks ran it out from Newberne and opened fire at us as
we crossed the railroad. The Yankee gunboat began to shell
us. A 150-lb. shell fell just in front of my regiment; buried
itself in the soft earth, and exploded. digging a nice well,
from which we got our supply of water!

The troops on our left flank had not been idle. They
had already captured one fort and sixty prisoners. Preparations were now in full progress to make a general attack
on the Yankee works all along the line, when orders came for
us to withdraw and hurry back to Kinston. We were needed
in old Virginia!

General Grant, who was now in command of the army
of the Potomac, had completed his plans for conducting the
campaign against "Marse Robert" in the Wilderness. The
army of Northern Virginia had never before had such numbers, and vast resources, to contend against. The official
return of the army of the Potomac, on May 1st, 1864, shows
present for duty, a total of 141,160 men of all arms. To
meet, and successfully resist this vast host, General Lee, by
official returns of his army, had only 63,984 men of all
arms: a difference in favor of General Grant, of 77,176 men;
or more than two for one I am thus particular in giving
the relative strength of the two armies, in order that the
reader may have a proper conception, and appreciation of
the difficulties that beset our great commander and the noble
men who fought under him. In addition to this force, Gen-

eral Grant had ordered General Butler (the beast) to leave Fort Monroe with 38,000 more, and land them on the James River, between Richmond and Petersburg, to capture one or both these cities if possible. It was to meet this attack of Butler's that we were ordered back to Virginia. Our return march was commenced from Newberne on the afternoon of the 5th of May and continued until the 8th, on which day we reached Kinston and halted. From this place we took the cars, passed through Greensboro, and on to Stony Creek, where we arrived on the evening of the 13th, and camped. The Yanks had been here and burned the bridge, and our train could go no further. A train of cars was sent out from Petersburg. This reached us on the morning of the 14th. We immediately got aboard and were soon in Petersburg. We were broken down and hungry, and had been told that the good people of Petersburg would feed us as we passed through the city. This was not to be. On our arrival we found the people much excited and no grub in sight Butler was then destroying the railroad between Petersburg and Richmond! We left the cars at Jarratt's Hotel in Petersburg and hurriedly formed line and away we went at the double quick down Sycamore street and across the Pocahontas bridge into the county of Chesterfield. We took up our line of march along the pike leading to Richmond. Not knowing exactly where Mr. Butler was, we threw forward skirmishers; and marched slowly behind them. When we began to close up on him, Mr. Butler found he was on the wrong road, and fell back toward the James river, thereby leaving the pike open to us to Richmond. We quickly availed ourselves of this error, and passed rapidly along his front, and halted at the "Half-way House" and went into line of battle along Deep Creek, and called check to his march on to Richmond. Here we remained in line of battle all night expecting an attack but none came. Old "Tin Ware" Wicker and myself were in the skirmish line that night and could hear the Yanks forming their lines and getting into position for tomorrow's fight.

Early on the morning of the 15th our skirmish line was drawn in without a fight. We had only nine thousand men in front of Butler's thirty-eight thousand. We were outnumbered more than four to one, but ready to put up a good fight, which Butler soon found out. Butler began to move and soon the fight was on. He threw a flanking column down our right, which we could not resist while in the works, so we vacated the line and gave them battle in the open field. Here too, they proved too many for us After a short and sharp fight, we fell back to our second line of works. Butler did not attack again that day. Early on the morning of the 16th we heard the pop, pop, of the skirmish line on our left, then the long roll of musketry as the infantry advanced. We at first thought it was the Yankees making the attack, but soon found by the firing that the Rebs were getting down to business and making things lively for Butler and his people Soon the order came for us to leap the breastworks, and charge the Yankees in our front, which we did in fine style, and with the old Reb yell We never stopped until we had cleaned them up. Our entire line, consisting of 9,000 men was advancing in good order, and fighting trim, on Butler's 38,000! Strange, but true, in less than two hours we had whipped them so bad they did not stop running until they reached the breastworks on the James river. Had General Whiting, who was near Petersburg, and in Butler's rear, done his duty, we would have captured Butler and his whole army.

We followed Butler's retreating forces until we had reached our former position near the Half-Way House. Here we again formed line of battle along our outer line of works, and remained during the night of the 16th On the morning of the 17th we resumed our advance toward Petersburg, and again formed line of battle along the pike. Soon the order came to move forward and we commenced the advance toward the James river, on which Butler had retreated under cover of his gunboats. We soon struck his skirmish line, which was driven back on his main line. Our line of battle was now up, and ready to grapple again with Mr Butler He did not wish to feel us again so soon, and withdrew his line nearer the river. We halted here and threw up a slight line of works. My company was now detailed, and thrown forward as skirmishers, in front of our regiment. We deployed to the front and commenced the advance again, leaving the other troops to complete the line of works. We advanced across an open field and entered a large body of woods. Here we felt sure we would run into the Yankees and again open up the fight, but they had continued their retreat and we failed to locate them. Night was now coming on, but we continued the advance for half a mile further and halted in position. We were now more than one mile in advance of our line of battle, and each of us selected the best possible position for the night's duty. We fully expected the Yankees would feel us out during the night and we were not disappointed About twelve o'clock they came up a wood, leading to our position. It so happened that old Bow Harvey's post in line was right in this road He saw the road suddenly darken in his front, not twenty yards off. He knew the Yankees were coming and, without a word, raised his musket and fired. My post was just ten feet to his left, and behind a big pine tree. I let drive at them, when the whole line opened. We fought them for half an hour, when they retired, but not yet satisfied. They wished to find out where our line of battle was, and in about an hour they advanced again. Everything was quiet along our line, but all on the alert. We could hear the tramp, but could not see them. It was cloudy. and very dark in the woods. Here and there we could hear the officer in command say to his men "Steady on the right; steady on the right." This gave us a cue as

to their distance from us. Captain Morrissette cautioned the
boys to hold their fire. We did so until they were within twenty-five yards, then our muskets began to talk in earnest. The
Yanks returned the fire at once. We now had the flash of
each other's guns to fire at, and the midnight fight waxed
warm and furious; the boys were there to stay; the Yanks
could not move them. After a half-hour's good, hard, stand-
up fight, they gave up the job and retreated. We made no
effort to follow them in the dark.

Early on the morning of the 18th, we were relieved and
returned to the line of battle. Our company had now been
on duty for twenty-four hours without sleep, and very little
of anything to eat, yet went to work on the breastworks as
soon as we reached the line, and worked until night, by which
time we had a very good line of works, and wanted the
Yanks to give us one fight from behind them. We never got
the chance. All our labor was lost. Early in the night of the
19th we were relieved by other troops, ordered to vacate the
works and march to Richmond, which we reached on the
morning of the 20th, got aboard the cars and started in the
direction of General Lee's Army. Arriving at Penola station we found Yanks in that neighborhood. We got off the
cars and prepared to fight My company was again detailed and thrown forward as skirmishers, and was ordered
to go forward and protect a railroad bridge about a mile below the station. Captain Morrissette placed a man in the
center of the track and deployed his men right and left,
using this man as a guide for the line. The command, "Forward; guide centre," soon came and off we went double quick
for the bridge. When within one hundred yards of the bridge,
we discovered the Yankees about the same distance on the
other side, coming up to the bridge. It was now a race as
to which would get there first. It fell to our luck, and we
opened a brisk fire on them. They returned the fire, but soon
fell back We now went to work digging rifle pits, and soon

had good ones. It did not take a Reb long in those days to wiggle a hole in the ground to hide his head. It was now quite dark. Bob Elam and myself decided to have a good cup of coffee; we had gotten some out of the haversacks of the dead Yankees on the 16th. We soon had a fire; boiled our coffee: ate what bread we had; and resumed our position near our rifle pit.

Late in the night we heard a heavy splashing in the river above and below us. For some time we could not make it out, and two men were sent to find out the cause. They soon returned and informed the Captain that the Yankee cavalry were swimming their horses across the river above and below and were then surrounding us. Captain Morrisette immediately drew in the boys from right and left, formed us in single file on the railroad, and ordered us to stick to the roadbed, but to git, and git fast. You bet we got, and got in a hurry. We succeeded in passing out just as their two lines were crossing to cut us off. They opened fire on us and we handed them a few in return, but kept "a gitting" all the same. Reaching the station where we expected to find the regiment, to our surprise not a man was there; not even one to direct us the way they went! We were in a pretty fix Had the Yankees now come up, they would have gobbled up the last one of us Lucky for us, the moon was now up and, by getting close down to the ground, we discovered the way the toe marks pointed, and followed them as our guide. About day we came up with them, on the Telegraph road on which General Lee's army was moving to keep up with General Grant in his great flanking movement. We rested here while Lee's troops were passing, and fell in with the rear guard and marched to Hanover Junction

On the 23rd we marched to Andersonville during the night, halted there until the 27th, when we left, and made seventeen miles in the rain, and camped near Atlee's station The following day we passed the station and marched about

12 miles toward Hanovertown, and camped about three miles from Mechanicsville. On the evening of the 30th we reached the line of entrenchment near Cold Harbor. Here we had a very heavy fight with Grant's army, in which we lost many good men.

One June 1st there was heavy fighting on our right; also on the 2nd, when Gen. Early drove the enemy some distance. On the 5th more fighting in Kershaw and Hoke's front on the right. On the 7th, General Early's command drove in the Yankee skirmish line, taking about one hundred prisoners.

We were still doing duty with General Corse's brigade, and the boys were anxious to get again with our own, (Hunton's brigade) and requested Col. Carrington, who was in command of our regiment, to demand the same. Not many hours elapsed before the order came to fall in. We were satisfied orders had come for us to return to our brigade. The boys fell in with a yell. As we marched out we found "Old Puss in the boots," and many of his men had placed themselves along our line of march to bid us good-bye. As we passed, "Old Puss" stood with his hat off, and a smile on his face, and said, "God bless you, boys." We halted, gave the old man three rousing cheers and passed out. On arriving at our brigade camp we found everything ready for our reception. General Hunton and the boys had turned out to welcome us back, and with cheers, hand-shaking, and kind words, we resumed our position with the old war brigade once more.

On the morning of the 13th, we found the enemy had left our front, and were moving toward the river. At an early hour we started, marching in a parallel line with the enemy, passing over the old battle-field of Gaines' Mill, crossed the Chicahominy river over McClellan's bridge, near Seven Pines, and halted near the battle field of Frazier's Farm. On the morning of the 16th we started at daybreak, marched to Chaffin's Bluff, and crossed the James river on a pontoon bridge.

Passing over the battle ground of Drewry's Bluff. we got on the turnpike leading to Petersburg. On arriving just opposite Chester, when quietly marching along, the head of the column was suddenly fired into by the enemy who had possession of the turnpike. We (Pickett's division) were then formed in line of battle and, sending forward our skirmish line, commenced to advance We drove the enemy back to the line of works we had thrown up just one month before, they having been vacated that morning by our troops, who had been moved to meet General Grant's army at Petersburg, leaving only one cavalry regiment, which was unable to hold the enemy in check. Night was now coming on. We halted at this line of works. My company was again thrown forward as skirmishers We advanced about half-mile to the front, halted, and established line for the night. We were relieved early next morning by Company B of our regiment. We reported back to our line Soon the order came to advance. General Pickett had determined to recapture a line of works which our troops had thrown up further on, and nearer the river. The pop, pop, of the skirmish line was heard. The line of battle now closed up at a steady gait Coming up with our skirmishers, we raised the old Rebel yell, and charged the enemy in our front. They couldn't stand the yell, and bullets proved too much for them. They broke and ran like sheep. With our line closing up after them, we soon had possession of our other line of works, and the halt was called. We had many good men killed and wounded in this charge. Tom Price was killed in this battle. Of the wounded, I remember O. T. Wicker, W. J. Nash, N. S. Morton, and. I think, O. F. East. It afterward appeared that General Lee did not intend to carry on the attack to such an extent, and sent his aides to stop the charge, but they were too late, the charge had been made, and the work well done. However, he was satisfied with the result. He wrote the following letter to General Anderson after the charge.

"General:—I take great pleasure in presenting to you my congratulations upon the conduct of the men of your corps. I believe they will carry anything they are put against. We tried very hard to stop Pickett's men from capturing the breastwork of the enemy but could not do it. I hope his loss has been small.

(Signed) R. E. LEE, General."

Official   G. M. Serrel, Lieut.-Colonel, Acting Adjutant-General.

On which General Anderson endorsed.

"For Major-General. Geo. E. Pickett, Commanding Division."

The Richmond Examiner, at this time stated in one of its issues, that General Lee had given orders for long-tail coats to be issued Pickett's men to hold them back while charging.

After getting in those works, we moved up and down them for several days, getting the brigades of divisions in their positions, from right to left, reaching from the Howlett House on the James river, to the mouth of the Appomattox river. Between these points we now had Butler's force bottled up, and General Lee meant to keep the cork in.—the cork was our division and pretty hard to move. We now settled down to prepare for the long siege.

There was but little fighting along this line during this campaign. We did camp and picket duty on the skirmish line for some months. Winter was now coming on and we began to build huts and dig holes to protect us from the cold weather. While on parapet duty one day I looked to my right hand and saw Generals Lee, Pickett, and Hunton coming down the line of works. As they passed my post I halted and presented arms, they saluted and passed just beyond my post and halted. General Lee was inspecting our lines. At this time the Yankee skirmish line was not more than one hundrd and fifty yards from where they stood. Of course, our skirmish line was between them and the Yankees, but the Generals were in full view of the enemy, and could have been easily killed by their sharp-shooters. Our skirmish lines were so close to each other I could have shot a gravel from one to the other without effort. In fact we often exchanged tobacco for coffee with the Yanks. We would toss to them a piece of tobacco and they would toss back a small bag of ground coffee in exchange. General Lee remained here for some time examining the Yankee works through his field glass. My beat ran beyond where they were standing, and in walking it, I passed and repassed them many times Always on the lookout, I, of course, caught a little of their conversation. General Lee finally turned to General Pickett and said: "General, those people are too close to your works. You must move them." I did not hear Pickett's reply, but knew those Yanks had to get further After coming off duty I told the boys what I had heard They agreed with me.

We always relieved the skirmish line at sundown. A few days after General Lee had left the skirmish line, we doubled. We knew this had its meaning. After getting on the line we were told by the officer in command that when "taps" were sounded at the works, which was always done at nine o'clock, we should immediately leap the pits and charge the Yankees in our front without further orders The time soon came. Taps sounded and over the pits we went The Yankees were more than surprised. They fired but few shots before we were upon them and over their pits. We captured many of them and advanced our line further on, and halted to dig the new line of pits. The Yanks did not like this much. While we were digging away, they threw forward a new line of battle, charged our skirmishers and drove them back to the old line of pits. Everything now remained quiet for a few days.. Tom Dowdy of my company was wounded in this charge. Pickett was not satisfied,—General Lee's orders had not been carried out. Preparations were again made to charge the line   This time the effort would be made at daylight, so that we could see what we were doing. General Hunton came on the line to look after the work, gave orders to double the skirmish line, and to charge just at daybreak, which we did, again driving the Yanks out, and advancing our lines two hundred yards. Here we dug new pits, and General Hunton threw forward his line of battle to protect us until the work was finished. The Yanks, seeing the line of battle in the field, concluded to let us remain. It was on this new line, but not at this time, that Charlie Richardson and Tom Weaver were killed. This was our skirmish line so long as we remained at this point. Winter was now on and wood very scarce. We had used up all between us and the works. There was a small piece of woods between our line and the Yankee skirmish line. Both were afraid to cut it   The weather began to pinch us pretty tight   Both wanted that wood, so an agreement was made that each side should send out a detail of men, under guard, just before night, cut. and divide the wood   I have seen a Yank and a Reb cutting on the same tree and divide equally. The wood secured for the night, each would return to the pits, and ready to fight again if necessary. At this time the pickets were not firing at each other at all, although we were within speaking distance. I have stated we relieved the picket line at sundown every day. The Yankees did the same. I have seen the two details marching along their respective lines relieving the men in the pits, the lines being from fifty to seventy-five yards apart, and not a shot fired! In fact, we got to knowing each other by name! I have often heard a Yankee calling out: "Say, Johnnie, is Captain Nash on duty this morning?" Everything worked like this for a long time; in fact till the Yankees withdrew the whites, and put negro troops, in our front. This kicked up the devil, and the killing of everything in sight began again. There was no hold up now; the pop, pop of the guns was heard day and night. There was no rest for the negro; if he exposed any part of his body it was immediately shot at. Many were killed and wounded, but few of us were hurt Bob Meadows and myself were one day on the right of our line, sharpshooting, in front of Stewart's brigade. There were three negroes in a pit, but rather too far off for Stewart's boys to do much with them. Bob and I decided to turn our attention to them; they were about two hundred yards to our right, and in a half-moon pit. Our position gave us an enfilade fire along this pit, and we arranged a small log of wood to prevent the Yanks on our left and front from seeing us Elevating our rifle sights to two hundred yards, we awaited our time, agreeing that he would shoot the centre man, and I the one on the left of the pit. We did not wait long before we saw their heads coming up from behind the pit; we took deliberate aim, and, at the command from Lieut Murray, fired. At the crack of our guns the two fell back dead on the outside of the pit, and remained in full view from about ten o'clock in the morning, until dark. The other gentleman in that pit did not show himself again during that day, though we tried very hard to make him do so, by firing across his pit. I suppose he thought two dead niggers in one pit would do for one day. This firing was kept up for about three weeks, when, before day one morning, we were surprised by hearing a Yankee calling out "Hello, Johnnie, don't shoot! There are no negroes on this side, this morning" Dougherty, an Irishman belonging to our company, replied. "We will wait until day and see." Between daybreak and sun-up we called and asked them to show up. Immediately three white men to each pit jumped out in full view, not a shot was fired, and quiet was restored along our

whole front again. We chatted with them, swapped tobacco for
coffee, exchanged papers, and had a good time generally.
During the month of December we were relieved and withdrawn from the line, and marched to Richmond, and from
this point sent to Gordonsville, to meet a Yankee raid on
that place. We succeeded in checking this, and returned to
our lines again.

On the 22nd of January, 1865, our gunboats
came down the river to the Howlett House battery. Their
intention was to shell Butler's observatory, pass along down
the river in the rear of the Yankee line, and destroy the
enemy's shipping at City Point. In the attempt to pass
the obstructions in our front, all, except one, the "Fredericksburg," ran aground She succeeded in doing considerable
damage to the enemy's vessels. During that night a heavy
demonstration was made by our troops, and the next day the
enemy's monitors arrived, and opened fire on our iron-clads
which were aground in the river. A small wooden gunboat,
the "Drewry," was blown up by them. The firing was very
lively, the forts on both sides taking a hand in it About
the middle of the day, our boats succeeded, without material
loss, in retiring to the rear of Fort Howlett, and at night
they returned to Richmond.

In this connection permit me to narrate a little personal
experience. On the night of the gunboat expedition it fell
to my lot to do vidette duty between the lines. Right here
permit me to explain.   In this day none but old soldiers
would know what a vidette was. In approaching our line
of battle, at night from the rear, you would first strike the
the line of battle, then the skirmish line, next the vidette
post The post was next to, and as close as you could get it, to
the enemy's line They were thus placed, in order to observe
and report any movement of the enemy. In case of advance
on the part of the enemy, their orders being to fire and fall
back on the skirmish line, the skirmish line reserving their

fire until the videttes were all in. On this occasion I was left vidette for my line, with orders to hold my post until the Yankees advanced, then to fire and fall back. Those orders were given me by Lieut. Fitzgerald of Company "I," who was in command of the skirmish line that night. I had been on but a very short while when firing commenced on my left next to the Howlett House, nearly one mile away. I paid no attention to this at first, but gradually the firing extended up the line and toward my position. Having orders not to abandon my post unless the enemy advanced, I of course, held my ground as no enemy appeared. Yet I knew when the 8th Virginia opened fire on my left, to remain I would be in great danger, both from the Yankees and my own men, yet orders must be obeyed and, as there were no Yankees advancing on my front, I held my post. The boys in my rear lost their heads, and, forgetting that I was still in their front, they opened fire. The enemy opened also, thus placing me between the fire of the two lines. I placed my gun on the ground and laid down beside it, expecting that one side or the other would soon kill me. I could hear the singing of the bullets from either side, but was not hit. As soon as the fire slacked, I returned to the line of skirmishers; Lieut. Fitzgerald ordered me back to the vidette post; I refused to go; he said he would put me in the guard-house; I told him to do so, and be d—d, as I would no longer do duty for an officer who would place a vidette on post with orders to hold the same until the enemy advanced, then to fire and fall back; and he, being in a safe place, would permit his line to open on the enemy, with that vidette still in front. I jumped in a pit, and Fitzgerald did not arrest me, nor did I go on vidette duty again that night. I had fully made up my mind never again to serve as vidette with Lieut. Fitzgerald in command of the line, and I never did

After the white troops were put back in our front, with the exception of a few skirmishes in which we partici-

pated, we had a quiet time on the skirmish line Drilling,
guard and picket duty, and working on the fortifications,
were our principal occupations. The men had now learned
the value of being protected by the shelter of earthworks,
and they did a big lot of that kind of work.

On March 5th, our (Pickett's) division was relieved by
Mahone's division, and put in the field for active duty. Now
our troubles began again. We marched out and halted near
the turnpike, within two miles of Chester station. While in
camp without any shelter, a cold rain set in and continued
for two days On the 8th General Pickett held a grand
review of his division. On the 10th Stewart's and our (Hunton's) brigade marched to Manchester, where we got aboard
the cars, (old freight cars) on the Richmond and Danville
railroad and came to Burkeville. Here our trains, in
three sections, were transferred to the tracks of the
South Side railroad, now a part of the Norfolk and Western
system, and started for Lynchburg. We of course passed
through old Farmville On reaching here all the people
turned out and gave us all we could eat and drink, the boys
got "how come you so" in a hurry, but we soon were off again.
On arriving at Pamplin City we learned that Stewart's brigade had stopped off at Farmville and gone into camp We
were taken off at Pamplin's and camped in a piece of woods
just to the right of where the pipe factory at that place now
stands. We now heard that the object of our move was to
assist General Early in heading off, and thrashing, General
Hunter, who was making an effort to capture Lynchburg.
The old General had gotten afoul of him that morning,
cleaned him up, and was now in hot pursuit of him down
the valley, and did not need us. We took the cars again the
next morning and, headed again for Richmond, passed
through Farmville but did not stop Arriving at High
Bridge we stopped, got off, and went into camp near the
dwelling of Mr. Madison; the place is now owned by our
townsman, C. W. Blanton.

Soon after getting into camp, a lot of us came back to old Farmville, and were painting the old burg red. About one o'clock we were passing the Randolph Hotel where General Pickett had his headquarters, when Charlie Pickett our Adjutant General, called, and informed us that marching orders had come, and we must get back to the bridge as soon as possible, or we would be left behind. We now struck back to the railroad and counted sills at the double-quick We arrived on time, the boys were all on the cars, and only awaiting orders to steam out. It soon came and we were off for Richmond, where we arrived on the morning of the 14th. We started about 12 o'clock and marched within four miles of Ashland, where we halted in line of battle. General Longstreet was in command of the force of which our division was the main part On the next day, the 15th Virginia, had a sharp skirmish with Sheridan's cavalry at Ashland. At night we were changing our position, moving toward the right, halting now and then expecting an attack, but none came. The next day we reached the Pamunkey river and built a bridge. Here our pursuit after the enemy's cavalry stopped, as they had disappeared from our front. We now returned to the lines near the Nine-Mile road.

On the 23rd there was another grand review of our division by General Longstreet. On the 25th, Terry's, Stewart's, and Corse's brigades of our division, were ordered to Richmond, thence to the right of General Lee's army at Five Forks. Why we left I can't say. We did not move until the morning of the 30th, when orders came for us to march We moved to Richmond and took cars for Petersburg. We left the cars a few miles before reaching that city, and marched across to the South Side railroad. On reaching this point, our column was turned to the right, and marched up the roadbed for several miles, when we turned to the left, crossed Hatcher's Run on a bridge of loose logs near an old mill. Here we again filed to the right, and were soon in line of battle behind breastworks which had been thrown up before our arrival. It had been raining very hard all day, and we were wet to the skin, hungry, and muddy. We remained behind these works all night with skirmishers out to the front, and orders were to sleep (if we could) with guns in hand, as the enemy might attack our position at any minute. The night passed without any advance on the part of the Yanks.

The next morning, 31st, we were formed behind the works and orders came to right face, counter march, by file right. We marched down the works for half-mile, when we filed to the right, and passed to the front, forming line of battle along the White Oak Swamp (I think it was) Here we found some Georgia troops deployed as skirmishers to our front, in an open field Everything being so quiet some of us took off our shoes, and began bathing our feet in the puddles of water left by the hard rain of the day before, and, while engaged in this, the pop, pop of the guns of the skirmish line in our front was heard. You bet those shoes went on our feet quick, and the boys were in line, ready to meet the attack. The Yanks came charging over the hill and closed on our skirmish line in a hurry. A Lieut of the 8th Virginia regiment, seeing the danger to the line in front, called out in a loud voice: "Boys, they will capture our skirmishers; charge them." Without further orders, the boys raised the old yell, and at them we went on the run, with guns at the trail. Nearing them we opened fire, but continued to advance. The boys in blue stood it for a while, but, finding that we were closing in for a hand-to-hand fight, they broke and ran, we at their heels yelling like devils, and burning powder for all we were worth. Running them into a large body of woods, we found another line formed to meet us. We did not stop, but charged into, and broke this line also, and continued to advance. About a quarter-mile from this point we discovered their third line. By this time we were all broke up, and orders came to halt and reform the line, which we did in a few minutes although under fire. Orders now came to charge the third line, which we did in fine style, breaking it up in short order. We now had three lines of battle of the enemy, running in our front, we following on the run, yelling, shooting and killing all we could. This was all very nice, and we enjoyed it, but the Yank's time was now to come. We succeeded in driving them back nearly to the Jerusalem plank road, our ranks growing weaker and thinner at every step The enemy had massed a very heavy force along the Plank road and put a stop to our advance. On nearing this position we were halted and ordered to reform line, but our boys, having already broken three lines of battle, were very much scattered, and before we could line them up, the Yanks charged. It was impossible in our con dition, to successfully resist this counter-charge, and the boys began to fall back; slowly at first. The Yanks, seeing how few we were, began to crowd us, and we broke into a run, and made back to our starting-point, and, this being the Yanks' time, they gave us "hail Columbia" before we reached the White Oak Swamp Road; but here we halted and stood at bay;—they could drive us no further! Right here the heavy fighting done at Hatcher's Run ended; about dark we withdrew and fell back again behind our works In this charge my company had killed: Elam, Boatwright, Harvey, Jackson, and Dougherty; wounded: Stratton, and Tompkins; captured· Harrison Walthall. A sad day's work for old Co. F: five killed, two wounded, and one captured. Elam was a brother of our townsman D. T Elam.

There was no better soldier than Bob Elam. I have often heard him say, if the Confederacy must fail, he wanted to die in the last fight. The noble boy nearly got his wish.

There were but few fights after Hatcher's Run, 31st day of March. Soon after getting behind the works that night, Col. Carrington, who was in command of my regiment, sent for me, and I reported immediately. He informed me that all his staff had been killed or captured in our charge, and I must remain with him to carry orders. I placed two rails on the works, over which I stretched an oil-cloth, and then placed our blankets under them, and I laid down to rest. We had been fighting all day without one mouthful to eat, and now, the fighting over, we had not even one cracker to appease our hunger. We did not mind this much as we had become accustomed to it. We only drew the cartridge box belt the tighter and kept going. It was raining, and the night was very dark. Soon after we had stretched out to rest, we heard an orderly enquiring for Col Carrington. I called him, and found he was one of General Hunton's orderlies. He gave Col. Carrington some orders from General Hunton for the officer in charge of our skirmish line. The Colonel said to me: "Sam, you have heard the orders, go out to the line and deliver them to Lieut. Murray who is in command." Our line was about 250 yards in our front, and in a body of woods. The woods in front of our works, for a distance of two hundred yards, had been cut down, lapped and interlapped, until a rabbit could scarcely get through it. Now you can imagine what a time I must have had in going to the front in such darkness. I mounted the works and struck out the best I could, stumbling here, falling there, and sometimes walking upright, then on hand and knees, I finally worked my way to the edge of the woods in which our line was posted I now thought my trouble was over, but not so; the Yanks got it into their heads to advance and drive out our boys, and the pop, pop, of the guns soon began again. I could hear the zip, zip, of the bullets, as they passed right and left, and I got behind a tree and awaited results. The Yanks soon found out that our boys were there to stay, and after firing a few rounds they fell back. I now advanced toward our line, and it was so dark I could not see a man. The men being deployed, I passed them without knowing it, and was on my way to join the Yankees, when I heard someone say in very low tone: "Halt! Who goes there?" I recognized the voice of Sam Moore, a member of B Company, and a most excellent soldier. I told who I was, and he said: "You spoke in time; I was about to pull down on you." I asked him where Lieut. Murray was. "Gone to the left," was his reply, so I went to the left too, and soon found Murray, and gave him the orders, and started on my way back to the works. Somehow I got completely turned around in those woods, and when I reached the cut down timber I was lost good. But I knew our works were in the direction I was going, so kept steadily on and finally reached them fully one mile below our regiment. I was now among some Georgia troops, who told me that my brigade was on their left higher up. I got on top of the works and found them again. On reaching the Colonel he said: "Sam, where have you been?" I replied: "Lost, but Murray has his orders." This satisfied him and we went to sleep No more orders that night, except to sleep on arms.

April 1st, about day, orders came to march by the right flank, and we marched in the road, through fields, in the woods, taking all the near cuts. in order to get to, and reinforce, the other three brigades of our division, who had been cut to pieces the day before by Sheridan's cavalry and Warren's corps, at Five Forks. We joined them about dark, but found them falling back slowly, before five times their number. About nine o'clock we halted, formed line of battle to fight again, but the Yanks thought better of it, and did not attack. Early on the morning of the 2nd we began to fall back again, crossing the South Side railroad at Church Roads, just above Petersburg, and continuing the march, halted near Exiter Mills, on the Appomattox river, having marched about twelve miles that day. But there was no rest for the weary and hungry! We were soon on the march again. The division, now about 2,200 strong, moved to

Deep Creek, which we reached that night. Here we put up
a pretty little fight, stopped the enemy's advance, then continued the retreat, without rations

Constant marching and fighting without food, shelter,
or sleep, began now to tell seriously on that grand old division. The boys were worn almost to a frazzle, but with a
determination to do or die, they held the Yanks. Now and
then we would pass a poor fellow who could hold out no
longer, and had dropped by the roadside, to be picked up
by the Yankee cavalry, who were constantly pressing our
rear. With cheerful and loving words we would pass our
dear comrade by, telling him to make one more effort and
come if he could. When the lines were broken near Petersburg, our division, with some other troops, were cut off from
our main army. Sheridan put his whole corps of cavalry
after those few men and tried to capture them before they
could rejoin Lee. Sometimes he would attack our front:
sometimes our rear. He hung a snag We whipped him
every time, and succeeded in rejoining General Lee at Amelia
Courthouse. at which point General Lee had ordered rations
for his army. None had been sent, consequently the army
moved off again without rations This was very hard to
bear, but there was no grumbling among that noble band of
men. They knew it was no fault of General Lee's and you
could hear them say: "We will follow Marse Robert to the
end, I will be the last spoke in the hub when the wheel fails
to turn "

From Amelia Courthouse our division headed for
Painsville, marched in that direction about two miles, when
we counter marched by file left, came back to the Richmond and
Danville railroad, up which we marched for several miles,
then struck off to the right, and passed through Deatonsville,
and reached Sailor Creek during the morning of 6th of
April. Somewhere along the line of march, Colonel Carrington sat in a corn-house door and gave each man as he

passed three ears of corn, which he said was for three days rations. The head of our brigade had halted near Sailor Creek, and this placed our regiment in the road opposite Capt. Hillsman's dwelling. I got in his yard, kindled a fire, and with a half of a canteen was parching some of my corn While doing this William Wilkerson, who now lives with me in my factory, came to me. He belonged to the 19th Va., Regt. We were discussing the question of coming by home, when I happened to look over to the left and discovered a Yankee cavalry crossing an open field and passing rapidly to our front. I called his attention to them and he said they were not Yankees I told him they were, and that I would know that flag if I saw in it perdition. General Pickett was sitting on his horse nearby. I called his attention to them and he immediately gave orders for us to cross the creek. We did so, and marched about 100 yards up the road, filed right and formed line of battle along the edge of a piece of pines. In our front was an open field about seventy-five yards across, then came a body of oak woods. We had been lined up but a few minutes, when the Yankees lined up along the edge of the oak woods. They were mounted, and we did not wait for any orders, but gave them a solid volley of musketry, and charged across the field. They gave way and we continued to follow, yelling and shooting. I had gotten about 25 yards into the woods, standing loading my gun, when a shell exploded very near me, a piece of which passed through one of my limbs, giving me a serious wound, which kept me on crutches for seven months after the war closed. I was placed on a stretcher and taken to the rear, where Dr. Berkeley dressed my wound, and sent me over the creek to a spring I was not here long before the Yankee Infantry in line of battle, came up. I was of course made a prisoner.

I knew it was getting serious for our boys now. With infantry in our rear, and on both flanks, and their cavalry in our front, it would be a hard matter to hold our own against

such odds. The boys would not yet give up; they formed
hollow square, and continued the fight until late in the afternoon, and were forced to surrender. I have heard that we
had about 12,000 men in this fight, against 52,000 of the
enemy, yet we held our ground for five hours! Could men
do more?

It were enough honor to have shared the fortunes of
any of those regiments. During the night I was taken up
by the enemy and carried to Capt. Hillsman's yard, which
was full of wounded Yanks and Rebs. Many died during
the night. I was very weak from loss of blood and thought
many times that night, while hearing the constant cry of the
wounded. and the last gasp of the dying, that I too, would
soon be marching in the silent army, but the good Lord ruled
otherwise, and I am here to-day to recount to you those
scenes of long ago.

The next morning a Yankee Sergeant, who had been
left in charge of us, drove a cow in the yard and shot her
for those hungry, wounded men After skinning her, he
would cut a big chunk of the flesh, with the blood dripping
from it. hand it to the boys, who, like dogs, ate it raw   I
very well remember I thought it the sweetest piece of meat
I ever ate.

On the 9th a Federal surgeon came along with a lot
of ambulances, examined, and dressed the wounds. put the
boys in the ambulances. and sent them on to prison. When
he got to me, he examined my wound very carefully. and
said "Johnny, you are very badly shot, and, if I start you
back, you will die between here and Burkeville." I said:
"Doctor, let me die here; I will die that much nearer home."
He asked me where my home was, and I told him, Farmville. He soon left with his ambulance train, leaving me
alone in Hillsman's yard I now made up my mind to get
to Mr. Creed Farley's if possible, and in this I succeeded,

and was never better treated or looked after in my life.
While going over to Mr. Farley's I had the good fortune to
run across a Yankee soldier, William Ferris, by name. He
was from New York city, and belonged to the 6th army
corps. He was a man with a big heart; and, had I been
his brother, he could not have done more for me. He
dressed my wound twice regularly every day, and remained
with me until I came home. We corresponded for a number of years after the war. I wrote him last at St Louis,
Mo., but he has never replied, and I fear he has answered
his last roll-call and is now marching with the silent army.
He it was who first informed me of General Lee's surrender,
and the assassination of President Lincoln.

On the 27th, it having been twenty-one days since I was
shot, the Federals sent an ambulance from Farmville for
me   I bid my good friends. the Farley's and Ferris. good-
bye, and started for home with brother Henry, who had come
down with the ambulance for me.   On our way, arriving at
Mr. Walthall's, we found Miss Sallie Reives, who afterwards
married Mr William Daniel, and who now lives a few miles
from town.   She wished to return to her home in Farmville
with us, and we gladly consented, and had the pleasure of
her most excellent company from there home.   We left her
at the residence of Mr. Joe Wiliams, who was her step-
father, and drove to my own home. where there was great
rejoicing over the return of the young, wounded soldier.

That night I had a fall from our front porch which
came very near terminating my life   My wound was all torn
open again, and it was thought I would bleed to death, but,
as heretofore, I managed to pull through, and, as many of
my friends will admit, am here yet, and hope to remain for
many moons to come.

As before stated, I was shot and captured on the 6th of
April. at Sailor Creek, about twelve miles below Farmville,

and left on the battle field, where, what was left of our division, stood as a forlorn hope to save Lee's wagon trains, and those who did their duty on that day, were either killed, wounded, or captured, almost to a man. Here my own experience as a soldier of the army of Northern Virginia, ended. I can now only state what others have said as to the final march, and end, of that noble army.

From Sailor Creek, General Lee continued his retreat in the direction of Lynchburg, passing through Farmville He pressed on as fast as the condition of his men would permit, fighting every inch of ground, until he reached Appomattox Court-house. Here he found himself, and his little army, surrounded by Grant and his vast host. Up to this point he had managed to check their pursuit from time to time, and to continue his retreat. On the 7th of April, General Grant sent the following communication to General Lee.

General: The result of the last week must convince you of the hopelessness of further resistance on the part of the army of Northern Virginia, in this struggle. I feel that it is so, and regard it as my duty to shift from myself the responsibility of any further effusion of blood, by asking of you the surrender of that portion of the Confederate States army known as the army of Northern Virginia.

U. S. GRANT,
Lieutenant General.

General Lee did not think as General Grant did. He replied on the same day, April 7th, as follows.

General: I have received your note of this date. Though not entertaining the opinion you express on the hopelessness of further resistance on the part of the army of Northern Virginia, I reciprocate your desire to avoid the useless effusion of blood, and therefore, before considering your proposition, ask the term you will offer on condition of its surrender.

R. E LEE,
General.

General Fitz. Lee says the next communication from General Grant was received by General Lee "at a large white farm-house at Curdsville." It would be interesting to know who resided at that "white farm-house" then, and who occupies it now. I trust some old resident of Curdsville will give the information. The two notes read as follows:

April 8, 1865.

General: Your note of last evening, in reply to mine of the same date, asking the condition on which I will accept the surrender of the army of Northern Virginia, is just received.

In reply, I would say that, peace being my great desire, there is but one condition that I would insist upon, namely, that the men and officers surrendered, shall be disqualified for taking up arms again against the government of the United States until properly exchanged. I will meet you, or will designate officers to meet any officers you may name for the same purpose, at any time agreeable to you, for the purpose of arranging definitely the term upon which the surrender of the army of Northern Virginia will be received.

U. S. GRANT,
Lieutenant General.

To which General Lee replied:

April 8, 1865.

General: I received at a late hour your note of to-day. In mine yesterday I did not intend to propose the surrender of the army of Northern Virginia, but to ask the terms of your proposition. To be frank, I do not think the emergency has arisen to call for the surrender of this army, but as the restoration of peace should be the sole object of all, I desire to know whether your proposal would lead to that end   I cannot therefore meet you with a view to surrender the army of Northern Virginia, but as far as your proposal may affect the Confederate States forces under my command, and tend to the restoration of peace, I shall be pleased to meet you at 10 a. m., tomorrow, on the old stage road to Richmond, between the picket lines of the two armies

R. F. LEE,
General.

On the next morning General Grant dispatched another note to General Lee, as follows·

April 9, 1865.

General Your note of yesterday is received I have no authority to treat on the subject of peace I will state, however, General, I am equally anxious for peace with your-self, and the whole north entertains the same feeling The terms upon which peace can be had are well understood. By the South laying down their arms they will hasten that most desirable event, save thousands of human lives, and hundreds of millions of property not yet destroyed Seriously hoping that all our difficulties may be settled without the loss of another life, I subscribe myself, etc.

U S. GRANT,
Lieutenant General.

General Humphrey sent this note forward by Colonel Whittier, his Adjutant General, who met Colonel Marshall, of Lee's staff. by whom he was conducted to the general To this note Lee replied:

April 9, 1865.

General I received your note of this morning on the picket line whither I had come to meet you and ascertain definitely what terms were embraced in your proposal of yesterday, with reference to the surrender of the army. I now ask an interview in accordance with the offer contained in your letter of yesterday for that purpose.

R E. LEE,
General.

Grant, who received this note eight or nine miles from Appomattox, at once answered it.

April 9, 1865.

General R. E. Lee, Commanding C. S. A ·

Your note of this date is but this moment (11:50 a. m.) received. In consequence of my having passed from the Richmond and Lynchburg road to the Farmville and Lynchburg road, I am, at this writing about four miles west of Walker's church, and I will push forward to the front for the purpose of meeting you. Notice sent to me on this road when you wish the interview to take place, will meet me.

Very respectfully,
your obedient servant,

U. S. GRANT,
Lieutenant General.

General Fitz. Lee says this reply was sent direct to General Lee by Colonel Babcock. Our noble old leader was obliged to confront a painful issue. His duty had been performed, but so earnest was he in trying to extricate his troops, and carry them south, that he failed to recognize the hopelessness of further resistance, or the emergency that called for the surrender of his army. At the suggestion of some of his higher officers, General Pendleton, the commander of his reserve artillery, went to Lee on the 7th to say that their united judgment agreed that it was wrong to have more men on either side killed, and that they did not wish that he should bear the entire trial of reaching that conclusion But Lee replied, that he had too many brave men, to think of laying down his arms, and that they still fought with great spirit; that if he should first intimate to Grant that he would listen to terms, an unconditional surrender might be demanded, and "sooner than that I am resolved to die." General Lee had not altogether abandoned the purpose to march south, even after the notes of the 7th and 8th had been exchanged. Longstreet, Gordon, and Fitz. Lee, commanding his corps, were summoned to headquarters on the night of the 8th, near Appomattox Courthouse. The situation was explained free-ly, and the correspondence with Grant alluded to, yet "Marse Robert" was not ready, without one more effort, to surren-der those noble boys who had served him so faithfully.

So it was decided that Gordon and Fitz Lee should attack Sheridan's cavalry at daylight on the 9th, and open a way; but in case the cavalry was reinforced by heavy bodies of infantry, the commanding general must be at once notified, as surrender was inevitable The attack was made at sunrise, and the Federal cavalry driven back with the loss of two guns, and a number of prisoners The arrival at this time of two corps of Federal infantry, necessitated the re-tirement of the southern lines. General Ord, who commanded one of the corps of Federal infantry, states that he was "barely in time, for, in spite of General Sheridan's attempts, the cavalry was falling back in confusion." The die was cast; the last gun fired; and a white flag went out from the Southern ranks; the war in Virginia was over !

Colonel Babcock, the bearer of General Grant's last note, found General Lee near Appomattox Courthouse lying un-der an apple tree upon a blanket spread upon some rails; from which circumstance the widespread report originated that the surrender took place under an apple tree.

General Lee, Colonel Marshall of his staff; Colonel Bab-cock of General Grant's staff, and a mounted orderly, rode to the village, and found Mr. Wilmer McLean, a resident, who, upon being told that General Lee wanted the use of a room in some house, conducted the party to his dwelling. General Lee was ushered into a room on the left of the hall, and, about one o'clock, was joined by General Grant, his staff, and Generals Sheridan and Ord. Grant sat at a marble-topped table in the centre of the room; Lee at a small oval table near the front window. Generals Lee and Grant had met once, eighteen years before, when both were fighting for the same cause in Mexico After a pleasant reference to that event, Lee promptly drew attention to the business before them; the terms of surrender were arranged; and, at General Lee's request, reduced to writing as follows·

APPOMATTOX COURTHOUSE, VA.

April 9, 1865.

General: In accordance with the substance of my letter to you of the 8th inst., I propose to receive the surrender of the army of Northern Virginia on the following terms, to wit· Rolls of all the officers and men to be made in duplicate, one copy to be given to an officer to be designated by me, the other to be retained by such officer, or officers, as you may designate. The officers to give their individual parole not to take up arms against the government of the United States until properly exchanged, and each company and regimental commander to sign a like parole for the men of their commands. The arms, artillery, and public property, to be packed and stacked, and turned over to the officers appointed by me to receive them. This will not embrace the side arms of the officers, nor the private horses or baggage. This done, each officer and man will be allowed to return to his home. not to be disturbed by the United States authority so long as he observes his parole, and the laws in force where he may reside.

U. S. GRANT,
Lieutenant General.

He then said to General Lee, "Unless you have some suggestion to make, I will have a copy of the letter made in ink and sign it " This gave Lee the opportunity to tell him that the cavalrymen and many of the artillerymen, owned their own horses, and wished to know if those men would be permitted to retain them. General Grant said he would give instructions "to let all men who claim to own a horse or a mule take the animal home with them to work their little farms."

April 9, 1865.

General: I received your letter of this date, containing the terms of the surrender of the army of Northern Virginia as proposed by you As they are substantially the same as those expressed in your letter of the 8th instant, they are accepted. I will proceed to designate the proper officers to carry the stipulations into effect.

R. E. LEE.
General.

The formalities now concluded, his thoughts now turned to his hungry veterans, and to his prisoners; he said to General Grant: "I have a thousand or more of your officers and men, whom we have required to march along with us for several days, and I shall be glad to send them to your lines as soon as it can be arranged, for I have no provisions for them My own men have been living for the past few days, principally upon parched corn " General Grant suggested that he would send him twenty-five thousand rations. He told him it would be ample, and assured him it would be a great relief. He now rode away to break the sad news to the brave troops he had so long commanded. His presence in their midst was an exhibition of the devotion of soldier to commander. They pressed up to him, anxious to touch his person, or even his horse, and tears washed from strong men's cheeks, the stains of powder. Slowly and painfully he turned to his soldiers, and with voice quivering with emotion, said: "Men we have fought through the war together, I have done my best for you, my heart is too full to say more " It was a simple, but most affecting scene to see those iron-hearted men, whose eyes had been so often illumined

with the fire of patriotism and true courage; that had so
often glared with defiance in the heat and fury of battle; and
so often kindled with enthusiasm and pride in the hour of
success; moistened now with the deep love and sympathy
they each had for their beloved chief. He soon sought respite from those trying scenes and retired to his private quarters. On the next day a formal leave of his army was taken,
in these never-to-be-forgotten words:

HEADQUARTERS ARMY OF NORTHERN VIRGINIA,

April 10, 1865.

After four years of arduous service, marked by unsur-
passed courage and fortitude, the Army of Northern Virginia
has been compelled to yield to overwhelming numbers and
resources. I need not tell the survivors of so many hard-
fought battles who have remained steadfast to the last, that
I have consented to this result from no distrust of them, but
finding that valor and devotion could accomplish nothing
that could compensate for the loss that would have attended
the continuation of the contest, I have determined to avoid
the useless sacrifice of those whose past services have endeared
them to their countrymen. By the terms of agreement, officers and men can return to their homes and remain there
until exchanged. You will take with you the satisfaction
that proceeds from the consciousness of duty faithfully performed, and I earnestly pray that a merciful God will extend to you his blessing and protection. With unceasing
admiration of your constancy and devotion to your country,
and a grateful remembrance of your kind and generous consideration of myself, I bid yoo an affectionate farewell.

R. E LEE.

General.

And then in silence, with lifted hat, he rode through a
weeping army. Thus terminated the career of the Army of

Northern Virginia—an army that was never vanquished, but that, in obedience to the orders of its trusted commander, who was himself yielding obedience to the dictates of a pure and lofty sense of duty to his men and those dependent on him, laid down its arms and furled the standards never lowered in defeat.

Now, Mr. Editor, my task is advancing to its close; before doing so permit me to offer an excuse for reproducing the correspondence which passed between Lee and Grant, prior to the surrender In my conversation with many of my old comrades I have found but few who ever saw it in print. If this be true, then very few there must be among our young people who have seen it. For their benefit I ask that you publish it. There is one historical fact, pertaining to the surrender, which I think all should know. It is this· the vast discrepancy in numbers and resources we were contending against at this particular time. On April the 10th, one day after the surrender, General Meade called to pay his respects to General Lee. The conversation naturally turned upon recent events, and he asked General Lee how many men he had at Petersburg, at the time of Grant's final assault. General Lee told him in reply that, by his last returns, he had 33,000 muskets General Meade then said· "You mean that you had 33,000 men in the lines immediately around Petersburg." To which Lee replied, "No:" that he had but that number from his left in the Chickahominy, and to his right at Dinwiddie Courthouse. At this General Meade expressed great surprise, and stated that he then had with him, in one wing of the Federal army which he commanded, over 50,000 men. Now, remember, General Lee had for months, kept up his line of defense before Richmond and Petersburg, a distance of more than thirty miles, with an army of 33,000 half-starved men, in the face of General Grant and his vast army of well-fed men. The last returns on March 1, 1865, of Grant's army, gives the total of all arms, at 162,239 men. Col. Walter H. Taylor, who was Lee's Adjutant-General, says: "When General Lee withdrew his army from the lines during the night of the 2nd of April, he had of all arms, not over 25,000 men who began the retreat that terminated at Appomattox." Think of it! 25,000 men fighting and retreating before 162,000 and for several days succeeded in checking and driving back every attack, and at last with only 8,000 muskets in ranks, surrendered!

Charges were now withdrawn from the guns, flags furled, and the Army of the Potomac, and the Army of Northern Virginia, turned their backs upon each other, for the first time in four long, bloody years. The Southern soldiers, wrapped in faded, tattered uniforms, shoeless and weatherbeaten, but proud as when they first rushed to battle, returned to their desolate fields; homes in many cases in ashes, blight, blast, and want on every side! Grand, glorious, and noble body of men, your deeds of bravery and self-sacrifice to duty and your fair Southland, will go down the ages in history and in song, never, no never, to be forgotten!

Now, Mr. Editor, as my task is drawing to its close, my heart throbs and thrills; again my blood courses rapidly through my veins as I hear in imagination the old Rebel Yell, and recall the many deeds of daring of my old and much-loved comrades in gray. How I love that grand old army and the noble band who filled its ranks! And it fills my heart with joy when I feel and know that we

"Who fold this love with rapture nearer our heart,
Believe that some-where, some time, we will meet and
never part."

LOCAL WAR HISTORY

The following very interesting paper was read before the Pickett-Thornton Camp, Chapter 16, of the Daughters of the Confederacy, at Farmville, Va., by the late Dr. James L. White, and reported in the Farmville, Va , Herald of July 9, 1897. Dr. White died June 26, 1909, aged 76 years, and lies buried in the Cemetery at Farmville. This very suggestive inscription is inscribed on his tombstone there · "The Beloved Physician."

At the request of some of the members of your organization, and after reading the second letter from Prof. T. J. Garden, addressed to you, it has occurred to me that I might, from my personal recollection, add some items of interest and information to the history of the Confederate General Hospital, located at Farmville during the late war.

After participating as Surgeon in the celebrated campaign in the Valley of Virginia in 1862, I was ordered to report for duty to the surgeon in charge of the General Hospital at Farmville, and did so about the middle of December of that year. I remained on duty at the General Hospital at Farmville until January '64, when I was transferred to field service and ordered to report to Gen. Longstreet, whose corps was then occupying the eastern portion of Tennessee. In the latter part of the spring of that year, Longstreet's corps was ordered to return again to Virginia, and I served as Brigade Surgeon to Bryant's brigade, of Kershaw's Division in the campaign of 1864, from the battle of the Wilderness to the front of Petersburg.

I remained with Longstreet's corps until the early fall of 1864, when I was again transferred to hospital duty at Lynchburg, and served as Surgeon in charge of one of the General Hospitals until February, 1865, when I was again transferred to Farmville, and took charge of my old division in the General Hospital, and served in that capacity till the termination of the war.

Pardon me for alluding to this much of my war history. It is only referred to because, to some extent, it is connected with the history of the General Hospital at Farmville.

The General Hospital at Farmville was organized in the year 1862, under the supervision of the late Dr H D. Taliaferro, who was surgeon in charge from its organization to the termination of the war. Its capacity was about 1,200 or 1,500 beds, which were occupied chiefly by cases of chronic diseases, and convalescents from the hospitals in the cities, and others near the field of active operations.

The buildings used for hospital purposes were the several tobacco factories and warehouses in the town, which constituted the 1st and 2nd divisions, together with ten or twelve new wards erected, and located to the west of the corporate limits, and directly on the line of the N & W. railroad, which constituted the 3rd division of the General Hospital

Drs. Walton and Tuft were in charge, respectively, of the 1st and 2nd divisions, and I was assigned for duty in charge of the new wards, or the 3rd division Those wards became the property of the United States at the surrender, and, after being occupied as hospitals, and deposits of distribution of rations and other supplies to our indigent colored friends of this and the several adjacent counties, under the auspices of the Freedman's Bureau for several years, were sold in 1870, or at the time this department was discontinued at Farmville. Soon thereafter they were all torn down and removed, with the single exception of the extreme western ward, which is even now, at this writing, partly intact, and used as a dwelling.

The office of the surgeon in charge of the 3rd division

and the dispensary (which was in charge of the late Mr
L. W. Williamson, a very competent druggist, who died a few
years ago and is buried in the Farmville Cemetery), together
with the bakery and the commissary department of that division, are still standing and occupied as dwellings. They
are the buildings in the rear of the residence and garden of
our worthy fellow-citizen, ex-Governor McKinney, on the
south side of the N & W. R R., and were opposite the
wards which were located on the north side, with their gables
and main entrance fronting the road, and extending back in
their length from 100 to 150 feet towards the river.

Dr H. D. Taliaferro had been previous to the war, surgeon in the United States Navy. He was a good organizer,
a splendid executive officer, well up in his profession, an af-
fable and kind-hearted gentleman, and well qualified for the
position of Surgeon in charge of the General Hospital at
Farmville to which he was assigned. After the close of the
war he returned to his former home in Orange, Virginia, and
after a few years went thence to Richmond, and finally returned to Farmvile, where he resided and practiced his profession until his death, which occurred in January, 1891.
He was buried in the Farmville Cemetery. The other surgeons in charge of divisions were Dr. R. H. Walton, and
Dr. Tuft respectively of the 1st and 2nd divisions. Each
of the division surgeons had under their direction a number
of assistant surgeons who had charge of the several wards in
the respective divisions. Among those associated with me in
the 3rd division were Drs Boatwright, Chandler, Mathews,
Garden, Ladd, Grayson, etc. In the other divisions the
ward surgeons were Drs. Carter, Boykin, Russell, Hancock,
Tatum, and others whose names I cannot now recall. Revs. Osborn, Langhorn, and McIlwaine were Chaplains. The Quar-
termaster and Commissary departments were in charge of
Major R. B. Marye, with several assistants. It was a pleasant military family and every branch was in harmony, and

satisfactory to the citizens and refugees, of whom there were a great many temporarily residing in Farmville at that time.

There were none among us who at that time entertained any other idea than that the independency of the Confederacy would be ultimately established; but as time lengthened into years, we became more and more convinced that our cause was slowly but surely waning in its strength and resources, and that we had jeopardized our all, save honor and love of tradition and section, in the uncertain balances of war, which would end ere long in disaster to our homes and loved ones. We were not therefore, altogether surprised at the news which reached us on the 3rd of April, 1865, that the overwhelming Federal forces, which had been besieging Petersburg for nearly a year, had at last succeeded in breaking through the attenuated lines of our half-clad, and half-fed Confederate heroes, driving them from their strong and fortified position in the front of that city and necessitating the evacuation of Richmond, which was the seat of the Confederate Government.

Then began that sad, but stubborn and celebrated retreat of the Confederate forces which terminated in the surrender, on the 9th of April, at Appomattox Courthouse   The sad and terrible scenes witnessed during that short week of the retreat of the Confederates, and those which followed for many days and weeks thereafter, will long be remembered by the citizens of Farmville. Especially will be remembered the days of the 6th and 7th of April, for those were the days and nights our famished soldiers reached our town. All day and all night long the worn and weary column dragged its slow length through our streets; all day and all night long did our generous people, with open doors, distribute such provisions of food and comfort as they possessed, to this almost famished and heart-broken army

Early in the morning of the 7th, I think it was, Gen-

eral Lee, weary and worn with loss of sleep and the great
responsibility of his position, entered our town and, ascer-
taining the whereabouts of Generals Breckenridge, Lawton,
and St. Johns, respectively the Secretary of War, Quarter
Master General, and Commissary General, who had spent the
night, but not in sleep, at the residence of Mr P. H. Jackson,
held an interview with them. He remained but a short while
and, after taking a CONFEDERATE cup of coffee, which
was sent to his room, parted from those gentlemen at the
yard gate. This, perhaps, was the last meeting, or official
consultation, held betwen General Lee and any of the cabinet
officers of the Confederate Government Generals Breckenridge and Lawton turned their course toward Danville to
join President Davis and the other members of the Cabinet.
who had gone by rail directly from Richmond to Danville,
and General Lee, in the opposite direction, crossing the
bridge over the Appomattox river at this place, joined the
Confederate column in Cumberland. which had been drawn
up in line of battle from the point of woods near the
railroad bridge crossing the hill near the Lithia Springs,
thence across the old plank road near the toll house and beyond the dwelling on the Bazarre plantation The Federal
column occupied the hills to the south and east of the town
At one time, early in the day, it was thought that a general
engagement would take place, and the citizens were ordered
to leave the town. Many of them, especially the women and
children, did so, but there was nothing more than an exchange of a few artillery shots between the two opposing lines
of battle, which resulted in no damage, though some of the
houses within the corporate limits were struck, and the
marks of the shots may be seen on them even at this day.
Later in the afternoon, that portion of the Confederate
forces which had been engaged at the High Bridge, crossed
to the north side of the river at that point, and after uniting
with the main body opposite the town, took up again their

march. In the meanwhile the Federals, so soon as the Confederate forces began their march, threw a pontoon bridge across the river, (the wooden bridge having been burned by the Confederates early in the day) and crossing to the Cumberland side of the river, made an attack. They were repulsed and made no further advance till near sunset.

The night of that day our citizens were again kept from sleeping and in an anxious and alarmed state, by the continuous passing of the Federal forces through the streets None but those who were present can imagine the horrors of that miserable night to our people. Closed doors were but little protection from the swarm of the Federal host that crowded our yards and streets, and none at all from the horde of lawless thieves and boomers who followed in the wake of the victorious army. We were indeed in a pitiable condition. Martial law, however, was established the following day, and guards of protection were given those who applied for them, and though we were prisoners in our own homes, still we felt less alarm, and made ourselves more comfortable. We knew nothing of the events transpiring at the front Hopeful we were, but ignorant as to whether our people had succeeded in reaching and uniting with others of our Confederates at Lynchburg, or had encountered irreparable disaster. Sunday morning however, the various Church bells and others in the town, began ringing, and we were told it was to announce to all the surrender of General Lee at Appomattox Courthouse.

Thus ended with us the entire movements of the war, but for days and weeks and months we had to submit to military government in our town and vicinity. A provost marshal with a military company to assist him, held us in submission for eighteen months or two years, and we had no liberty or freedom of action until the last blue coat of our conquerors had disappeared from among us.

This much of the local history of our town during the last days of the Confederacy I have thought would be of interest to you. None but those who witnessed them can ever realize how terrible was our everyday life. Our domestic living and home rule, underwent a sudden and deplorable change. With no financial resources, and our provisions all exhausted, many of our citizens were compelled to accept the *GENEROUS BOUNTY* of dry codfish and hardtack from our aggressors.

(NOTE· This article was continued in a later issue of the Herald, but this much is perhaps sufficient for our present purpose.—C. E. B.)

Chapter Nine

Prince Edward County in the Re-construction Period

PRINCE EDWARD COUNTY IN THE
RE-CONSTRUCTION PERIOD

The War was ended! It had ended disastrously for the South! Virginia, battle-ground of the hostile forces, was devastated! Her soldiers came back to their homes, if indeed they had any homes to come back to, and, settling down to peaceful pursuits with the same determination with which they had addressed themselves to the war, began the sterner struggle with poverty.

There was not enough seed left in Prince Edward with which to plant the first crop; neither was there money with which to buy seed had it been obtainable. Their hands were tied in many trying ways, yet they bent to the new tasks with a cheerfulness that was inspiring.

Freedmen's Bureaus were set up by the conquering North and officials with shoulder straps and brass buttons abounded. They were sent into every County with authority to look after the late slaves; "wards of the nation," as they were then called.

The negroes were organized into "Union Leagues." They were not eager for work. The difficulty of obtaining labor was added to the other troubles of the people. Depraved men, some of them alas, citizens, many of them a low type of Northern new-comers, entirely ignorant of the negro and his ways, and of the problems of the South; "Scalawags," and "Carpet-baggers" they were called, respectively, went among the negroes and did what they could to incite them to tumult and riot.

To the everlasting credit of these negroes, be it said, that, though accepting their freedom as a great boon, and relying with childlike faith upon the promises of these northerners, most of them continued to be orderly, respectful and industrious. Thus was the previous kind treatment they had received from their Virginia masters vindicated. Yet, even in spite of their admittedly difficult position, it cannot be said that Prince Edward County, had even then, any greater "labor problem" than has been experienced by her in recent years.

We must not neglect to note in this connection, the fact that the city of Baltimore came to the aid of Virginia in this time of tremendous need like a veritable Ceres sowing seeds of hope, and offered to furnish seed on security of the crop to be planted, and marketed. This offer was most gratefully accepted, and everybody took fresh courage. There was pulsing life once more in the land; peace brooded over all. Alas it was not to go on uninterrupted! The horrors of the reconstruction were coming on apace. Prince Edward shared in the hope that came with the generosity of the city of Baltimore; she was to share in the turmoil of the reconstruction days. The eager cormorants from the north were getting hungry and were already demanding their sop.

In 1870 the new Constitution of Virginia, framed in 1867-68, by what is known in history as the "Black and Tan," or "Underwood" Convention, became effective. Virginia was "readmitted into the Union;" that Union she had been foremost in forming and in establishing, and that Union she had been loathe to leave. Under these new conditions, each county was laid off into townships, and the County Courts, almost coeval with the Colony, were abolished, and the office of County Judge was created.

Boards of Supervisors were created at the same time. Grave apprehension was felt lest the negroes, then constituting the majority of the registered voters, might work great havoc in the fiscal matters of the county by electing a majority of the newly created boards. The whites, however, so arranged their forces that these fears were never seriously realized, and the minimum of disorders occurred.

From about 1870 matters have gone on in regular and orderly routine, with nothing of particular moment calling for the attention of the chronicler of the Reconstruction Days.

Further light is shed on these strange days in the chapter on the judiciary, to which the attention of the reader is specifically directed

Chapter Ten

Prince Edward County in the World War

1. Introduction.

2. Red Cross activities.

3. Muster Roll of the Farmville Guard.

4. List of white men from Prince Edward county in the service.

5. List of colored men from Prince Edward county in the service.

PRINCE EDWARD IN THE WORLD WAR

INTRODUCTION

In this chapter we shall endeavor to give, with some reasonable accuracy, the story of the part played by Prince Edward county in the great war of 1914-18. Of necessity the recital must be somewhat curtailed, for space is not available in which to tell of the multitudinous war activities of the people of this part of the State. Then, too, the lists appended are subject to further revision for errors. It is too much to expect that, in the mad whirl of war's turmoil, all names shall be properly recorded or transcribed. Many of the men went by "nicknames" and these occasionally got into the records Difficulty was encountered also, in keeping the names of white and colored soldiers separate. Reasonable accuracy has, however, been attained, due in no small measure to the splendid work of Mrs. Roberta Large of Farmville, who, at much expenditure of time and labor. has done so much to keep our county records straight.

Much additional and valuable information upon this topic will be found included in chapter eleven of this work, in the war activities of the Churches of the County.

THE RED CROSS

The following brief statement respecting the work of the Prince Edward County Chapter of the American Red Cross, is taken from a careful report of the work of that organization during the great war, prepared by Senator R. K. Brock of Farmville, and filed at the Court House·

The local chapter was organized at Farmville, August 31, 1917, largely through the efforts of Dr. T. G. Hardy, supplemented by a visit to Farmville of Col Henry W Anderson, later head of the Red Cross Mission to Roumania.

At the organization meeting the following officers were elected:

Chairman: Robert K. Brock.
Vice-Chairman· Mrs. J. L. Jarman.
Treasurer: J. L Bugg
Secretary· Rev. C. P Holbrook.

Executive Committee: the Chairman, Secretary, and Treasurer, ex-officio; W. S. Weaver. Rice, Va.; E. S. Taylor, Prospect. Va.· Mis. T. P. Singleton, Darlington Heights, Va; E S. Martin, J. L Jarman, Mrs. R. B Tuggle, Mrs. A. T. Gray. Mrs J. L. Jarman, and Mrs. W. P. Richardson, all of Farmville, Va

A Membership Committee, composed of Dr. J. L. Jarman, Mrs A. T Gray. Mrs R. B. Tuggle, Mrs. Thos. G Hardy and Miss Sue Gray Flippen, was appointed by the Chairman, and the membership was rapidly increased.

The officers and the Executive Committee, as well as the Committee on Membership, are people of standing in the community. The Chairman is a lawyer by profession and a former member of the Virginia Senate; the Vice-Chairman, wife of President Jarman of the State Normal College for Women at Farmville, occupies a place of great prominence in the social and civic life of the community; the Treasurer is Cashier of the People's National Bank, one of the leading banking institutions of this section, and Chairman of the third, fourth, and fifth Liberty Loan Campaigns, bringing his county well over the top each time: and the Secretary is Rector of Johns Memorial Episcopal Church, Farmville, who has had wide experience in many forms of social welfare work, and brought with him an enthusiasm for the great work he was espousing

The Women's Work Committee, headed by Mrs. J. L. Jarman, amongst much other invaluable war work made the following articles:

Surgical Dressings	21,660
Hospital Garments	825
Hospital Supplies	520
Refugee Garments	818

Reclamation Work done for Soldiers at	
Camp Lee	1,368
Comfort Kits	1,100
Christmas Packets	50
Property Bags	50
Linen Shower	350

In addition, the Knitting Committee completed the following:

Sweaters	248
Socks	286
Mufflers	11
Wristlets	18
Afghan	1

Branch Chapters were organized in the following places: Rice Branch, W. S Weaver, Chairman; Meherrin Branch, M. E. Gee, Chairman; Darlington Heights Branch, Mrs. T. P. Singleton, Chairman; Prospect Branch, T. J. McIlwaine,

Chairman, suceeeded by W. C. Chick; Sandy River Branch, W. B. Bruce, Chairman; Abilene Branch, Miss Annie McGehee, Chairman; Felden Branch, Miss Marie Allen, Chairman: Hampden-Sidney, Miss Susie Venable, Chairman; Five Forks Branch, Mrs. Norvell Crute, Chairman   There is also a Colored Branch in Farmville, and colored members elsewhere in the county, who did fine work.

The Chapter was not organized when the first drive for funds was inaugurated, but in the second drive in the spring of 1918, with Dr. Jarman as Chairman of the War Fund, the quota of $2,800 was more than doubled, the sum of $6,250 being raised. This was accomplished with the splendid organization perfected by Dr. Jarman.

The Home Service Section was organized in the early summer of 1918, with Dr. J. M. Lear as Chairman, and Miss Mary Dupuy as Secretary. Miss Dupuy was succeeded by Mrs. Roberta Large, who has performed wonders in securing and perfecting the records of the individual personnel of the men who went into service from Prince Edward County.

The Junior Red Cross, under the leadership of Miss Ilma Von Schilling did wonders and forwarded the following articles to the Red Cross Headquarters:

Property Bags	200
Layettes	1 Box
Garments	145
Scrap Books	180
Gun Wipes	500

The local Chapter is still (1921) maintaining an existence, as a permanent organization.

IN SERVICE DURING THE GREAT WAR

MEMBERS FARMVILLE GUARD

J. Watson Anglea; John W. Almon

J. E. Baldwin; S. Blanton Badgett; Charles Boyd; Lloyd Bullock; Otis Bowman; Robert Stanley Baldwin; Henry Bailey

D. J. Carroll; *Alfred Coleman; J. Vernon Collins; John Hughbert Cocks; Wirt Cardwell; William Haislip Crenshaw; Fields Cobb; Granville Chappell; Mack Cowan; W. C. Collins; Guy J. Crenshaw; Felix Cline; C. E. Chappell.

Harry Dix; *Hershel Dix; W P. Davis; F. L. Dietrick; Ruben Daniel; W. D. Druen; R. C. Dodl; J. F. Dodson.

Littleton Edmunds; Charles F. Eifert; J. F. Echols; Decker Emerson.

R. H. Foster; George Fitzgerald; J W. Fers.

Thomas Greenalls; *John N. Garland; J. H Gilliam; J. E. Garnett; R. R. Gilliam; W S. Gilliam; J. W. Goodman: Walker M Gray.

H. H. Hunt; Goode Hundley; L. L. Haymaker; *W. W. Hillsman; J. Ashley Hurt; Meband Harper.

John N. Irving; Linwood Irvine; Courtney Irvine.

Emerson Jarman; Joseph Jarman.

Henry A. Kelsey; A. G. Kelsey; *Finney Kernodle.

Joseph E. Lowe; James E. Lipscomb; Guy F. Lancaster.

Horace H. Moorefield; Richard K. Marsh; Rupert F. Mann; Frank L. McIntosh.

T. A. Perrow; D. W. Paulett; Raymond Phillips.

Robert B. Rodgers; Lucius R. Reedy; Charles W. Rafferty; Spottswood B. Robinson.

*Millard Guy Smith; H. B. Shultz; Emmett Sheppard;

Joel Sheppard; Bryant Sheppard; Melvin T. Smith; Blanch-
ard Skillings: Frank E Slaughter

J. C. Terry; Lawrie W. Thompson; Thomas F. Taylor.

Cunningham Watkins; T. H. Whitlock; J. A. Whitlock;
James Leigh Wilson, Jr., W. H. Waters; Ernest Woodall:
T. H. Williams; Sam Webster; *John Woodson Webster;
Henry Wood; Carl Wilck; Paul Wilck; George W. White:
Homer F Wilkinson; Stanley Watkins; Wallace J. Wilck,

*Signifies those who died in Service.

LIST OF WHITE MEN IN THE SERVICE FROM PRINCE EDWARD COUNTY

Paul T. Atkinson; William Scott Addleman; Henry Guthrie Allen.

*Paul Simpson Barrow; Owen Hall Bliss; Samuel W. Bondurant; William T. Bondurant; Charles Richard Bugg; K C. Bliss: J. M. Brightwell; W. R. Berry; John W. Brandon; T. L. Bliss; Everett Bailey; John Barton; J. T. Baker; Norman Berry; R A. Brisentine; W. D. Brisentine; C. H. Borum, J. E. Booth; Willie Brooks; Rush W. Bondurant; Robert N. Bradshaw; William H. Bondurant; Charles D. Beck; Nathan Baker; Oscar Borum; John Clarke Bondurant.

Charles M. Clarke; Frank B. Chernault; M. B. Coyner; T. H. Crenshaw; J. C. Crawley; J. L Calhoun; H W. Covington: F. B Cale; *R. C. Cheadle; L. B. Carwile; Baudie G. Carter; Charles Booker Cunningham; Albert Casey; John D. Cobb; Jasper S Carter.

Leon Lonsdale Duncan; L. W. Drummeller; T. B. Daniel: Harry S. Durfee; W M. Davis; Linwood Dalton; Shirley E. Dowdy; W. M. Dickerson.

Claude M. East; Russell East.

Andrew Jackson Fears; Sam. S. Flippen; J. N. Foster; H. Leonard Fulcher; Roland Scott Franklin; H. T. Ferguson; John W. Ferguson; *Henry Fowlkes.

William Gaunce; James Sherman Goodrich; Watson Womack Gray; Thomas H. Garnett; H. A. Glenn; N. I. Gibson; N. C. Gallier; I. Peyton Glenn; F. T Glenn; Ulysses O Gunter; Isaac C. Glenn.

E. H. Herzig; Thos G. Hardy; W. A. Holt; W. W. Hughes; J. C. Hopkins; W. Edward Hines; W. Eleaser Hughes; J. B. Holt; Harry E. Hamilton; B. G. Hood; Henry Hancock; Alfred E. Inge; L. P. Inge.

R. W. Jones; J. N. Jennings; Ernest L Jennings; Edward L. Jennings.

G W. Kennedy.

W. E. Lee; Berry Lee; J. V. Lewis; Joseph H. Lewis, Jr.; Herman Levy.

Richard Lee Morton; Mark A. Moffett; R. E. Moffett; M. R. Mays; T. J. McIlwaine; W. H. Mason; Charles W. Mason; R. F. Mann; William Conway Morris; D. C. Morris; John A. Morris.

C. M. Noel; Finley N. Nelson.

F. L. Orange; J. J. Overton; L. N. Oliver; Otto Oliver.

William R Price; C. A. Price, Jr.; Joseph A Poole; M. M. Ponton; G D. Pickett; Haywood Pollard; Robert H. Phillips.

Gates Randolph Richardson; Joe Edmund Rogers; James G. Redford, Sam H. Rodgers

Willie Mann Scott; T. B. Scott; Frank Commer Shultz; William Thomas Straley; L. D. Simpson; F. G Shultz; *Phil B. Swan. L. A. Snow; G. E. Shorter; C. L. Stuart; Hutch Stowe; Nunnally Smith.

John Daniel Thomas; W. E Tomlinson; Pitzer S Turns; Oscar Thompson.

James B. Vaughan.

Robert Earle Warwick; Thomas Edward Webster; Harry Eastley Whalley; John Hugh Whalley; Lee Carrington Whalley; Oscar Hamet Whitten; James William Wilson, Jr.; Howard F. Weaver, Cecil F. Walker; Charles T. Walker; H. E Walker; G. L. Walker; S. N. Wood; Gene B. Walker: Sam M. Weaver: Alfred Wolter.

*Signifies those who died in Service.

WHITE MEN OF THE COUNTY WHO ENLISTED
ELSEWHERE

Ernest Allen; Jean Anderson; Willie Adams.

J. P. Bondurant; Charles Bates; Richard B. Bates; Eugene Budd; J. Spencer Burger.

W. G. Carter; James Cowan; Melvin Childress; Robert T. Cocks; Morris Conway; Leslie Carwile; Martin Covington; J. G. Crenshaw; Charles B. Crute; A. B Crawley, A. L. Crawley.

Berlin Driskill; W. G. Dunnington; Wallace Duvall; A. R Dunkum; W. C. Davis; E. M. Dickerson; Jack Dunnington.

Reid Edmunds; J. Watson Elliott

Pierce Farr; H G. Farley; James D Fowlkes

Ernest Garland; T. A. Gray, Jr.; Thomas D Glenn; Everett Garber.

T. A. Hubbard; H. J. Hubbard; C W. Hubbard; C. A. M. Hubbard; Hunter C. Harris; Willard Hart; Robert Hundley.

Jack Irving.

Hicks Ligon; Massie Lowe; Hatcher Layne; Haynes Lancaster; Clarence F. Lynn; Stanley R. Legus.

*Dan A. McIntosh; Henry L. Moore; Percy Moring; Cumfy Mottley; McGinnis.

Bernard Oliver; Walter Overton.

Walter A. Palmore; Thomas G. Price.

J. Maxwell Robeson; Clyde V. Ransom; Robert Richardson; Walter Richardson; *Dewitt Riggins; Floyd Rosser.

Ed Shorter; Joel Sheppard.

Elmer R. Tomlinson; Henry C. Thompson; T. A. Tweedy.

Petit Venable; Reginald Venable; W. A. Vernon; A. E. Vaughan.

Frank Nat Watkins; Sam W. Watkins; Louis Whitlock; E. Dixie Wilkinson.

Earle Homer Young.

*Signifies those who died in Service.

IN STUDENT ARMY TRAINING CORPS FROM PRINCE EDWARD COUNTY AT HAMPDEN-SIDNEY COLLEGE

*F. A. Allen; R. W. Bugg; J. S. Q. Carson; G. E. Coffman; K. Drummeller; T. J. Headlee; J. A. Jones; R. C. Moore; J. W. Putney; W. E. Smith; J. M. Watkins.

*Signifies those who died in Service.

COLORED MEN IN THE SERVICE FROM PRINCE EDWARD COUNTY

William H. Anderson; James Armistead; C. H. Anderson; Luther Allen; J. N. Anderson.

Wesley Bedford; Leonard P. Bedford; Willis Berry; Henry T. Brown; Charles William Brown; Lancaster Brown; Fred Baker; John Baker; Phillip Bland; Wesley Brown; Floyd Brown; John Brown; Howard Brown; Archer Brown; Hunter Brown; R. W. Brown; J. H. Brown; S. J. Brown, Eddie Brown; Percy Brown; Royall Brown; Thomas B. Blue; Clarence Blanton, Eddie Berry; Edward Beverley; Willie Baker; Charles Banks; Waverley Burr; J. C. Berryman; Robert Baldwin; Ernest L. Berryman; William Beasley; *Richard Lee Biggers; Vernon Bartee; Cavel Barksdale; Norvel Brown; William Booker.

Roy Carthorn; John Cheatham; James Clarke; Berkley Carthorn; Joe Coles; William Clarke; J. H. Cromwell; Paul Coleman; Emmett Crute; James Carter; Albert Casey; Willie Clark; Morton Couch.

Amos Dickerson; James S. Doswell; George Daniel; H. A. Dodson; Edgar Durphey; Champ Dupuy; Walter Davis.

Willie Ellis; Willie Ellis; Tom Evans; Charles Ellis; Paul Ellis; Johnny Evans; Alfred Eggleston.

Fletcher Felton; Clinton Felton; Jeff Foster; Henry Foster; Sam Foster; Spencer Flournoy; Peter Freeman; Robert Foster; George Fultz; William Ford; Robert Fowlkes; Robert Flournoy; James Ford, John L. Fears; Solomon Fore; Lewis Flagg; Frank Farley; W. L. Fowlkes; John Freeman; Edward Flagg.

James Gans; Floyd Glenn; Phillip Alex Green; Lewis Washington Green; Ederick S Green; Wiley Ghee; John H. Giles; Herbert Green; Laban Green; Horace Green; John Goode; Frank Gales; Reese Gordon; John D. Thomas Galher.

Nathan Harvey; Clarence O. Hilton; Philip Arlie Hilton; Richard Arthur Hilton; Walter Samuel Hurt; Floyd Harris; Vernon Haskins; *Charles Harris; Wiley Haskins; Charles Haskins; W. Sanders Hines; James Hicks; John Haskins; Pompey Harrison; J. W. Holmes; Randolph Harrison; Johnny Hurt; Spencer Hurt; Simie Holley; Walter Hayes; Adam Hicks; John S. Hendricks.

George James, John Jeffries; John Henry Jordan; Mathew Johnson, Tom Johnson; Wiley Johnson; Joe Johnson; Herman Johnson; Albert Johnson, Jr.; C. T. Johnson; Henry Johnson; Johnny Johnson; George Johnson; Clem Johnson; Elijah Johnson; Benj. F Jones; Henry T. Jones; Henry Jones: Thomas Jones; Jim Jenkins; Nineveh Jones; Eddie Jones; J. H Jones; Alex Jones; Jasper Jones; Champ Jones: Charles Jones; H. E. Johns; Durvan Jackson; Nelson Jeffries; Lee Jackson; Ulysses Jackson: Clinton Jackson; Chester A. Jeffries; Emmett Jackson, J. M. Jackson.

Willie Knight; Homer Kelsor.

Freebelle Lee, Lightfoot Lacy; Robert Lacy; Armistead Lambert; James A. Lewis; C. Henry Lewis; George Lucas; Bascom Ligon; G. H. Ligon; Herman Ligon; Thaniel Lockett; Frank Lile, Jesse Logan.

Walter A. Marshall; Edward Marshall; Racey Matthews: Every Morton; William Morton; Junius Morton; Fred Morton; Taze Morton; Floyd Morton; Edward Miles; Clyde Mayo; Vanderbilt Miller; N. P. Miller, Ned Marshall; John Marshall; T. H Matthews; Joe Moore; David E. Moseley.

John Clarence Paige; Joe Pascal; Richard Payne, Warren P. Pryor; George T. Pryor; Waverley Pryor; James Pryor; H. T Patterson; Oscar Palmore; William Payne.

Hairson Randolph, Frank James Redd; Moses Randolph; Ulysses Joe Randolph; Henry A. Redd; Romeo Ran-

dall; John Richardson; Robert Rux; C. H. Robinson; Frank
J. Redd; Flan Redd; James Redd; Thomas Redd; Ed Redd;
Sam Redd; John Robertson; James H. Reed; Sam Reed.

Lurtie Scott; Henry Scott; Edward Scott; Albert Scott;
Prudential Scott; Cleveland Scott; Matthew Scott; Richard
Scott; Richard Scott; John Smith; George Smith; Sam
Simms; George Street; Vester Smith; Tom Stith; Oakley
H. Sanders.

Ellis Thomas; James Thornton; *Henry Threat; Watt
Threat; Warren P. Thompson; Fred Taylor; McKinley
Tucker: John Trent; Robert Terry; John P. Towns; Sam
Trent; Frank Topp.

Jimmy Venable.

Henry Watkins; Alex Watson; Truly Watson; William
Whit; Harrison Williams; Percy C. Womack, Willie Woodson; Cleveland Walker; Wiley Walker; John Wingfield;
Monroe Watkins; Walter Watson; Bennie Walden; H W.
Walker: Ed Williams: Norfleet Ward; Stardie Ward: Richard Woodson; Harrison West; Clem Warren; Emmett Warren; Hilary Wilson; Robert Winston, Edmund Watson; Edward Winston; Dennis Walker; Branch Washington; Charles
Watson.

Willie Young

*Signifies those who died in Service.

COLORED MEN OF THE COUNTY WHO ENLISTED ELSEWHERE

Dorsey Anderson; Paul Anderson; Claud M Allen.

Nelson Baker; Charlie Baker; Willis H. Branch; Harvey Brown; Anderson Brown; Dominion Brown; Herbert Brown; Robert Booker; Wesley Booker; Wayman Brown; John Sim Bolden.

Charles Cooper.

Henderson Davis; Edward Davis; Jack Dupuy.

W. D. Elam; Robert Anderson Ellis.

Samuel Fowlkes.

Levi Green; Burnett Griggs; A. S. Green.

Norman A. Hairston; Lindsey Hays; Spencer Hurt; Herbert Hines· George Hill; James Hall.

Ernest L. Johns; Mesles Johnson; Neal Johnson; James Johnson: Cleveland Johnson; Nelson Jordan, Jr.; Arthur Jenkins

Coley Lewis; Paige Lancaster; Daniel Logan; Wm. H Logan; Paul Layne; Joe Ligon.

James Miller; Preston Miller; Haskins Mosely; LaFayette Munford; Sam Matthews.

Olney Pryor.

Munford Richardson; Lud Roberts.

Sam Sims.

Charles Terry; Alfred Thornton.

Thomas Watts; Joseph Walker; Shirley Walker; Pernell Watkins; Harry Watkins; Jefferson J. Wilson; Burley Wilson; Leonard Wilson; Nat Ward; *Dick Ward; C. H. Wade; Robert Womack, Clyde Woodson; Howard White.

*Signifies those who died in Service.

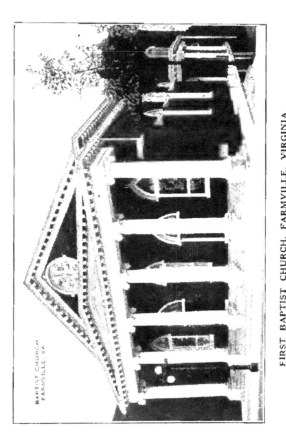

FIRST BAPTIST CHURCH, FARMVILLE, VIRGINIA

C. Edward Burrell, LL. B., D. D., Minister

See Page 213.

Chapter Eleven

The Churches of Prince Edward County

1. **The Baptists in Prince Edward County. (General History)**
   The Farmville Baptist Church.
   Pisgah Baptist Church. (Rice.)
   Mount Nebo Baptist Church.
   Sharon Baptist Church. (Sandy River.)
   Spring Creek Baptist Church.
   Bethpeor Baptist Church.

2. **The Episcopal Church in Prince Edward County. (General History.)**
   John's Memorial. (Farmville.)
   Five Forks

3. **The Methodist Episcopal Church in Prince Edward County. (General History.)**
   The Farmville M. E. Church
   The Prospect M. E Church.
   Olive Branch M. E Church.
   Salem M. E. Church. (Rice.)

4. **The Presbyterian Church in Prince Edward County. (General History.)**
   The Farmville Presbyterian Church.
   College Presbyterian Church. (Hampden-Sidney.)
   Jamestown Presbyterian Church. (Rice.)

5. Disciples of Christ. Liberty Church.

6. Colored Churches.

THE CHURCHES OF PRINCE EDWARD

BAPTISTS IN PRINCE EDWARD COUNTY

The first Baptist Church established in Virginia, was the Burleigh Church in Isle of Wight County (now known as the Mill Swamp Baptist Church), organized in, or about the year of 1714. (McClothlin.)

Long before the Revolutionary War, the Baptists in Virginia had reached considerable numbers and had attained some prominence and prestige.

The following from the Manuscript Journal of the House of Delegates, 1773-1774, suggests something of the prominence they had already attained:

Thursday, the 12th of May, 14 George III., 1774.—"A petition of sundry persons of the community of Christians called Baptists, and other Protestant dissenters, whose names are thereto subscribed, was presented to the House, and read, setting forth that the toleration proposed by the bill, ordered at the last session of the General Assembly to be printed and published, not admitting public worship except in the daytime, is inconsistent with the laws of England, as well as the practice and usage of the primitive Churches, and even of the English Church itself that the night session may sometimes be better spared by the petitioners from the necessary duties of their callings, and that they wish for no indulgences which may disturb the peace of Government," etc.

What action the House took on the Petition is not stated in the Journal.

That they, at that time, interested themselves in questions of public moment is evident from an Address presented by them to Patrick Henry upon the occasion of his first elevation as Governor of Virginia Of all the congratulatory messages received by him at that time, probably none came so straight from the heart as did this one from the distressed and persecuted dissenters in Virginia, called Baptists, who had learned, in many an hour of bitter need, to look upon him as their strong and valiant champion, in the Legislature and in the Courts. He was not of their persuasion, being himself an Episcopalian, nevertheless, on August 12, 1776, "the ministers and delegates of the Baptist churches" of the State, being met in Convention at Louisa, sent him the following Address:

"*MAY IT PLEASE YOUR EXCELLENCY,*—As your advancement to the honorable and important station as Governor of this Commonwealth affords us unspeakable pleasure we beg leave to present your Excellency with our most cordial congratulations.

"Your public virtues are such that we are under no temptation to flatter you. Virginia has done honor to her judgment in appointing your Excellency to hold the reins of government at this truly critical conjuncture, as you have always distinguished yourself by your zeal and activity for her welfare, in whatever department has been assigned to you

"As a religious community, we have nothing to request of you. Your constant attachment to the glorious cause of liberty and the right of conscience, leaves us no room to doubt your Excellency's favorable regards while we worthily demean ourselves

"May God Almighty continue you long, very long, a public blessing to this your native country. and, after a life of usefulness here, crown you with immortal felicity in the world to come.

Signed by order: Jeremiah Walker, Moderator.
John Williams, Clerk."

To this loving and touching address, the Governor replied, on the very next day, in an off-hand letter, showing deep feeling and a very natural gratification:—

"TO THE MINISTERS AND DELEGATES OF THE BAPTIST CHURCHES, AND THE MEMBERS OF THAT COMMUNION.

"GENTLEMEN,—I am exceedingly obliged to you for your very kind address, and the favorable sentiments you are pleased to entertain respecting my conduct and the principles which have directed it. My constant endeavor shall be to guard the rights of all my fellow-citizens from every encroachment.

"I am happy to find a catholic spirit prevailing in our country, and that those religious distinctions, which formerly produced some heat, are now forgotten. Happy must every friend to virtue and America feel himself, to perceive that the only contest among us, at the most critical and important period, is, who shall be foremost to preserve our religious and civil liberties.

"My most earnest wish is, that Christian charity, forbearance, and love, may unite all our different persuasions, as brethren who must perish or triumph together; and I trust that the time is not far distant when we shall greet each other as the peaceable possessors of that just and equal system of liberty adopted by the last convention, and in support of which may God crown our arms with success.

"I am, gentlemen, your most obedient and very humble servant,   P. Henry, Jun.

August 13, 1776"
(American Arch., 1 905, 906.)

The Baptist churches of Prince Edward county, maintain membership in the Appomattox Association. This Asciation grew out of the old Middle District Association, which, at a meeting held at Rice's station (its second) on May 9, 1785, sent out the Mcherrin, and the Appomattox Associations, itself retaining the name of Middle District Association.

The first meeting of the newly formed Appomattox Association was held in Prince Edward county, at Walker's Church the same year. Four of the churches forming the new Association were located in Prince Edward; viz. Rocks, organized 1772; Appomattox, 1773; Sailor Creek, 1781; and, Mountain Creek, 1788. Of these four, only Rocks and Appomattox remain, but are now, by reason of a later county division, both in Appomattox county.

The meeting house of Sailor Creek Church was located about one-half mile from Rice on the road leading to Farmville. It was destroyed by a cyclone in 1832. On August 15, 1857, Pisgah Church, (Rice) was formed at Union, and, in 1881 moved to their present building at Rice's Station Pisgah is thus the lienal descendant of Sailor Creek Church.

The Mountain Creek Church has passed out of the memory of the present generation. The Church building is supposed to have stood about two and a half miles northwest of Green Bay station, in Prince Edward county.

It is considered probable that Sandy River Church, (Sharon) formed in 1827, and situated about five miles distant, absorbed the membership of the Mountain Creek Church.

A severe controversy arose in 1832-1834, between the Methodists and the Baptists, over the building occupied by the Baptists at Sandy River, which ended by the Baptists retaining possession.

The following Baptist Churches are located in Prince Edward county:

Bagby Memorial.

Bethpeor.

Farmville.

Mount Nebo.

Pisgah.   (Rice)

Sharon.   (Sandy River)

Spring Creek.

BAGBY MEMORIAL BAPTIST CHURCH

For several years prior to 1903 preaching services were held at a little schoolhouse hard-by the site upon which stands the place of worship of this congregation. It is known that J. R. Doan, now pastor of the Baptist Church at South Boston, while pastor of the Burkeville Baptist Church, and F. W. Moore, now pastor of the Second Baptist Church, Petersburg, Virginia, both went time and again to preach at this school house. Especial interest was shown in the spiritual needs of the people of this neighborhood, by Dr. George R. Bagby, while he was pastor of the Baptist Church at Farmville, Virginia

On April 18, 1903, Rev. Dr. W. J. Shipman; Rev. W Moseley Seay; and F. L. Overton, effected the organization of a Baptist Church here, to be known as the Bagby Memorial Baptist Church, the name being given in honor of Dr. George R. Bagby, of Farmville. Mr. Seay became the first pastor of the new Church. The Rev. W B. Daugherty followed Mr. Seay and served during 1904-5. Then followed Rev. Z. J. Edge, 1906; Rev W. T Woodhouse, 1907-8, returning to serve from 1910 to 1917. The Rev. Dr. J. M. Pilcher was supply pastor for a term of months in 1909 Beginning November 1, 1917, the Rev. Dr. John E. White has been the pastor

The Church had but few charter members and was admitted into the Appomattox Association of Baptist Churches in 1904

The first deacons were. J. C. Moring; P. N. Jenkins; W. V. Clements; and W. T. Gibbs. Its present deacons are C. L. Elliott; G. P. Nunnally; J. R. Moring; E. P. Johnson; and A. Lee cook.

The present membership of the Church is ninety-nine

The Church building occupies a desirable and well located site, about three and a half miles from Burkeville and near to the road which leads from that town to Farmville, and is valued at about $850.

The Church was represented by three of its young men in the great war. Daniel K. Harris, son of the Rev. D. J Harris. went to Camp Lee, but was soon transfered to a hospital suffering with tuberculosis. Later he returned to his father's home in Prince Edward county, and early in 1920, died in Roanoke, Virginia.

James Oscar Thompson enlisted at Farmville, September 10, 1918, and saw service in France.

J. Grady Redford entered Camp Lee in September, 1917 In February, 1919, he was returned from France, having been severely wounded in the right shoulder and arm. He was discharged from the hospital in August, 1919. He was with the 318th Infantry Regiment, 80th Division

FARMVILLE BAPTIST CHURCH

The Farmville Baptist Church was organized, November 25, 1836, by the Rev. William Moore, who remained its Minister from that date until 1840. In a brief historical sketch by the late Dr. Peter Winston, it is noted that Sam and Phil White (colored) were the first members of the Church.

B. M. Robertson; Frank Robertson; W. Nunnally; and G. Nunnally were the first deacons of the Church, and the following were registered as charter members:

Benjamin M Robertson;
Mrs. E. R. Robertson;
C. E Chappell;
Mrs A. B. Chappell;
Miss Mary Harwood:
M. Grigg,
Mrs. Edith Mann;
Mrs. Jane Williams;
Granville Nunnally;
Mrs. Betsy Nunnally;
Washington Nunnally;
Mrs Judith Nunnally;
Jeremiah Porter;
Mrs Jeremiah Porter;
Reuben Seay;
Royall Godsey;
Mrs. Delilah Godsey;
Thomas J. Valentine;
Shelton Davis;
Mrs. Mary Davis;
Mandy Porter;
Samuel White; (colored)
Phil White; (colored). 23 in all

The Rev. William Moore, the first pastor, was assisted

in the organization of the Church by the Revs. Daniel Witt, and Elijah Roach.

The Church building was finished within a year and in 1837, was formally dedicated to the worship of God, by the celebrated Rev. Daniel Witt, whose remains lie buried in the little graveyard of the Sandy River Baptist Church, some eight miles distant from Farmville.

The first Church building, a modest structure, continued to meet the needs of the new congregation until 1856, when, during the pastorate of the Rev. James Hay, a new building was erected on the present site, and formally dedicated in February of that year by the Rev. Dr. T. G. Jones.

This second building continued to serve the needs of the congregation until 1912, when the present beautiful and finely equipped Church building and Sunday School plant was erected during the pastorate of the Rev. Willis L. Wayts, and formally dedicated to Divine worship on November 1, 1914, by the Rev. Dr G W. Perryman, of Norfolk, Va , who offered the dedicatory prayer and preached the sermon of the day. Dr. Perryman was assisted in these impressive services by the Rev. H. M. Fugate, a former pastor, and by the then pastor, the Rev. Willis L. Wayts The total cost of the plant, according to a minute upon the Church Register of January 3, 1915, was $24,033.93, without pipe organ and other furnishings Under the same date there is an entry regarding a payment on pipe organ and furnishings of $1,255.32, in a report presented by Mrs. (Dr) R. L. Hudgins, treasurer of the Pipe Organ Fund.

From the completion of the new Church building, the congregation has enjoyed an almost phenomenal growth, so that the premises are already too circumscribed for the large congregations. The property is situated on Main Street, in the very heart of the business section of the city.

The current issue of the minutes of the Appomattox Association of Baptist Churches gives the following interesting figures regarding this Church as reported at the Associational Meeting held with the Maple Grove Baptist Church, July 19-20, 1921:

Membership of the Church	504
Baptisms for the year	56
Total new members received during the year	101
Sunday School enrollment	397
Sunday School income ̣ ϩ	430 57
Church income, total from all sources	14,014.00
Benevolence, (included in above total)	3,755.62
Per capita, (including all depts.) .	27 80
Value of Church building	35,000
Value of parsonage	8,000
Total .	$43,000

The following ministers have served the Church since its inception

Rev William Moore, 1836-1840. Organized the Church and built the first Church building, 1836.

Rev. James H. Fox, 1840-1842.

Rev Thomas W Syndor, 1842-44.

Rev. James W. Goodman, 1844-1846

Rev. Robert Nowlin, 1846-1848.

Rev. William Sedgwick, 1848-1849. Served only six months.

Rev. William Tyree, 1849-1852.

Rev. James Hay, 1852-1858   It was during his pastorate that the second Church building was erected, 1856.

Rev. S. C. Boston, 1858-1859

Rev. A. J Huntington, 1859-1862.

Rev. Robert East, 1862-1865.

Rev. S. C. Boston, 1865-1867. Second pastorate.

Rev. N W. Wilson, 1867-1869. Died of yellow fever in North Carolina.

Rev. H. J. Handy, 1869-1875. Died in Maryland

Rev. James Nelson, D. D , 1875-1885. Was the organizer of the State Normal School for women, Farmville, and later was President of the Woman's College, Richmond, Va Died, 1921.

Rev. W. F. Kone, 1885-1891. Died in Kentucky.

Rev. George F. Bagby, D. D., 1891-1899. Died of cancer.

Rev. Samuel H. Thompson, 1900-1904. Died of cancer.

Rev. R. A. McFarland, 1904-1906. Went to Seminary.

Rev. J. D. Harte, 1906-1907 Served for only four months. Resigned; ill-health.

Rev. Henry M. Fugate, 1907-1911.

Rev Willis L Wayts, 1912-1915. Resigned; ill health. It was during his pastorate that the present edifice was erected.

Rev. Cosby M. Robertson, A. B , B. D., 1916-1918 Resigned to enter Navy as Chaplain during the Great War.

Rev. C. Edward Burrell, LL. B., D. D., 1919. Came to the Church from Camp Lee, where he served as Chaplain during the Great War, and is still with the Church.

The present officers of the Church (1921) are:

Rev. C. Edward Burrell, LL. B., D. D., Minister.

Dr. J. H. Cocks, Clerk.

R. C. Gilliam, Corresponding Secretary.

L. A. Smith, Treasurer.

C. A. Kennedy, Financial Secretary.

E L. Erambert, Honorary Deacon.

J. A Armisted; E. W. Sanford; C. M. Smith; Anderson Ligon; Frank Pillow; Dr. J. H Cocks; W. C Fallwell; T.

H. Fallwell; R. W. Noel; O. S. Mann; S. W Putney; L A. Smith, Deacons

Mesdames J. L. Horner, R. W. Noel, J L Putney; E. W. Ellington. Colin Stokes, J A. Armistead; W. P. Gilliam, Deaconesses.

Mrs. W B. Hobson, Organist

T H Fallwell, Missionary Treasurer.

J. L. Putney, Chairman Finance Committee.

William H Crenshaw, Chairman Property Committee

G. S. Thomas, Chairman Missionary Committee.

E W. Sanford, Chairman Music Committee.

Fred Butcher, Chief Usher.

M W. Whitlock, Assistant Chief Usher.

R C. Gilliam and S. W. Putney, Auditors

W. C. Fallwell, Sunday School Superintendent.

This Church had sixteen (16) men in the various branches of the service during the great war, 1914-1918

The Rev. Cosby M Robertson, B. A ; B. D., pastor of the Church at the outbreak of hostilities, resigned his pastorate to become Chaplain in the Navy, in which position he served throughout the war, with the rank of Captain

Dr. J. H Cocks, the Clerk of the Church, entered the service with the rank of 1st Lieutenant He was later transferred to the dental branch He received his commission as Captain, on the field during the fighting in the Argonne Woods, where he was wounded.

William H. Crenshaw, received his commission as 1st Lieutenant, from the Officers Training School but did not succeed in getting overseas.

Henry A Kelsey was appointed Sergeant.

Lawrie W. Thompson was made a Corporal

The following served as Privates: T. H. Crenshaw: Garland Hurst; Walter S. Overton; Peter Raymond; Harry S. Thompson; Cary M. Smith. Jr.; John W. Webster: M. Guy Smith; T Elbert Osborne; F. L. Magann, J. W. Mottley; C. M. Noel.

All these men, save Lieutenant William H. Crenshaw, and private Cary M. Smith, Jr., F L Magann, and C M. Noel, saw service overseas.

Privates Guy M Smith, and John W. Webster were killed in action, and T Elbert Osborne died of wounds received in battle.

The present pastor of the Church, the Rev Charles Edward Burrell. LL. B , D. D , was stationed at Camp Lee during 1918-19 in the capacity of special Camp Chaplain

One of the women of the Church, Miss L. Wheeler, saw service overseas with the Red Cross

Throughout the war the general attitude of the Church was fervently patriotic All Federal requests for announcements and discourses were most heartily responded to. Special prayers for soldiers and sailors were continually offered and several patriotic services were held. A service flag was erected and there was a formal dedication of the same, and the national colors were displayed The Women's Organizations, together with the Men's Bible Class, co-operated in welfare work for men in uniform. A special memorial service for those who died in service was held. Food conservation was urged from the pulpit and practised by the membership of the Church in a general way, and they participated most heartily in the work of war charities, both at home and abroad, by way of special offerings, collections, etc.

This Church was the first in the county to fittingly commemorate the service rendered by the members of its congregation in the war. This was done by the erection of a suitable tablet in the main auditorium of the building. Excerpts from the report of the unveiling ceremonies, which appeared in the Farmville "Herald" of November 18, 1921, follow: "On last Sunday afternoon at 3.30, very appropriate services were held at the unveiling of the tablet dedicated to the boys who were in the service during the late war. A beautiful service was conducted by the American Legion, accompanied by the Farmville Silver Band, the Farmville Guard being the guard of honor. * * * The tablet is made of white Rutland marble, twenty inches wide and four and one-half feet long. The names of Millard G. Smith, John W. Webster and Thomas Osborne, the three boys from the Baptist Church who made the Supreme Sacrifice, are carved in gold. Those in the service were, Revs. Robertson and Burrell, J. H. Cocks, W H. Crenshaw, Henry A. Kelsey, Lawrie W. Thompson, Thos. H. Crenshaw, Raymond E. Phillips, Dallas G. Hurst, Walter S. Overton, Peter Raymond, Henry S. Thompson, Cary M. Smith, Jr., Joel W. Mottley, and Charles M. Noel

"The presentation address was delivered by Dr. J. D. Eggleston, of Hampden-Sidney College, who paid tribute to those who had so nobly served their country, and the many who had died to save Christianity, Democracy and the world from the despotic heel of an unscrupulous beast. * * *

"The Star Spangled Banner was rendered by the band, following which the American Legion Service was continued, including acceptance address by Commander J. H. Cocks, prayer of dedication by Chaplain Burrell, and dedication by Commander J H. Cocks. The services concluded with the benediction by Chaplain Burrell."

The tablet was unveiled by the Misses Lucy Lee Webster and Blanche Smith, sisters of two of the men who were killed in battle.

Others to take part in the service were, the Rev Dr. E. G. Gammon, the Rev. Dr. George Spooner, and the Rev. Frederick Diehl. The Baptist Church Choir, Miss Evelyn Barnes, and Joseph A. Poole, rendered special music.

PISGAH BAPTIST CHURCH, RICE

Only the most meagre outline of the history of Pisgah Baptist Church, Rice, Va., is available, all Church records prior to about fifteen years ago being lost. Much of the incidental history regarding Baptist work in this section of the county is, however, given in the general article on Baptest churches in the county The following brief sketch is furnished by Mr. J. R. Weaver, one of the oldest surviving members of the Church.

Pisgah Church was constituted at Union Church, in Prince Edward county, about two miles east of Rice Station, in 1857.

Union Church was known as a free Church, that is, it was free to all denominations. The celebrated Daniel Witt, D. D , was the pastor until his death in 1871.

1872. Rev. S J. Adkins was pastor for five or six years.

1878. Rev J. H. Newbill was pastor for two or three years.

1880 Rev J A Leslie was pastor for about five years It was during the ministry of Mr Leslie that the Church moved to Rice and erected a new house of worship there They have since then retained the property then purchased.

1886 Rev. W. B. Haislip was pastor for two or three years.

1889 Rev. J W. Wildman was pastor for about four years

1894 Rev. W. R. D. Moncure was pastor for two or three years.

1896. Rev E. M Dowley was pastor for two or three years

1898. Rev. A. B. Rudd was pastor for five months, resigning to accept Missionary work in Porto Rico.

1898. Rev. G. F. Bagby, D. D., was pastor for about two years.

1901. Rev W. J Shipman was pastor until his death, August, 1915.

From 1915 the Church was served by supplies from various sources, until 1917, when, January 1st of that year, the Rev Horace J. Parker assumed the pastorate, remaining until June 30, 1920. The Rev George F. Cook assumed the pastorate on September 1st, 1920 and resigned, September 26, 1921.

The present Church officers are Trustees· J. S. Bradshaw, B. J. Olgers, and J. R. Weaver. Deacons· J. S. Bradshaw, S. D Hubbard, B. J. Olgers, R B. Walthall, J. R. Weaver, and J W. Bradshaw.

Treasurer S. D Hubbard.

Apportionment Treasurer. J S. Bradshaw.

Sunday School Superintendent: B J. Olgers.

Clerk: J. R. Weaver.

The following report of the war activities of the Church was furnished the War History Commission. by the then pastor, the Rev. H. J. Parker "There were seven men who served in the Army from this Church, and their names are as follows: William T. Bondurant, John C. Bondurant, William Hester Bondurant, R Melve Bradshaw, Herbert Guy Farley, Thomas Howard Garnett, John Edward Garnett.

The only one in the Navy was James W Wilson, Jr.
Herbert Guy Farley saw active service and was slightly wounded at Argonne Forest. Thomas Howard Garnett and John Edward Garnett also saw active service.

The general attitude of this Church was one of loyalty toward war activities. The members united heartily in the

National Prayer Observance and other Spiritual activities. Federal requests for anouncements were frequently made by the pastor at the regular preaching services There was displayed in the main auditorium, a service flag.

The Church heartily participated in war charities at home and abroad by way of specal collections Members of the congregation strictly observed set rules in order to conserve food and fuel during the war."

MOUNT NEBO BAPTIST CHURCH

This Church is situated near the Abilene Post Office, on the county line road, between Prince Edward and Charlotte counties.

A partially successful attempt was made to organize on the 29th of November, 1903, but the organization languished until a more thorough organization was effected on the 1st of July, 1904.

The following pastors have served the Church·

Rev. J B Williams; June, 1904-July, 1906

Rev. George R. Pankey; November, 1906-January, 1910

Rev J. E. Tucker; March, 1910-May, 1911.

Rev. P. H Dalton; June, 1911-August, 1911

Rev. John E. White; February, 1912-January, 1916.

Rev. J. A. Barnhardt; April, 1916-March, 1920.

Rev. W. F Hunt; May, 1920-August, 1920.

Rev. G. A. Harris, present supply.

The Rev. W E. Warren was serving the field when the Church was organized, 1903.

Deacons· J. R. Pollard; J. W. Pankey; T B. Yeamen; and P. A. Denton.

Clerk: O. L. Vassar.

Treasurer: C. E. Bagby.

These officers are serving the Church at the present time.

The present membership of the Church is 72.

The following is the charter membership list of the Church as of November 29, 1903:

T. B. Yeamen, L. J. Yeamen, W. J. Yeamen, E. T. Yeamen, J. R. Pollard, J W. Pankey, J. W. Bagby, J. W. Allen, D. C. Allen, Mrs. J. R. Pollard, Mrs. J. W. Bagby,

Mrs. Mary J. Driskill, Mrs Nolia Baker, Mrs. Lizzie A. Nelson, Mrs Bettie Womack, Mrs. J. W. Allen, Mrs. D. C. Allen, Mrs. Emma Daniel, Carrie Yeamen, Sallie Yeamen, Pearl Yeamen, Mary Sue Yeamen

SHARON BAPTIST CHURCH   (SANDY RIVER)

Most of the subjoined material respecting this splendid old Church was supplied by Professor W A. Harris of Richmond University. The old records of the Church have all been either lost or destroyed so that recourse had to be had to the Baptist archives in Richmond and Dr. Harris undertook an exhaustive search of the materials stored there He says:

"In speaking of Prince Edward county, Jeter says: "The eastern, or lower, end of the county was quite destitute of evangelical, especially Baptist, preaching. Sandy River Church, an old framed, dilapidated, but spacious, colonial house of worship, occupied a central position in this region. It was open for preaching by all Christian denominations, and was occupied alternately by Rev. Jno H. Rice, D. D., of the Presbyterian Church, and Rev. Matthew L. Dance, of the Methodist Church. Thither Divine Providence directed the steps of Witt. * * * His first sermon at Sandy River, as stated in the Memorial Discourse by Rev. T W. Sydnor, D. D., delivered before the Appomattox Baptist Association, was preached on the fourth Sunday in February, 1827."—Life of Daniel Witt, by J B. Jeter, pp 146-7.

"In 1828, Sharon is given, (in the Association minutes, for the first time) with Daniel Witt as pastor and 71 members. In 1829 there were 84 members, and in 1831, 226, and in 1833, 289 members. The number gradually increased until, in 1864 there were 606 members, white and colored. From then until 1871 the members reduced to 137. (Suggestive of the dire results of the war.—Ed.)

"Daniel Witt was pastor of Sharon from its organization to his death, November 15th, 1871. Witt was succeeded in the pastorate by Rev. J. H. Newbill in 1872.

"Under the caption: 'Concise View of the Churches,' I find these entries in the minutes of 1834-35:

1834—"Sharon is one of the most respectable churches in the upper country. Since its constitution, and the settlement of Elder D. Witt among them, it has been signally blessed But the sickness of the minister's wife, and the disagreeable contentions with the Methodists, seem to have stopped their onward progress. They report no baptisms, but a decrease "

1835—"They are an active people, forwarding the religious enterprises of the day. They have a temperance Society, a Domestic Missionary Society, a Foreign Missionary Society, and a Sunday School "

"The following is from Jeter's life of Witt, pp. 160-61: 'For many years' says Dr. Sydnor, in his Memorial Discourse, 'he was pastor at Jamestown, in Cumberland. and at Union in Prince Edward; and for a few years at Lebanon, in Nottoway,' the two latter of these churches, as well as the flourishing Church in the town of Farmville, claimed Sandy River; or Sharon; as their mother, and Dr. Witt as the principal agent in their organization "

The controversy with the Methodists, referred to above by Dr Harris, occurred in 1832-34, with respect to the building in which they had held their services jointly. During this dispute a line was surveyed directly through the building, the Methodists claiming one-half and the Baptists the other! Surely a difficult situation if the brethren were to dwell at peace in Zion! The Baptists retained possession of the property The matter was fully set out in a pamphlet of the day.

From this Church there were but three who served in the Army or Navy during the world war; viz: Heber Weaver and Moncure Weaver in the Army, and Carroll Melvin Bass in the Navy Heber Weaver saw active service in France.

The entire membership of the Church responded in a most fervent manner to all war appeals, and in observance of all conservation regulations

As this Church has been a part of the "field" with Pisgah Church of Rice, ever since the days of the saintly Witt, the same pastors have served them both, therefore a list of the pastors may be found in the sketch of the Pisgah Church.

The present pastor of both churches is the Rev H. P. Dalton, who came to them, April 1st, 1922, from Boykins, Va., in succession to the Rev G. F. Cook

The officers of the Church are:

John H. Bruce, Clerk.

D J. Weaver, Treasurer.

W. B. Gates, Sunday School Superintendent.

J. J. Gilliam, D. J. Weaver, W M. Gilliam, J. T. Bruce, C. M. Bass, and W. B. Gates, Deacons.

SPRING CREEK BAPTIST CHURCH

This Church was organized in 1823. Unfortunately, like so many other churches, this organization set so little store by its earlier records, that they have either been lost or destroyed Amongst its earlier ministers, were the noted Daniel Witt, D. D , and E. W. Roach, the last of whom served the Church for about forty years.

From records at present available, the following ministers have served the Church since 1875

Rev J H Newbill, July 3, 1875, to July, 1877.

Rev. S. J. Atkins, July, 1877, to July, 1880.

Rev. E S Taylor, 1880-1886.

Rev. S J Atkins, (second pastorate) 1887-1888

Rev W B Haislip, March, 1899, to October, 1889.

Rev. S. U Grimsley, 1890-1892.

Rev. J H. Couch, 1892-1903

Rev. J. B Williams, 1903-1910

Rev W. A. Pearson, 1910-1915.

Rev Vernon I'Anson, 1916-1918.

Rev. W. W. Hamilton, Jr , April to August, 1919 (Supply)

Rev Elbert Y. Poole, 1919-1922

During the pastorate of Rev. Vernon I'Anson a commodious parsonage was erected, and during that of the Rev. Elbert Y. Poole, a new and modern Church structure was built at an expenditure of a little more than $20,000.

The present officers of the Church are

Deacons: E. D Carwile, B L. Jordan, Hatcher Layne, A. L Dickerson, H. I Shorter, S A Wilkinson, and D G. Womack.

Clerk: Robert St. John

Sunday School Superintendent: E. D. Carwile.

The present membership of the Church is 303. Total amount raised for all purposes in 1921, $10,482 79.

The Church engaged heartily in all forms of war work during the great world war. The following members of the congregation served' in various branches of the service: Walter Chennault, Frank Chennault, Walter Overton, J. J Overton, Jr, Paul Layne, Hatcher Layne, D. C. Morris. W. C. Morris, Edward Shorter, Jr., Everett Garber, W A. Watson, Jr, Edward Roach, H. F. Hamilton, Leslie Carwile, W. M. Dickinson, John B. Cobb, Charles W. Putney. There were no causalties in the contingent supplied by this Church.

(Note: The foregoing sketch was furnished by the Rev E Y. Poole, the then pastor of the Church.)

BETHPEOR BAPTIST CHURCH

In 1913, the Spring Creek Baptist Church dismissed a number of its members to form the new Bethpeor Church, under the leadership of the Rev. W. A. Pearson, then pastor of the Spring Creek Church. Mr. Pearson served the two churches until 1915, when he was succeeded by the Rev. Vernon I'Anson, who served for two years, when he was succeeded by the Rev. Elbert Y. Poole, who resigned in the spring of 1922

The present membership of this Church is 79 In 1921 the sum of $1,049.37 was raised by them for all purposes. W. H. Gilliam is the Clerk of the Church, and Ray Mickle is the Superintendent of the Sunday School. The Chapel House is valued at $2,500.

THE ESPISCOPAL CHURCH IN PRINCE EDWARD

The Espiscopal Church of Virginia began with the first settlement of the first Colony in 1607. It immediately encountered immense difficulties from the scarcity of ministers of and character. The clergy of England were strangely reluctant to undertake work in the new mission field of America. Of those who did come, but few were faithful and duly qualified for the station. Indeed some them were men of very questionable character. given to swearing and drunkenness

By Act of the Assembly of 1755 the new Espiscopal parish of Prince Edward county was established under the name of Saint Patrick. The county of Prince Edward had been separated from that part of Amelia in which the parish of Nottoway was constituted, and the parish of Saint Patrick was made to correspond with the bounds of the new county of Prince Edward In 1788 the county of Nottoway was established substantially on what are its present lines. The Act of the Assembly speaks of two new churches being recently built in the lower part of Nottoway Parish, and requires that the Nottoway Parish refund a portion of the money which had been raised from the whole parish before the division, for the building of these two churches, to the new parish in Prince Edward county Services were held irregularly until 1779, when for a time, Saint Patrick's had no representative, either clerical or lay, in any convention of the Church. During this initial period the parish was served in turn by the Rev. James Garden, and the Rev. Archibald McRoberts. During Mr. McRoberts' time there were three churches in Prince Edward, viz: The Chapel, or Watkin's Church, situated about eighteen miles from Prince Edward Court House, on the Lynchburg Road; it was this congregation that followed Mr. McRoberts when he relinquished his Episcopal ministry to form an Independent Church in 1799; French's Church, situated about a mile from the Court House; and Sandy River Church, about eight miles from the

Court House on the Petersburg Road. None of these churches have survived to the present. Of course, in these early days, the Episcopal Church in Virginia occupied the same relation to the Government as did the Episcopal Church in England; it was the established Church; all others were known as Dissenters

The decline of the Episcopal Church in Prince Edward was no doubt hastened by the defection of McRoberts; the questionable character of some of its ministers; and the rise of Hampden-Sidney College and the Presbyterian Church. Certain family connections made the decline certain. "Thus Anne Michaux, daughter of one of the original refugees, and who, having fled from France on the revocation of the Edict of Nantes, settled at Manikin, married Richard Woodson, Esq., of Poplar Hill, Prince Edward, sometimes called Baron Woodson, on account of his large possessions. This lady —— lived herself to a great age, but, of a numerous offspring, only two daughters survived, one of whom was married to Nathaniel Venable, son of that Alvan Venable —— one of the vestrymen of a parish in Louisa; — the other to Francis Hopkins, Esq., clerk of Prince Edward —— Joseph Morton, the ancestor of the most numerous branch of the Mortons, of Charlotte, married a sister of Richard Woodson. The progenitor of the Mortons of Prince Edward and Cumberland, married a Michaux. Other familes of Scots or Scotch-Irish and Huguenot race were settled in both counties." Thus the intermarriage of Episcopalians with these peoples, mostly Presbyterians, was the real basis of the decline of the Episcopal Church in Prince Edward, at this time.

The following entry in the minutes of the Assembly held at the capital at Williamsburg, November 22, 1781, is suggestive of the impending decline: "Sundry inhabitants of Prince Edward county pray that all the old vestries may be dissolved by the Act of Assembly and new ones elected by the body of the community at large, Dissenters to be equally competent with conformists to the post of vestrymen, and the sole proviso to be 'attachment to the present form of government.' Referred to the next Assembly, and, June '9, 1782, rejected."

The following most interesting excerpts are taken from an historical sketch contained in the Parish Register of John's Memoral Church, Farmville, Va., and written by the Rev. Philip Slaughter, Historiographer of the Diocese, of St. Patrick Parish, and Witmer Parish, Prince Edward county.

"Saint Patrick should not be confounded with plain Patrick Parish, which is in the county of Henry, the latter county and parish dividing between them the honors of the name of the 'Forest-born Demonsthenes,' Patrick Henry. These names are redolent of the Revolution and of a new era: Prince Edward and Saint Patrick point to the old regime, when princes and saints were above par. Prince Edward county was taken from the county of Amelia by Act of Assembly, in 1753, and the Parish of Saint Patrick from the Parish of Nottoway, in 1755.

The first vestry met at the Court House, September 9, 1755. Present. Jno. Nash, Jno. Nash, Jr., David Flournoy; George Walker; Thos Scott; Jno. Leneve, James Wimbish; Thos Hawkins; Peter Legrand; and Charles Venable. These qualified by taking the oaths required by law in Court, subscribing to the test, and the promise of conformity to the Doctrine and Discipline of the Church of England. —— Hugh Challis was chosen Clerk and ordered to get a book in which to record the proceedings of the Vestry. —— This book lies before me, having been found (among the papers of Nathaniel Venable, a Secretary of the Vestry, in Colonial times) by Mr. A. P Venable, and kindly sent to the writer.

The next Vestry meeting was at Sandy River Church, December 3, 1755. The Rev. James Garden (who, as appears in the 'Lambeth Archives,' was licensed for Virginia by the Bishop of London, September 2, 1754), produced a letter from the Hon. Thos Dawson, Commissary for Virginia, recommending him to this Parish, 'upon which, and upon the knowledge of this Vestry, he is unanimously chosen Minister.' ——

The Wardens were order to pay £250 for 300 acres of land for a glebe when they were satisfied with the title, which came originally from J. Morton, Patentee. ——

In 1757 R. Burk; Philemon Holcombe; Jno Graham; R. Woodson: and Zachariah Leigh were added to the Vestry, and Nathaniel Venable made Clerk

In 1760 Obadiah Woodson was added to the Vestry, and the keys of the Glebe houses were received from P Legrand and delivered to the Rev. Mr. Garden. The following minute occurs at this date: 'Whereas, the upper Church is situated among the Dissenters, the Vestry think that service should cease there from this time.'

3rd December, 1761, the Vestry ordered new churches on the land of Messrs. Buchanan & Co., Merchants of Glasgow, near Robin's Spring; the other near where Sandy River Church now stands, dimensions 48 ft., by 28 ft., and that £100 per year be levied for building these churches. 1762 a chapel was ordered on O. Woodson's land in the upper part of the Parish. Col. John Nash and P. Legrand were given leave to build pews in the upper Church with windows. John Nash, Jr, was given leave to build a gallery for his family in the upper Church, and John Leigh, one in Sandy River Church.

1763. Three acres of land were bought for Sandy River Church.

1766, Peter Johnston, Vestryman, in place of Woodson, deceased.

1766. Dials on good posts were ordered at each Church; service to begin at 11 o'clock a. m.; April to October, and at 12 o'clock the rest of the year; and the Communion administered at Christmas, Easter, and Whitesuntide; a gallon flagon, pint cup, and salver of silver, with table cloth and napkin to be provided.

1772. 'Ordered that Peter Johnston import superfine crimson broadcloth, to be made up with silk lace and tassels, and proper cushions, for the use of the Church'

Rev. James Garden died, Feb., 19, 1773. On the 10th of August, the Revs Moss; Ogilvie; Saunders; and McCartney's names were before the Vestry, which chose the Rev. James McCartney 'in consideration of the character given him by gentlemen from North Carolina.' At this date, David Rice was Clerk (Lay Reader) of Sandy River Church, which was about eight miles from the Court House on the Petersburg Road; Richard Byrd was Lay Reader at French's, sometimes called 'Middle Church,' one mile from the Court House; and John Crockett of the Upper Chapel (Watkins) about eighteen miles from the Court House on the road to Lynchburg. When the minister attended one Church, Lay Readers served the others. Buffalo Church had disappeared from the record.

Sandy River Church, after the Revolution, became the source of a bitter contention between the Methodists and the Baptists, the details of which may be seen in a pamphlet of the day. The dispute was referred to Judge Bouldin and Mr. Charles Smith. The Baptists, I believe now hold it.

The latest record in the old Vestry Book is December 1774; many leaves having been torn out. We know from other sources that the Rev. Archibald McRoberts was minister of the Saint Patrick, 1777-78. (There is a deed recorded in Prince Edward of date, August 14, 1778, from Thos. Scott; Benjamin Haskins; Thos. Haskins; John Nash; Peter

Johnston; Peter Legrand; Philemon Holcomb; and William Bibb, Gentlemen Vestrymen of Saint Patricks Parish, to Archibald McRoberts, conveying 500 acres of land, adjoining Nathan Venable and Daniel McGehee)

In 1779, when the Church of England was tottering to its fall, he deserted the sinking ship, and set up an 'independent' Church at the Upper Chapel, which soon came to grief, and he joined the Presbyterians, who were then riding the top of the wave in Prince Edward. —— Many Episcopalians became trustee of Hampden-Sidney College, and one (Cushion), at a later period, presided over it. Two Presbyterian waves, one from Hanover, and the other from the Valley, met and culminated in Prince Edward, and many Episcopalians, (sheep without a shepherd) were carried away by them The Episcopalian Church having never been allowed to have an American Bishop to watch over and confirm its members and ordain its ministers, and having now cut off from the Church of England, was in a state of supended animation, from which many thought she never would be awakened.

Rev Devereux Jarrett of Bath Parish, one of the few burning and shining lights of that dark day, sought by his evangelistic fervor and electrical eloquence to keep alive the smouldering embers upon her altar. Outside of his own Parish he traversed twenty-nine counties in Virginia and North Carolina, lifting up his voice like a trumpet; prophesying that the old Church was not dead, but sleeping, and would again rise from the dust and be a praise in the land. In 1781-82 Jarrett preached at Sandy River and French's. Saint Patrick's sleep has been long and deep; quite, or nearly a century! —— One cannot but think that the descendants of the Woodsons, Reades; Venables; Wimbishes; Flournoys; Scotts; Nashes; Goodes; Haskins; Leighs; Legrands; Holcombes; Byrds; Berkleys; Johnstons, Buiks, and scores of other names recorded in this book, whatever may be their present connection, will look —— with approving eye and helping hand at the effort to resuscitate the Church of their fathers."

John's Memorial Church, Farmville, is the only Episcopal Church now surviving within the bounds of Prince Edward county.

Property is still held for Church purposes on the road leading from Hampden-Sidney College to Pamplins, on which stands a modest meeting house known as Saint Ann's Church, or Spring Creek Mission. Occasional service is conducted by the Rev. Thomas H. Lacy, of Richmond, Virginia, though there is no Church organization and no Church members there now. It appears that a party of English people, from Dorsetshire, settled in that part of the county sometime shortly prior to 1870, and these gave land for Church purposes and erected a modest building, and, among them, maintained the Church. They later returned to England and from there deeded the property to the Church, as appears from a deed recorded in the Clerk's Office at Farmville, in Book 31, page 257, the purport of which is that T. A. Homer. and W. C. Lacy, Dorsetshire, England, convey to John Siddons and Henry Jacob of Prince Edward county, Virginia, trustees of the Spring Creek Episcopal Mission Fund, one-half acre of land in Prince Edward county, and described as follows "Fronting 275 links on the public road leading from Hampden-Sidney College to Pamplins depot, and extending 185 links back on each side, being part of the tract of land formerly owned and occupied by Henry Collett, and now occupied by Thomas Homer." The deed was signed by T A. Homer, W. C. Lacy, and was dated May 10, 1874, and acknowledged by them in England before one, Cam Lyker, a Justice of the Peace, on May 23, 1874.

JOHN'S MEMORIAL EPISCOPAL CHURCH, FARM VILLE

The Church known locally as Saint John's Protestant Episcopal Church, but properly, John's Memorial Protestant Episcopal Church, was organized in 1880, in the house then occupied by Mr. L. M. Blanton, and now occupied by Dr. L. D Whitaker. For a time, services were held in the Court House. During the year of the organization; 1880, the present Church property was purchased, as appears by deed dated October 1st of that year and recorded on page 30 of book 34, in the land books in the Clerk's office. As there recited, one-half acre of land was conveyed by Ellen W. Berkeley, widow, through R M. Dickinson, Commissioner appointed by the Circuit Court of Prince Edward county at the September term of the court of that year, to James M. Johns, by whom it was conveyed to the members of John's Memorial Church for purposes of public worship.

By the same instrument Alfred Moth, L. M Blanton and L. C. Irving were constituted trustees to the use of the Church. The price paid for the land was $400.

The instrument is signed by:

R M. Dickinson, Commissioner;

Ellen M. Berkely:

J. M. Johns;

Pauline C. Johns, wife of J. M. Johns.

The present rectory property was acquired under a deed dated March 27, 1883, and appearing on page 198 of book 35, in the Clerk's office at the Court House. No price is stated in the deed. The premises were formerly occupied by Colonel R. A Booker, and are located at the corner of St. George and High Streets.

Thus the efforts of several years, to establish an Episcopal Church in Farmville were at last being rewarded.

In March 1879, the Rev. Frank Stringfellow became Rector of the Parish, and it was as a result of his labors that the Church was organized and the Church property bought. The first building was erected under his supervision. He was sent to Farmville with the hearty approval of Rt. Rev. F. M. Whittle, D. D., Bishop of Virginia, and his short ministry was eminently successful.

Rev. F. D. Lee was his assistant for a year. Rev. Arthur S. Lloyd was placed as Deacon in charge of the Parish in 1880. He resigned to go to St. Luke's, Norfolk He was followed by the Rev. J. W. Ware, who resigned to go to Saint James, Ashland, Virginia.

Rev. Baker P. Lee, deacon, was sent to the Parish in 1896, by the Bishop. In two years he was followed by Rev. Walter B. Capers, deacon.

July 1, 1901. Rev. Stephen O. Southall accepted a call to the Parish, and took charge. April 1, 1903, he resigned and accepted the Rectorship of Bath Parish, Dinwiddie County.

In January, 1904, Rev. Randolph Royall Claiborne of Forest, Va., (Saint Stephens Church) was called to this Parish. March 1st he accepted the call and took up the work, which also included the country work; All Saints, Grace, and Guinea. December 25, 1906, he resigned to go to Saint Francisville, La.

The Church then remained without a rector until July 1st, 1908, during the greater part of which time the Rev. George G. Matchetts, (perpetual Deacon from the Dioscese of Pennsylvania) acted as supply.

On July 1st, 1908, the Rev. Dudley Boogher, of Saint Andrews Church, Clifton Forge, Virginia, took charge of the work in Farmville. (the churches of Cumberland county being ministered to by the rector of Powhatan Court House) and continued until June 5, 1914, when his resignation was accepted that he might take charge of the Church of the Good Shepherd, Parkersburg, W Va

In November, 1914, Rev Frederick Diehl, rector of Saint Paul's Church, Wellsboro, Pa , was called. He accepted the call and began his rectorship, January 13, 1915. In the meanwhile the rectory was enlarged and much improved. Mr. Diehl left February 1, 1917, to take charge of the Church of the Good Shepherd, Rocky Mount, North Carolina

The Rev. Charles Pay Holbrook, rector of Saint Andrew's Church, Beacon, N. Y., was called on May 6, 1917, and began his work in Farmville, June 10, of that year In 1918 two flags were placed in the Church; the National Colors on the Gospel side of the arch, and a service flag, with ten stars, on the Epistle side These ten stars represent the following sons of the Parish ·

Chaplain J. M Robeson, who was later wounded in battle.

Lieutenant W. P. Hazelgrove.

Charles R. Bugg

Robert E. Warnick.

John N. Garland, killed in action, October 1918

Robert B Rogers.

Guy Lancaster, wounded in battle

Junius Wilson.

March Moffett.

Haynes Lancaster.

In July, 1918, four more stars were added for

Roy Moffett.

Joseph A. Poole

M. B. Coyner.

C. F. Walker.

In September, 1918, another star was added for

Robert W Bugg, member of the Student Training Corps, of Hampden-Sidney College.

Mr. Holbrook resigned on May 1, 1920, to take charge of the new mission work in the suburbs of Norfolk

Upon the resignation of the Rev. Mr Holbrook, the Vestry called the Rev. Frederick Diehl, rector of the Church of the Good Shepherd, Rocky Mount, North Carolina, who accepted the call, and began his second rectorship of the Farmville Church on October 1, 1920.

The value of the property, including both the Church and the rectory, is set down as $19,000.

The membership, in September, 1921, was given as 95, and the total income from all sources, as $3,126.00

The following are the officers for the current year, 1921.

Vestrymen Charles F Bugg; George M. Robeson; J L Bugg; J. A. Garland; A. T. Gray; Fred. M. Bugg; W. C. Newman.

Senior Warden. Charles F. Bugg.

Junior Warden: George M. Robeson.

Treasurer: J L. Bugg.

Secretary: J. A. Garland.

Sunday School Superintendent: J. L Bugg.

President, Women's Auxiliary Mrs. W. C. Duvall

President, St. John's Guild: Mrs. J. A Garland

President, Junior Auxilary. Miss Ilma Von Schilling.

President. Little Helpers: Miss Virgilia Bugg.

Organist. Mrs. Roberta Large.

Choir Mother: Mrs. Munro Gordon Jones.

President, Ladies' Aid Society Mrs Carrie Taliaferro.

Sunday School Teachers: Miss Virgilia Bugg; Misses Edith, Maud and Carrie Taliaferro; Miss Mary E. Peck; Mrs. R. E. Duvall. The Rev. Frederick Diehl teaches the Bible Class.

THE METHODIST EPISCOPAL CHURCH IN PRINCE EDWARD COUNTY

Methodism was slow in entering the State following after the Episcopal, the Presbyterians, the Quakers, and the Baptists had obtained a more or less secure footing in Virginia.

To the Rev. Robert Williams belongs the honor of planting Methodism in Virginia He was born in England He had labored extensively in Ireland. He received from Mr. Wesley a license to preach under the authority of the regular Missionaries in the new American Mission field. He was extremely poor, so that his passage to America was paid for him by a Mr Ashton, who came over in the same vessel.

Williams landed at New York in the fall of 1769. He thus came in advance of Messrs. Boardman and Pillmoor. He continued his labors in the city of New York until the close of the summer of 1771. In the meantime Boardman and Pillmoor had arrived in the new world, having landed at Gloucester Point, in New Jersey, on the 24th of October, 1769, from whence they went to Philadelphia. Williams visited Philadelphia and received a general license to travel and preach, from the hands of Pillmoor. After a visit with Strawbridge, the father of Methodism in Maryland, he, in the spring of 1771, returned to New York city.

The date of the beginning of Williams' work in Virginia, is 1772, when early in that year, he landed at Norfolk, and at once opened his mission. He preached his first sermon at the door of the Court House in that city. He mounted the steps and sang a hymn, which resulted in a curious crowd gathering to see what it was all about. The hymn finished, he knelt where he was and prayed. He then announced his text and proceeded to preach to a most disorderly crowd of people, quite unused to such a spectacle. Owing to the extreme plainness of his diction, he was charged with "swearing." This grew out of his frequent use of the words. "hell," "devil," "damned," etc   He was voted "crazy" by the frivolous people who heard him.

However, a few hearts were touched, and these sincere people received him into their homes and cared for him.

"The tree of Methodism was thus planted in an uncongenial soil, but, watered from on high, it struck its roots deep, and put forth goodly branches, bearing much fruit."

After this beginning in Norfolk, Williams went over to Portsmouth and, under a couple of persimmon trees, preached the first Methodist sermon ever heard in that town. Among those converted under his ministry in Norfolk, was Isaac Luke, a citizen of Portsmouth, and a member of the Episcopal Church, who invited him to come over to Portsmouth, and who befriended him in his work in the two cities.

As to how long Williams continued his labors in Norfolk and Portsmouth, we have no accurate information, but, in the fall of 1772, he was joined in his work there by William Watters, who accompanied him on his return from a visit to Maryland. On their journey from Baltimore to Norfolk, the two held a meeting at King William Court House, in the home of a Mr. Martin who had kindly entertained them overnight. Along the entire route of three hundred miles, they preached at every convenient place and opportunity, finding everywhere an appalling lack of "experimental religion." They were the first Methodist preachers who ever passed through this part of the new world

Weary and worn with toil, they at length reached Norfolk to take up again the work begun there. They found the field a most difficult one. After spending the winter of 1772 in Norfolk and vicinity, Williams went, in February, of 1773, to Petersburg, and introduced Methodism officially into that town. He was invited there by two citizens of the place whose names will ever remain identified with the beginnings of Methodism there; Gressett Davis and Nathaniel Young. As elsewhere, so here, the other denominations were found fairly well entrenched. Williams preached his first sermon in the theatre, which had been opened for religious services through the instrumentality of Davis and Young.

After laboring in, and about the town for several weeks with but little to encourage him, Williams was furnished a horse by his two young friends and set out, in true Methodist fashion, to preach in the country round about the city. In a short time a generous revival rewarded his work in the country, which was destined to spread Methodism over every part of the State of Virginia and North Carolina In this part of the State, Williams was much encouraged in his work by the sympathy of Archibald McRoberts and Devereux Jarratt, ministers of the Episcopal Church.

On the 14th of July, 1773, the first American Conference of the Methodist Episcopal Church, assembled at Philadelphia, when the whole number of members was reported as 1160, viz· New York 180, Philadelphia 180, New Jersey 200, Maryland 500, Virginia 100. Six circuits were formed and ten preachers appointed. Virginia appears in this entry: "Norfolk, Richard Wright; Petersburg, Robert Williams."

The whole of 1773 was spent by Williams in preaching and forming Societies in that part of the State south of Petersburg, during which time the Lee family was received into the Society; Jesse Lee being a conspicuous representative of that noble family.

On the 26th of September, 1775, this splendid "soldier of the Cross" entered into "that rest that remaineth for the people of God." In his "Journal" Bishop Francis Asbury thus refers to the event: "Tuesday 26, Brother Williams died. The Lord does all things well; perhaps Brother Williams was in danger of being entangled in wordly business, and might thereby have injured the cause of God. So he was taken away from the evil." On Thursday, Bishop Asbury preached his funeral sermon. Every trace of the burial place of this pioneer of American Methodism has been lost. Not even the rudest stone is left to mark his resting place.

Robert Williams preached the first Methodist sermon on Virginia soil; formed the first Methodist Society; printed the first Methodist book; was the first Methodist Minister to marry; aided in building the first Methodist Church building; made out the plan for the first Methodist circuit; was the first Methodist minister to "locate;" the first to die; the first to be buried in Virginia soil; and was the first Methodist preacher to enter heaven from Virginia! A pioneer in things Virginian, surely!

At the Christmas Conference, held in Baltimore, December 25, 1784, the Methodist Societies definitely took the form of a Church organization, in the strict and proper sense, with the title, "The Methodist Episcopal Church." Francis Asbury and Thomas Coke were, at this time, elected to the office of "Superintendents of the Methodist Episcopal Church in America," the first in a long and honorable line.

The "O'Kelly Schism" that had so long agitated the body, and that finally culminated in the "Christian Church;" the body possessing the proper legal right to the use of that title; came to a head at the Baltimore Conference of November 1st, 1792, when O'Kelly and his immediate adherents withdrew from the Conference to establish the "Republican Methodist Church," as it was at the first called. In 1801, O'Kelly changed the name of his party, by formally renouncing the first name chosen and announcing the new name to be "The Christian Church."

The question of slavery agitated the Methodist Church long before it became a national question under the impulse of northern propaganda, and many efforts were made by the young Church to stamp it out, at least in as far as it affected Methodists. The movement that ultimately resulted in the emancipation of the slaves, was in reality a southern movement, in which the Methodists had an high and honorable part, later taken up by northern agitators. At the annual Conference, held at New Bern, N. C., February 10, 1813, the following series of resolutions were adopted:

"1. The preachers shall instruct the colored people in the principles and duties of religion.

2. To search out and pay particular attention to all the classes of colored people in the bounds of their stations and circuits.

3. If any member of the M E. Church be found guilty of carrying on, directly or indirectly, the trade of slave speculation, he or she shall be expelled the Church." Bishops Asbury and McKendree presided over this Conference

The first instance on record of the elevation of a colored man to ministerial orders by the Virginia Conference, occurred at the Petersburg Conference of the 18th of March, 1824, when David Payne, of Richmond, a free man of color, was graduated to the office of Deacon. Payne subsequently went to Liberia as a missionary, where he died at his post of duty.

Methodism was slow in taking root in Prince Edward County While great progress was being made in virtually all the surrounding counties, Prince Edward seemed to remain comparatively neglected until a rather late date This was partly owing to the fact that in the east and west journies of the Apostle of Methodism, Francis Asbury, and his co-workers, the line of travel seemed to take them either to the north, through Dinwiddie, Amelia, Buckingham; or to the south, through Brunswick, Lunenburg, Charlotte. Whatever may have been the cause, it remains a fact that Prince Edward County appears but rarely in the earlier records of the Church In 1805, on their journey to the Conference at Granville County, N C., the two veterans, Francis Asbury and Richard Whatcoat, passed through Prince Edward County, doubtless exhorting the saints on their way. At a later date, while Presiding Elder of the Meherrin District, the celebrated John Early held a remarkable Camp Meeting at Prospect, where, it is said, that in seven days about one thousand persons professed conversions.

In a mere sketch of such a mighty movement, it is obviously quite out of the question to go into details, hence the progress of Methodism in the County will be best followed through the brief historical sketches of the local churches of the county.

THE METHODIST EPISCOPAL CHURCH SOUTH, FARMVILLE

The following sketch of the early history of the M E. Church, Farmville, was made by the Rev. Staunton Field, November 7, 1846, and is to be found in an old Registry Book of the Church.

"A brief history of the rise and progress of Methodism in this place may not be without interest and importance for future reference when the present generation shall have passed away.

Up to the year 1833 this was merely a casual preaching place for the Methodist Ministry. In that year, under the administration of the Gospel, by that evangelical and zealous Minister, the Rev. William B. Rowzer, who had charge of the Prince Edward Circuit, the first class was formed, and Methodism formally introduced and established. From this time Farmville appeared upon the plan of the Prince Edward Circuit, up to the "Great Revival," as it was called, of 1837.

It seems from the best information we can obtain, though it appears somewhat remarkable, that the first house of worship was commenced in 1831, and completed in '32; a year previous to the formation of the first class. The Rev. John Early was at this time Presiding Elder of the District, then included in the Lynchburg District, through whose active instrumentality, no doubt, the building was commenced and finished.

In the year 1837, as above mentioned, under the ministry of the Rev. John W Childs; Dr. A. Penn, Presiding Elder, it pleased Almighty God to visit the infant Church here, with a powerful and sweeping revival. The meeting was continued from day to day successively, for several weeks, and resulted in the conversion of many souls. It may be recorded as a remarkable fact, that the store doors were closed, and business generally suspended, during the exercises of the meeting. This circumstance will go to show the extraordinary character of that revival, and is a lasting memorial of the deep and pervading interest which must have been experienced by the whole community. Many who are on their way to Heaven, and some who have already reached that happy place, will, throughout the dateless periods of eternity, look back upon that occasion as the brightest era in their existence

This revival so fully and firmly established Methodism here, that the brethren, believing that it would be important to its further prosperity and success, requested to be set off as a station, distinct from the Circuit, which was accordingly done in the following year, and the Rev. Jesse Powers was appointed the first stationed Minister in this place. By his zeal and piety as a Christian Minister, and especially as a Pastor, the station was sustained, and abundantly blessed of the Lord

The following year, 1839, the church being too small, in the estimation of many, and without a suitable place for the accommodation of the colored people, it was thought advisable that a new and more commodious house should be erected. Accordingly, the present house of worship was commenced in '39 and completed in 1840.

The Rev George W. Blain, of precious memory, succeeded Bro. Powers, and at the Conference of 1840, which assembled in this place, was returned in charge of the station. With alternate successes and reverses, the cause of Methodism moved on, without any great display of Divine power in the conversion of souls, up to the year '42, at which time, under the administration of the Rev. Jacob Manning, Pastor, and the Rev. H. B. Cowles, Presiding Elder, the Church was again visited with a "season of refreshing from the presence of the Lord." Many valuable members of the Church were brought in at that time, and many, we trust, will remain pillars in the temple of the Lord, to go out no more forever.

The Rev. Thomas H. Jones succeeded Bro Manning in the charge of the station. Nothing of special interest occurred during this year. There were some few conversions and accessions to the Church. The Rev. J. L. Knight was the next preacher in charge of the station for the year 1845. There was no revival this year and no incident which we have gathered up worth recording. These are some of the most prominent circumstances and events connected with the growth of Methodism in this place, set forth hastily and in the most simple and unvarnished manner, and may serve, if for no other purpose, to give some data upon which to construct a more comprehensive and extended account, by some more able or competent pen."   S FIELD,

Farmville, Nov. 7, 1846

In connection with the notable fact, cited by the above historian, that the first building was erected before the formal organization of the Church, the transfer of the property, lot 19, in the plan of the Village of Farmville, from James Madison and Susan his wife, to Thomas Scott, John A. Scott, John Clarke, Nathaniel Jackson, Charles Venable, Joseph E. Venable, and Thomas Almond, Trustees of the M. E Church, South, is recorded, under date of February 6, 1833, in Book 21, at Page 183, in the Registry Office in Farmville. The consideration was the sum of $150. The Church has retained the original site to the present day

The membership in 1846 had reached the respectable total of 118, many of whom, however, were colored. Both white and colored were members of the same Churches in those days. Discipline was very rigorously enforced as evidenced by notations set opposite many names, such as: "Expelled for dancing;" "Expelled for intemperance;" "Withdrawn in preference to standing a trial "

The following note occurs during the ministry of the Rev. Frank Stanley, 1860: "I leave Farmville tomorrow for

Conference, and have transferred from the Richmond Church Advocate, my letter of 22nd of last March, and have only time to record my sense of gratitude to God and my thanks to all the members of this Station, and, indeed to all the people, for their uniform kindness to myself and family; for the ample support they have given us, notwithstanding they have this year expended about $4,000 in improving the Church, have paid the Conference Collection, and given liberally for missions and to the poor. This has been one of the happiest and most successful years of my ministry. This book will show a large increase of members. May God make them perfect in holiness and keep them all blameless unto the Day of Christ I pray my (unknown) successor not to let the numerous Class of colored Catechumens be neglected "

FRANK STANLEY,
Farmville, 14, Nov., 1860.

The membership at this time was 155.

List of Ministers With Notes

1838. Jesse H. Powers.
1839. George M. Blain.
1840. Benjamin B. Miles.
1841. Jacob Manning
1842. Thomas H. Jones.
1843. Wm J. Norfleet. Deceased, Jany. 1881.
1844. J. L. Knight.
1845. Stanton Field.
1846. Wm. H. Rohr.
1847. J. C. Garlick
1848. J D. Blackwell
1849. J. C. Newberry.
1850. Josephus Anderson.
1851. Josephus Anderson.
1852. Oscar Littleton.
1853. Charles H. Hall. Died, 1872.

1854   Wm. W. Berry

1855.   Joseph J. Edwards.

1856.   Joseph S. R. Clarke.

1857.   Joseph S R. Clarke.

1858.   John S. Rees   Died in 1861.

1859.   Frank Stanley.

1860   Nelson Head

1861.   Nelson Heal.   Died in Baltimore Conference 1903.

1862-1865.   Wm E Judkins.

1865-1866.   Jacob H Proctor.

1866-1867.   C. C. Pearson.   Left the Church for Episcopal

1867-1869.   Oscar Littleton   Died July 31, 1910. Buried at Farmville.   For 60 years a member of the Virginia Conference.

1869-1870.   Wm. E Edwards.   Died in 1902.

1870-1872.   F. M. Edwards

1872-1873.   George M. Langhorne

1873-1876.   James F. Twitty, D D.

1876-1880   Leonidas Rosser, D. D.

1880-1882.   Joshua Hunter.

1882-1886.   Wesley C. Vaden.

1886-1889.   W. E. Evans, D. D

1889-1890.   T. McN Simpson, D D.

1891-1894.   James Cannon, Jr., D D. Later Bishop.

1894.   R. H. Bennett, D. D. (3 months.)

1894-1895.   G. W. Wray

1895-1899.   T McN. Simpson, D. D

1899-1901.   J. S. Hunter.

1901-1903   T. N Potts, D D.

1903-1905.   J. B. Winn, D. D.

1905-1909.   S. C. Hatcher, D. D.
1909.   W. T. Green.
1910-1911.   W. R. Proctor.
1911-1912.   W. G. Porter.   ·
1912-1913.   S. A. Donahoe.
1914-1916.   G. H. Lambeth, D. D.
1916-1919.   Jno. T. Bosman, D. D.
1919.   G. H. Spooner, D. D.

This Church had in the various branches of the service during the Great War, forty men.

Captain H. H. Hunt went overseas as Captain of a Company from Farmville, served at the front and was made Major.

Dr. C. B. Crute volunteered, June 21st, 1917, and was appointed 1st Lieutenant in the Medical Department, and was attached to the British Forces overseas and was promoted to be Captain. He saw service in France, Belgium, Italy, Egypt and India. After two years service overseas, he returned to America, and was stationed at Fort Whipple Barracks in Arizona, and later was transferred to Fort Mc-Pherson, in Georgia, from whence he received his discharge and returned to Farmville to re-enter his profession as a private citizen.

Dr. T. G. Hardy volunteered in June, 1917, and saw service overseas as 1st Lieutenant in the Medical Department in France, both at the front and in hospital work. He was discharged in January 1919, and resumed his private practice in Farmville.

Dr. J. S Burger enlisted in the Medical Department with the rank of 1st Lieutenant, and served at Camp Meade throughout the war.

Paul Barrow enlisted in the Navy and died in Hampton Roads of pneumonia.

Walker Paulett enlisted as private, and was promoted to be 1st Lieutenant and, in the fight in the Argonne Woods, led his company for many days with conspicuous bravery.

Edward Davis enlisted as a private, was promoted to be Sergeant and, when all his superior officers were killed, wounded or captured, led his Company, reduced to a handful, for days in the thickest of the fight

Emerson Jarman volunteered early and was assigned to the regular army, and promoted to be 1st Lieutenant. He did not get overseas.

Joseph Jarman, James Cowan, Mack Cowan, F. Lawrence Orange, James Lipscomb, Henry Wood, Zenas Chappell, Walker Drummeller, and Howard Whitlock, saw service in the ranks overseas

Willard Hart saw service overseas as an expert marksman with the Marines.

T A. Gray, Jr., C. B. Collyer, R. H. Paulett, and Gates Richardson, saw service with the Aviation Corps, but did not get overseas.

John Foster saw service with the Wireless Department overseas.

Walter Gray got as far as England, but did not succeed in getting to the trenches.

E. A. Chappell, J H Lewis, Jr , F. L. Carter, Harry Mottley, John A. Morris, Wallace Duvall, Lewis Whitlock, and C. B. Cunningham saw service in the homeland.

Womack Gray was detained in America in preparation for work in the Medical Department.

O. H Whitten saw service in the navy but did not succeed in getting overseas.

Among the Student Army Training Corps, were W P. Venable, Jr , J. B. Wall, Jr., Archer Paulett, Reginald Venable, and Ernest Garland

Judge J. M. Crute, from whose article this sketch is made, says: "At this late date (March 19, 1920), with all the records turned in, it is impossible to give a correct report Several of those across the sea were promoted to Sergeants and Corporals, who enlisted as privates."

Dr. T. G. Hardy, Dr. J. L. Jarman, Mrs. J. L Jarman, Mrs. T. G. Hardy, E. S. Martin, and Dr. J. M. Lear, were prominent in the work of the Red Cross in the county. The work of Mrs. Jarman with the women of the county was a notable contribution to the work of the Prince Edward Chapter of the American Red Cross

THE METHODIST EPISCOPAL CHURCH SOUTH, PROSPECT.—OLIVE BRANCH CIRCUIT

This is the oldest M. E. Church organization, in what is now Prince Edward county and is composed of two preaching appointments in the county, viz: Prospect and Olive Branch. It is the mother of Methodism in the county. Originally it was attached to the Lynchburg Circuit.

The Church organization was in existence for some considerable time before the property was secured, as a meeting house was already upon the land purchased for Church purposes by the Society in Prospect, July, 14, 1820. The land then purchased consisted of one acre and was conveyed by Robert Venable to Charles Venable, William Johnston, David, Anderson, Jesse Bradley and Samuel Venable, in trust for the M E. Church, for Church purposes. (See Deed Book 117, page 139, in the Clerk's Office at Farmville)

Approximately the same situation obtained at Olive Branch appointment, a meeting house being already upon the property, and in use for Church purposes, prior to the actual acquisition of the land by the Society. The property, one acre and building, was conveyed by Benjamin Boatwright and his wife, Mary W Boatwright, to Rev. William Johnson, Rev. James McNeal, Edwin Gray, Thomas Andrews, Joel Elam, John C. Owen, Charles W Wilkerson, James Martin and Charles Venable, in trust for the M. E. Church for religious purposes, July 9, 1829. (See Deed Book 20, page 242, in the Clerk's Office at Farmville.)   An additional piece of property was subsequently obtained for the use of the Society adjoining the first parcel, from the same parties, January 17, 1834, making up the present property.   (See Deed Book 21, page 196, in the Clerk's Office at Farmville.)

The present Parsonage property at Prospect was conveyed by James D. Crawley and his wife, Amanda M. Crawley, in trust, to Joseph W. Gills, Thomas H. Crawley, Thomas H Glenn, Joseph B. Glenn, George M. Gillespie, Robert N. Wilkerson, and W. E. H. Durphy, trustees, July 30, 1877, the consideration being the sum of $1,125. (See Deed Book 33, page 140, in the Clerk's Office at Farmville.)

There is a singular lack of available data relating to these early days of Methodism in this part of the county, the minute books of the Society being either lost or destroyed What information there is available serves to indicate that the work of the Circuit was pressed with great earnestness and with a gratifying measure of success.

For 1920-21 the Prospect Church raised for all purposes, the sum of $4,175.56, while, for the same period of time, the Olive Branch Church raised $1,845.92.

The present officers of the Prospect Church are.

Minister: Rev. R S. Baughan.

Stewards: T. S. Tweedy, I. H. Glenn, J. R. Glenn, B. T. Taylor, C. H. Rucker, C. W. Crawley, C. E. Chick, T. R. N. Cocks.

Trustees: G. R. Glenn, R. J Carter, E S. Taylor.

Sunday School Supt   B. T. Taylor.

President of the Woman's Missionary Society; Mrs R. S. Baughan.

———

The present officers of Olive Branch Church are·

Stewards: J. Hopkins Wilkerson. J Henry Wilkerson, W. W. Vaughan, R. H. Wilkerson, H. C. Elam, W. B. Binford, H. L. Moore, J. R. Fore.

Trustees: E. H. Gilliam, I. O. Reynolds, Emery Chick, G. D. Warriner, R. Lee Price, J. W. Davis.

Sunday School Supt.: W. B. Binford.

President, Woman's Missionary Society; Mrs. J. D. Carter.

———

The circuit was organized in 1870 with three churches, viz., Olive Branch, Prospect, and Pamplin. In 1873 Smyrna was added to the circuit, and later on Piney Ridge. In the year 1914 Pamplin and Piney Ridge were transferred to another circuit, leaving Olive Branch, Prospect, and Smyrna, which compose the present charge. The first pastor of Prospect Circuit was Rev Alfred Wiles, who was succeeded by Rev. J. Wiley Bledsoe. Revs. J. S. Hunter, W. C. Vaden, G. H Ray, H C. Cheatham, T. J. Taylor, J. E. Potts, R W. Watts, and J. H. Proctor were others of the early pastors.

With the passing of the years this charge has grown and kept pace with the progress of the times. It now has three good Sunday Schools open every Sunday throughout the year, three flourishing "Woman's Missionary Societies," with one young lady from Olive Branch preparing for work in foreign fields. The charge over-subscribed the Centenary quota by a good margin, and raised the full quota in the Educational Movement

The budget system has been adopted enabling the Stewards to meet all obligations promptly. The pastor is paid monthly and presiding elder quarterly.

Recently, a copy of the Advocate has been put in every home on the charge, totaling 175 subscriptions

The village of Prospect was named for the original Church, which stood on the site of the present cemetery. This building was burned in 1860, at which time it was being used as a school house

The present building was erected in 1859. During the

War between the States the Federal soldiers camped on the Church grounds and pitched one of their tents on the northeast side of the building. Needing a place to hang their clothing, they bored holes in the weather boarding and inserted wooden pins for clothes racks. These holes still remain.

The following constituted the first official board: Samuel T. Clark, Henry J. Venable, Thos W. Crawley, J. W Gills, James D. Crawley, and Robt. V. Davis. Records show that at this time there were only 96 members on roll.

In 1919 the old Church building was remodeled Eight Sunday School rooms were built and equipped, an attractive recess pulpit put in, furnace installed, and an imposing colonial front added

An Epworth League has recently been organized, which gives promise for splendid work in the future.

SMYRNA CHURCH

Smyrna Church is located at Sheppards in Buckingham county, about ten miles from Prospect. Prior to 1873 it was on the Buckingham Circuit. Since that time it has been a member of Prospect Charge.

The following article was supplied by the Rev. J. M. Moser, then pastor of the Prospect M. E. Church:

"The two churches, Prospect, and Olive Branch, of our Prospect Charge, sent twenty-one men into the various branches of service in the world war.

Husie Glenn to Camp Taylor, and oversea

Peyton Glenn to Camp Lee, was made Sergeant, and saw duty oversea.

Watkins Brisentine and his brother Allen were in Camps Lee, and Hancock.

Hunter Ferguson to Camp Lee, and made Sergeant.

Norwood Gallier was in Camp Lee, and was in action oversea.

Frank Glenn was in Camp Lee, and made Sergeant.

Leonard Fulcher in Camp Lee, and saw service oversea.

Claude East in Camp Lee, and saw action oversea.

Russll East first in Camp Eustis, and later in school and was training at University of Virginia.

Robert Cocks to Navy, and made storekeeper.

Robert Cheadle in Camp Lee. He died of pneumonia, following influenza.

Warren Tomlinson in automobile training, and saw service oversea

Elmer Tomlinson, helper in war shops, up east somewhere

Jake Hopkins in Camp Lee.

Isaac Glenn in school and war training at University of Virginia.

Bascom Taylor in school and war training at Randolph Macon College, Ashland, Virginia.

Phil Swan to Camp Lee, saw action oversea, and was killed in battle there.

John Fore, saw action oversea, and, after Armistice, did police duty in Germany.

Ernest Woodall, in action oversea, and was seriously wounded.

Henry Moore in the Navy.

Both these churches were, without exception, warmly patriotic   All seemed bent and determined to do their part in all the war activities without hesitation or stint.

During the whole time our boys were in camp and oversea there was not a single service in our churches without fervent, faithful prayer for them, that in body they might be protected by the Great, Good Lord of Hosts; that in soul they might be kept pure, in life clean, and that after they had won the victory and set the world free, they might return to us the same pure boys they were when they went away

We had no service flag, but we all kept and carried a service heart

Our boys were sent away with a farewell prayer service —a real overflow community prayer meeting. And, on their return, we called them together in the same Church in a gracious service of thanksgiving to our Father for His wonderful goodness and mercy to our boys, and to us and our Allies.

Our people were quite active and very generous in raising all war funds, even the children catching up the patriotic spirit, both buying, and soliciting War Saving Stamps with a zeal that called out our best praise; so that in Red Cross work, Y M C. A work, Liberty Loans, and War Saving Stamps, our people truly excelled. We are not able to give the figures, but verily they were far into the thousands. We feel safe in making the statement that our people never turned down a single call for War Charities. Our men, our women, our children, were always ready to give, and to do, for the war and for relief."

March 6, 1920.

SALEM M. E. CHURCH, SOUTH; RICE

This article was contributed by the Rev. O. M. Clarke, present pastor of the Church.

Salem M. E. Church, South, was organized in the fall of 1884, as the outgrowth of a Sunday School organized in 1883, at the home of Mr C L. Overton, by Mr. A W. Drummeller, of Farmville, and a revival meeting conducted at Rice, by Rev. J. S. Hunter of Farmville.

There were fourteen charter members, as follows:

Mrs M. J. Hubbard, Mrs M. R. Watson, Miss Betty Wade, John T. Branch, Mrs M B. Price, J W Garrett, Mrs. V. C Garrett, W. H. Hubbard, J. E Hubbard, S D Hubbard, Miss Nannie B. Hubbard, (now Mrs. Amos, of Roanoke,) Miss Mary Watson (now Mrs. Smith, of Cumberland) Miss Mary Watson (now Mrs. J. A. Hillsman,) Miss Anna Watson (now Mrs. John Morrissette).

The Church was assigned to Burkeville Circuit, with Rev. J. B. Askew as its first pastor, who served until 1887.

The following ministers have since served this Church: J. E. White, 1887, (died); W. E. Bullard, supply, 1887; T. M. Beckham, 1888-1890; F. B. Glenn, 1890-1892; R. L. Wingfield, 1892-1894; R. S. Baughan, 1894-1897; W. F. Hayes, 1897-1899; J. E. Oiler, 1899-1900; Dr. Leek Spencer, 1900-1903, (died); J. E. McCullough, supply; W. L. Jones, 1903-1907; T. E. Johnson, 1907-1909; W A. S. Conrad, 1909-1911; R. G. James, 1911-1913, W. A. S. Conrad, 1913-1917; T. H. Stimson, 1917-1918; O. M. Clarke, 1918, to the present.

Present officers:

Rev. O. M. Clarke, Postor.

J. E. Hubbard, Superintendent Sunday School.

W. D. Mason, Treasurer.

Stewards   J. E. Hubbard; George Frank; M. T. Garrett.

Assistant Stewards: W. D. Mason; H. H. Hubbard; W. H. Price.

Trustees. J. E. Hubbard; George Frank; W. D. Mason; W. H. Price; H. H. Hubbard.

The gross income for last year, for all purposes, was $1,125.

THE PRESBYTERIAN CHURCH IN PRINCE EDWARD COUNTY

Somewhere about the year 1740, reports came to Virginia of awakenings and revivals of religion occurring in the North, and some books, differing from those in common use, found their way for the first time into Virginia, and disturbed the minds of many persons in the counties of Hanover, Louisa. and thereabouts. Finding nothing corresponding with these teachings in the sermons of the clergy of the established, or Episcopal Church, and deeming them to be Scriptural, as opposed to that of the clergy, some of these people of the laity, separated themselves from the usual services, which by law they were bound to attend, and read sermons in private houses.

These things came to the ears of the then Governor of the State, Governor Gooch, and he became much offended, and, summoning a general court, delivered a charge complaining of the conduct of those laymen and preachers who, professing to be Presbyterians, yet utterly disregarded the Act of Toleration, and produced much discord in the colony. This charge was laid before the Synod of Philadelphia, by a messenger for Virginia.

The Synod, having considered the matter, sent the following address to the Governor ·—

"May it please your Honour, the favorable acceptance which your Honour was pleased to give our former address, and the countenance and protection which those of our persuasion have met with in Virginia, fills us with gratitude, and we beg leave on this occasion with all sincerity to express the same It very deeply affects us to find that any who go from these parts, and perhaps assume the name of Presbyterians, should be guilty of such practices, such uncharitable and unchristian expressions, as are taken notice of in your

Honour's charge to the Grand Jury. And, in the meantime, it gives us the greatest pleasure that we can assure your Honour that these persons never belonged to our body, but are missionaries. sent out by some, who, by reason of their divisions and uncharitable doctrines and practices, were, in May, 1741, excluded from our Synod, upon which they erected themselves into a separate society, and having industriously sent abroad persons whom we judge ill qualified for the character they assume, to divide and trouble the churches. And, therefore, we humbly pray, that while those who belong to us, and produce proper testimonials. behave themselves suitably, they may still enjoy the favor of your Honour's countenance and protection And, praying for the divine blessing on your Honour's person and government, we beg leave to subscribe ourselves your Honour's, etc etc.

ROBERT CATHCART, Moderator.

These persons, thus complained of, are identified by an address to the House of Burgesses, sent at about this time, as follows

"ADDRESS TO THE BURGESSES"

"To the Worshipful the Speaker and Gentlemen of the House of Burgesses.

"The humble petition of some of the clergy of this Dominion showeth

"That there have been frequently held in the counties of Hanover, Henrico, Goochland, and some others, for several years past, numerous assemblies, especially of the common people, upon a pretended religious account,—convened sometimes by merely lay enthusiasts, who, in these meetings, read sundry fanatical books and use long extempore prayers and discourses,—sometimes by strolling, pretended ministers, and at present by one Mr. Samuel Davies, who has fixed himself in Hanover; and, in the counties of Amelia and Albemarle, by a person who calls himself Mr Cennick, well known in England by his intimacy with Mr. Whitefield.

"That though these teachers and their adherents (except the above-mentioned Cennick) assume the denomination of Presbyterians, yet we think they have no just claim to that character, as the ringleaders of the party were, for their erroneous doctrines and practices, excluded from the Presbyterian Synod of Philadelphia in May, 1741, (as appears from an address of said Synod to our Governor,) nor have they, since that time, made any recantation of their errors, nor have been readmitted as members of that Synod, which Synod, though of many years standing, never was reprehended for errors in doctrine, discipline, or government, either by the established Kirk of Scotland, the Presbyterian Dissenters in England, or any other body of Presbyterians whatsoever. Whence we beg leave to conclude, that the distinguishing tenets of these teachers before mentiond are of dangerous consequences to religion in general, and that the authors and propagators thereof are deservedly stigmatized with a name (New-Lights) unknown till of late in this part of the world.

"That your petitioners further humbly conceive' that, though these excluded members of the Synod of Philadelphia were really Presbyterians. or of any of the other sects tolerated in England, yet there is no law in this Colony by virtue whereof they can be entitled to a license to preach, far less to send forth their emmissaries, or to travel themselves over several counties, (to many places without invitation) to gain proselytes to their way· 'to inveigle ignorant and unworthy people with their sophistry;' and, under pretence of greater degrees of piety among them than can be found among the members of the Established Church, to seduce them from their lawful teachers and the religion hitherto professed in this Dominion.

"Your petitioners therefore, confiding in the wisdom and piety of this worshipful House, the guardians of their religious as well as their civil privileges, and being deeply sensible of the inestimable value of the souls committed to their charge, of the infectious and pernicious tendency, nature, and consequences of heresy and schism, and of the sacred and solemn obligations they are under 'To be ready with all faithful diligence to banish and drive away all erroneous and strange doctrines contrary to God's word, and to use their utmost care that the flock of Christ may be fed with the sincere milk of the word only,' humbly pray that the good laws, formerly in that case made and provided, may be strictly put in execution; particularly that entitled 'ministers to be inducted.' And, as we humbly think this law still retains its primitive force and vigour, so we pray that it may on this occasion effectually exert the same, to the end that all novel notions and perplexing, uncertain doctrines and speculations, which tend to the subversion of true religion, designed by its admirable Author to direct the faith and practice of reasonable creatures, may be suitably checked and discouraged. And that this Church, of which we are members, and which our forefathers justly esteemed a most invaluable blessing, worthy by all prudent and honourable means to be defended and supported, being by us in the same manner regarded, may remain 'the pillar and ground of truth,' and glory of this Colony, which hitherto hath been remarkably happy for uniformity of religion.

"And your petitioners, as in duty bound, shall ever pray, etc

"D. MOSSOM,
"JOHN BRUNSKILL,
"PAT. HENRY, (REV)
"JOHN ROBERTSON,
"ROBERT BARRETT."

The result of this protest from these five clergymen, was that Mr. Davies was summoned to appear before the House and plead his own cause, which he did with such ability that he appears to have secured recognition, though not to the extent that he had hoped for. He was allowed to continue his work with some restrictions. His labors were confined to the Hanover Presbytery which embraced the territory afterwards composing Prince Edward county, most of his efforts being concentrated on that section of his territory. His zeal and eloquence attracted great crowds, and drew many from the Episcopal churches, which stirred up continual opposition to him He was more or less directly instrumental in the establishment of the Academy of Prince Edward, now Hampden-Sidney College. He was afterward President of Princeton College, New Jersey. How he obtained recognition from the Synod of Philadelphia does not appear, nor does it appear that he was amongst those originally expelled by that body.

The progress of the Presbyterians in Prince Edward county has been co-existent with the growth of Hampden-Sidney College and the reader is directed to the chapter dealing with that institution for further information, as touching those early days of the Church

Another factor in the decline of the Established Church that did so much to accelerate the growth of the Presbyterians in Prince Edward, was the defection of the Rev. Archibald McRoberts from the Episcopal Church and his adherence to the Presbyterian Church. This good man was ordained in 1763, and continued a minister of the Episcopal Church until 1779. When he withdrew, he was located in a parish in Prince Edward, and lived at Providence, on the glebe near Prince Edward Court House, from whence, on July 13, 1780, he wrote his friend Mr Jarratt, regarding the change he had made. In that letter he says:—

"Upon the strictest inquiry it appears to me that the Church of Christ is truly and properly independent; and I am a dissenter under that denomination. Ecclesiastical matters among the Presbyterians I find every day verging toward my sentiments, and will, I believe, terminate there. There is very little that divides us even now. They constantly attend my poor ministry. Several of Mr Sankey's people have joined my congregation, and I have lately had a most delightful communion-season at Cumberland, where I assisted Mr. Smith at the urgent request of himself and the elders Soon after my dissent, as my concern for the people had suffered no change, I drew up a set of articles including the essential parts of natural and revealed religion, together with the Constitution and Discipline of the Christian Church, and proposed them to their consideration; since which they have formed a congregation at the chapel, and a few have acceded at French's and Sandy River. I preach at the churches by permission, and intend to continue, God willing, until the first of January, at which time, if congregations should not be formed at the lower churches, my time will be confined to the chapel, and such other places as Providence may point out and the good spirit of God unite his people at "

He was a Scotchman by birth The following incident is related of him "Most of the able-bodied men of Prince Edward were off with the army, on duty elsewhere, when Tarleton, with his troops of cavalry made a foray through that and the neighboring counties. He visited sundry houses in Prince Edward, attempted to frighten women and children, destroyed much furniture, and otherwise did much wanton mischief. A detachment was also sent to the glebe, and Mr. McRoberts had hardly time to escape They ripped open feather-beds, broke mirrors, etc., and went off, having set fire to the house. It burned slowly at first, but the building would have been consumed had not a shower of rain come up suddenly and extinguished the flames. Mr. McRoberts, who regarded this as a special interposition of providence, called the place PROVIDENCE."

The name stuck, and such it was known ever after. Later on, the glebe became the property of Colonel Venable. (Meade, Vol. I, 448.)

It would appear that two of Mr. McRoberts' sons graduaated with the first class from Hampden-Sidney College.

The Rev. Richard Sankey, ordained in 1739 by the Presbytery of Donegal, in Pennsylvania, moved to Prince Edward county with his entire congregation, establishing his work at French's, a little to the northeast of Kingsville. He was the first regularly installed Presbyterian minister in the county. Other Presbyterian churches of these early days of the county, now extinct, were Briery, 1748; Buffalo, 1759; and Watkins, 1759.

THE FARMVILLE PRESBYTERIAN CHURCH

There is a tradition that the Farmville Presbyterian Church was organized in 1828, but that is not borne out by the facts, as the following paper discloses:

"Petition of the members of Hanover Church, worshipping at Farmville, Va., to West Hanover Presbytery, asking a division of Hanover Church, October 8th, 1844.

Farmville, Va., Oct 8th, 1844.

The Memorial and Petition of members of the Hanover Church, (Prince Edward county) usually worshipping at Farmville, to West Hanover Presbytery:

Your petitioners respectfully request that the Presbytery would divide Hanover Church, organizing one of the divisions at Farmville. The records of the proceedings of Hanover Church in reference to the desired division will accompany this petition, and we ask that the same be considered a part of this memorial. The representatives of the Hanover Church in Presbytery will give the necessary explanations in reference to the wishes of the memorialists

We are not advised that it will be contrary to the constitution, or form of Government of the Presbyterian Church, to permit the present pastor of the Church to have charge of the two churches and, as your memorialists do not desire a change in our pastoral relations, they ask that a division be made contemplating such an arrangement.

Your memorialists will only add, that the members of Hanover Church, usually worshipping at Farmville, are nearly, if not entirely unanimous in the request herein presented.

Respectfully submitted,

F. N. Watkins, M. A Watkins, C. R Barksdale, Ed M. Barksdale, John Dupuy, Ann Dupuy, Wm. C. Flournoy, (by

F. N. W.), M. W. Flournoy, M. R. Flippen, Caroline Flippen, Wm. M. Womack, N. D Price, M. T. Price, M. E. Venable (by F N. W. by permission), Mary C. Womack, Jacob W Morton, Mary Jane Morton, Wm. C. Chappell, A. W. Millspaugh, C. C. Read, A. E. Read, Mary P. Venable, Charles T. Carrington, C. Scott Venable, E. G. Venable, Mary E. Venable. Sarah S. Venable."

This paper, the original of which is now in the hands of Mrs. Henry Edmunds of Farmville, Va., reveals the fact, that the Church was organized in 1844 with twenty-seven charter members, and was set off from the College Church, which was then known as Hanover Church, and was served by the same minister as the College, or Hanover Church. The minister was Rev. Wm. C Scott, who seems to have served the Church till 1854. He was succeeded by Rev. Michael Osborne, who served till 1863. Then followed in succession, Rev. Richard McIlwaine, 1864-1870; Rev. H. H. Hawes, 1871-1885; Rev. W. H. Neel, 1885-1888; Rev E. H. Harding, 1891-1903; Rev. J. G. McAllister, 1903-1905, Rev. H. T. Graham, 1905-1909; Rev. W. E Hill, 1909-1912; Rev. Andrew Allen, 1912-1916; and Rev. Charles F. Rankin, to the present time.

At the time the Farmville Church was organized, West Hanover Presbytery was composed of thirteen churches, the oldest of which was Cumberland, organized in 1754, having had a history of nearly a century when the infant Farmville Church was born The Presbytery now has forty-eight churches on its roll.

The present house of worship at Farmville, is the original building, and the lot on which it stands, is said to have been given by Col. James Madison, grandfather of Mr. William G. Dunington. To the original building has been added the portico, and the Sunday School annex, which was built during the pastorate of the Rev. W H. Neel, and just now the congregation is preparing to add another wing to the building, containing eighteen class rooms, for the purposes of a modern Sunday School.

During its seventy-eight years of history, the Church has grown from a membership of twenty-seven, to an enrollment of three hundred and sixty; and, from the modest contributions of those early days, to an annual budget of about $12,000, and is now the second largest Church in the Presbytery, Charlottesville ranking first.

It would appear that the Farmville Church, before the War between the States, had an endowment, as was true of some other churches in this section, and that this endowment consisted largely in slaves; of course the Church lost its endowment with the close of the war. This perhaps, seemed a great loss to the congregation at that time, but, doubtless, was a great blessing in disguise, as has been proven in so many other cases where a Church has lost its endowment.

Many of the names of those twenty-seven charter members still appear on the roll of the Church, in their descendants, as officers and members of the Church, who are worthily carrying on the work which their fathers and mothers so bravely began. And this old Church, which has waxed stronger as the decades have gone by, bids fair to render a more glorious service in the future than it has in the past; for, to the manhood of old age, it adds the lustiness of youth.

(Note With some unimportant alterations, the above most excellent record was furnished by the Rev C. F. Rankin It would appear that some substantial grounds for the tradition that this congregation was formed in 1828, exists in the probability that that date is meant to mark the time when Presbyterian services were first held in Farmville in connec-

CHURCH COLLEGE HAMPDEN-SIDNEY COLLEGE, VA.

Rev. E. G. Gammon, D. D. Pastor.

See Page 284.

tion with the Cumberland, Hanover (or College) Churches; the erection of the independent Church taking the place in 1844, as stated above.—Editor.)

The following compose the official membership of the Church at the present time·

Pastor; The Rev. Charles F. Rankin.

Elders: Dr. P. A. Irving, Clerk of Session. W. D M. Stokes, E. A Richardson, Joel Watkins, Judge George J. Hundley, Judge Asa D. Watkins, J. J Adams, W. T. Clark.

Deacons: Capt. S. W. Watkins, Chairman and Treasurer of the Church; George Richardson, Assistant Treasurer of Church; R B. Cralle, F. H. Hanbury, C. W. Blanton, C. W. Harrison, Charles Scheffield, Horace Adams, R. B. Johns, A. V. Wade, J T Thompson, F. W. McIntosh, E. W. Husted, F. S. Blanton, B. M. Cox.

Superintendent of Sunday School: F. S. Blanton.

Officers of Women's Auxiliary:

> President: Miss Carrie Bliss.
> Vice-Pres.: Mrs. A. B. Armstrong.
> Secretary: Mrs. E. S. Shields.
> Treasurer: Mrs. P. A. Irving.

Circle Leaders of Women's Auxiliary:

> Mrs. George Richardson.
> Mrs. Henry B Smith.
> Mrs. C. A. Price.
> Mrs. George Rex.
> Mrs. S. W. Watkins.

COLLEGE PRESBYTERIAN CHURCH, HAMPDEN-SIDNEY

This Church was first organized under the name, "Hanover Church," which name was subsequently changed by the Presbytery to "College Church," and is located at Hampden-Sidney, in the immediate vicinty of the College, and is, of course, the College Church.

On the 20th of October, 1835, "Hanover Church," (the present "College Church") was organized under orders of Presbytery, by a division of "Cumberland Church," which formerly embraced the territory and the membership of the present "Cumberland Church," the "College Church," and the Farmville Church, with the following officers· First pastor, the Rev. Benjamin M. Staunton, D. D., who was ordained in 1835, ruling elders Major James Morton, Dr. Goodrich Wilson, Moses Tredway, Armistead Burwell, James Madison, John Rice, Silas Biglow, Clement C. Read, Samuel Lyle, Samuel C. Anderson.

This new organization included ruling elders. Dr. Goodrich Wilson, Col. James Madison, Col. John Rice, Clement Read, Samuel Lyle, and Samuel C. Anderson.

The Church thus organized embraced "College Church" proper, and the Farmville Church, and so continued until the 21st of December, 1844, when a portion of the members of this Church was organized as a Church to be known as the Farmville Church

On the 1st of May, 1840, the following were elected ruling elders: Henry E Watkins, Dr. Peyton R. Berkeley, Nathaniel E. Venable, and Thomas Flournoy, Mr. Flournoy subsequently removed to the neighborhood of Farmville, and it is believed, never acted as elder in the College Church.

On the 1st day of March, 1845, at a meeting of the Hanover congregation, held at College Church, agreeable to previous notice, the following were elected as ruling elders: Asa D. Dickinson, John Hughes, Dr B. F. Terry

In September of 1856, the following were elected deacons in this Church, being the first of that class of officers: Robert C. Anderson, James A. Womack, John A. Dalby. At the same time Abraham C. Carrington was elected ruling elder.

In December 1859, Edwin Edmunds, Henry C. Guthrie, and Henry Stokes, were elected ruling elders.

In May, 1860, A. R. Venable and Charles Baskerville were elected deacons. On the 12th of August, 1871, Louis L Holladay and Andrew R Venable were elected to the eldership, while Henry W. Edmunds and John M. Venable were made deacons.

The following have served the Church as pastors:

Rev. B. M. Staunton, D. D., 1835-1840.

Upon the death of Dr. Staunton, Rev. James W. Alexander of Princeton, N. J., was called but declined.

Rev. Patrick I. Sparrow, D. D., June 26, 1841-1847.

Rev. Benjamin H. Rice, D. D., ordained, June, 1848-1858, when he died.

Drs. R. L. Dabney and B M. Smith, joint pastors, 1858-1874.

Drs. Smith and Peck, supplied, 1874-1875.

Rev. Charles A White, D. D., 1875-1891, when he died.

Rev. Richard McIlwaine, D. D., 1891-1895.

Rev. James Murray, D. D., 1895-1907.

Rev. W. J. King, 1907-1917.

Rev. Edgar G. Gammon, D. D., 1917.

The following are the officers for the current year, 1921.

Session. The Rev. Edgar G. Gammon, D D., Moderator. A. W. McWhorter, Clerk; E. L. Dupuy, J. D. Eggleston, P. T Akinson, R. E. Stokes.

Deacons J. H. Rodgers, Allan Stokes, John Allen, T. J. McIlwaine.

Church Treasurer: E. L. Dupuy.

The total income of the Church for the current year, (1921) was $12,040 16.

The value of the Church property, including the fine new manse, erected in 1920, is approximately $50,000.

The Church has made marked progress under the pastoral charge of the Rev Dr. Gammon, a sketch of whom will be found in the chapter on "Who's Who in Prince Edward," in this work.

JAMESTOWN PRESBYTERIAN CHURCH, RICE
War Record.

This Church had but one representative in the Great War, Private James Blanton Vaughan, who trained at Camp Lee and served overseas. He was discharged on March 1st, 1919, from Camp Dix. The Church as a whole, responded to all calls throughout the war period, including war charities. Prayers were offered for the success of the Allies, and a fervent patriotism was in evidence. The minister of the Church, the Rev. F. W. Osborn, led his people in all their war activities.

DISCIPLES OF CHRIST,
LIBERTY CHURCH

The following article respecting Liberty Church, was furnished by the Rev F. W. Berry, present pastor of the Church.

This Church was first organized in 1847 Its first location was near the Richmond and Danville R. R., three miles N. E from Green Bay. There were twenty-three charter members, with two elders: S. H. Wootton, and William Walton

In the year 1881 the Church was moved to Green Bay, its present location. Since locating at Green Bay, the Church has furnished the charter membership for three Churches, namely, Beulah, at Rice; Bethel, in Lunenburg Co.: and Crewe.

The present membership is one hundred and four. The officers are:

Elders· L D. Jones; F. W. Berry.

Deacons· F. H. Jones; S. C. Coleman; G. W. Palmer

Secretary-treasurer: F H. Jones.

The total income for all purposes in 1921 was $450.

The following men from the congregation served in the world war: R W. Jones; L. A Snow; W. R. Berry; Thomas Weaver, overseas; S. S. Flippen and O. C. Bonner. at home

COLORED CHURCHES

The author is indebted for the following very excellent sketch of the colored churches of the county, to the Rev. P. W. Price, who, besides serving a group of colored Baptist churches, is the principal of a large colored school in Farmville. The sketch is presented almost verbatim as prepared by him.

There are at present in the county of Prince Edward, twenty colored churches, with an approximate membership of 5,665; namely: Alabama; Beulah A. M. E.; Calvary; First Baptist, Farmville; First Rocks; High Bridge; High Rock; Levi; Mercy Seat; Mount Zion; Mount Moriah; Monroe; New Hope; New Witt; Peaks; Prospect A. M. E.; Race Street, Farmville; Sulphur Springs; Triumph; and Zion Hill.

The oldest of these, and the churches from which most of the others sprang, are, First Baptist, Farmville; Mount Zion; Sulphur Springs; Triumph; and New Hope. These were organized by colored members from white churches of which they were members before the emancipation, and in some instances with the aid and advice of the white friends who were members of the churches from which they obtained their letters of dismission to form the exclusive colored churches.

The value of the colored church property is about $37,-000. These churches pay to their pastors about $5,300 annually To Foreign Missions they pay about $300, and to Home Misssions (most of which is used in the county to help build schools and pay teachers,) about $19,000.

A few of the consecrated pioneers who have nursed these churches during their earlier years, often men of limited education, but men with fixed faith in God, were Revs. John White; Carter Braxton; Robert Watkins; Armistead Burkley; and Nelson Jordan.

HAMPDEN-SIDNEY COLLEGE—Faculty and Student Body

See Page 304.

Chapter Twelve

The Schools of Prince Edward

1. Hampden-Sidney College.
2. Union Theological Seminary, Richmond.
3. State Female Normal School, Farmville.
4. Colored Schools.

THE SCHOOLS OF PRINCE EDWARD

HAMPDEN-SIDNEY COLLEGE

This institution, a College for men, originated as an Academy, established by the Presbytery of Hanover, 1774-1775, and known as "Prince Edward Academy," and formally opened, January 1, 1776.

The circumstances leading up to its establishment were briefly these

Virginia was at the first settled by Englishmen, most of whom were members of the Church of England, now called the Episcopal Church. Dissenters were very few in number, but grew steadily, so that some years previous to the Revolutionary War, they had become a rather considerable body. They possessed no independent institution of higher learning, William and Mary, then the only College in the state, being under the control of the Episcopalians.

At about this time, the Rev. Samuel Davies, of Hanover county, with other of like mind, formed the Hanover Presbytery of the Presbyterian Church   The bulk of the Presbyterians in the lower part of the state, were then residing in Prince Edward and the nearby counties. This newly formed Presbytery determined to found an institution more in sympathy with their ideals than William and Mary, and did so at about the above date.

The Academy was organized into a College and chartered in 1783. It received its name from those two valiant champions and martyrs of liberty John Hampden and Algernon Sidney. When established, it was dependent upon private munificence, and has continued from its inception to be supported by private benefactions. Next to William and Mary. it is the oldest College in the South.

The many fine buildings of the College, occupy an elevated, healthy, and attractive situation seven miles from Farmville and about eighty miles from Richmond. The village of Hampden-Sidney and the College buildings are lighted by electricity supplied from Farmville. At the present time there are seventeen buildings in the College group, residences included, and the grounds comprise some two hundred and twenty-six acres, with one hundred and thirty and six-tenths acres still to come from the Venables' estate.

It is said that more instructors have come from this institution, than from any other in the Southern States.

The Presidents of Hampden-Sidney College, since its inception, are as follows·

Rev. Samuel Stanhope Smith, D.D., LL.D., 1775-1779.

Rev. John Blair Smith, D.D., 1779-1789.

Rev. Drury Lacy, D.D., 1789-1797

Rev. Archibald Alexander, D.D., LL.D., 1797-1806.

Rev. Moses Hoge, D.D., 1807-1820.

Jonathan P. Cushing, A.M., 1821-1835.

Rev. Daniel Lynn Carroll, D.D., 1835-1838.

Rev. William Maxwell, LL.D., 1838-1844.

Rev. Patrick J. Sparrow, D.D., 1845-1847.

Rev Lewis W. Green, D.D., 1848-1856.

Rev. John M. P. Atkinson, D.D., 1857-1883.

Rev. Robert McIlwaine, D.D., LL.D., 1883-1904.

Rev. James Gray McAllister, D.D , 1905-1908

Rev. Henry Tucker Graham, D. D., 1908-1917.

Joseph DuPuy Eggleston, A.M., LL.D., 1919.

The broken periods in the above line were filled by Committees and Acting Presidents, the following serving in one or other of these capacites· William S. Reid, D.D., 1807; Messrs. M. Lyle, James Morton, William Berkeley, John Miller, J. P. Wilson, 1820-1821; George A. Baxter, D D., 1835; S. B. Wilson, D.D., F. S. Sampson, D.D., 1847-1848; Charles Martin, A.B., 1848-1849, 1856-1857; Rev. Albert L Holladay (Died before taking office), 1856; James R Thornton A M., 1904; William H. Whiting, Jr., A.M., 1904-1905, 1908-1909; J. H C. Bagby, Ph.D., 1906; Ashton W. McWhorter, A.M., Ph.D., 1917-1919.

Amongst the notable names in the long and honorable history of Hampden-Sidney, none shine with greater brilliance than that of the Rev. Samuel Stanhope Smith, to whom is given the credit for the founding of the original Prince Edward Academy. He was a native of Lancaster county, Penna., and a graduate of the College of New Jersey, of the class of 1769. He subsequently united with the Presbytery of Hanover, Virginia, and so pressed the cause of education as to make his name historic in the early annals of the Commonwealth. He was the first Rector of the Academy, and, under his control and direction and stirred by his almost magical influence. it attained a remarkable prosperity He resigned in October, 1779, in order to accept the professorship of Moral Philosophy in his Alma Mater in New Jersey, and his brother, the Rev. John Blair Smith, was appointed to succeed him. He was the last Rector of the Academy, and the first President of the College proper. These two remarkable men, brothers, exerted a permanent and lasting influnce upon the religious and the educational life of the Commonwealth.

It is worthy of note that not so much respect for "moral

suasion" was entertained at Hampden-Sidney in those early days, as to exclude at least occasional recourse to corporeal punishment. This form of punishment was generally reserved for the members of the grammar school, but the superior dignity of the Sophomores and the Juniors was not always safe from invasion, though the Collegiate classes were usually exempt.

It is also worthy of note that in the early financial problems of the institution, the trustees did not hold back from accepting the friendly aid of the lottery schemes, at that time flourishing At so late a date as 1797, at a meeting of the Board, upon the occasion of the installation of Dr. Archibald Alexander, afterwards the founder of the Theological School of Princeton, as President of the College, a petition to the General Assembly of the state for a lottery to be conducted in favor of Hampden-Sidney, was most gravely approved and recorded!

From 1776, through to 1820, the Academy, and later the College, were enabled to exist through the union of the pastoral office with the Presidency of the school; the President of the College being later installed as Pastor of the Prince Edward and Cumberland Churches. In 1820 that union was permanently dissolved.

The Hanover Presbytery was determined in its choice of the site for the school, by the liberality of Peter Johnston of Prince Edward county, who donated about one hundred acres of land in his county for the purposes of Prince Edward Academy The land was situated in the tobacco-growing section, where money currency had but limited circulation This Peter Johnston, of Longwood, was a Scotchman, and a member of the Scottish Episcopal Church He was the friend and correspondent of the father of Sir **Walter** Scott, and was the adjutant of General Lighthorse Harry Lee's famous Legion during the Revolutionary War. His son, Peter Johnston, was a member of the first class of the institution, and was the father of the famous Gen Joseph E. Johnston of Virginia fame.

Among the Trustees of the original Academy may be noted the names of James Madison (1751-1836) fourth President of the United States, and Patrick Henry (who is believed to have drafted the college charter) subsequently Governor of Virginia. These names, amongst others, indicate that the institution was a product of the struggle for religious and civil liberty.

The legislative government of the College was originally vested in twenty-seven Trustees, who had authority to fill all vacancies occurring in their own body The following is a partial list of the original incorporators and trustees: Richard Sankey, John Todd, Samuel Leake, Caleb Wallace, Peter Johnston (donor of the land), Col. Paul Carrington, Col. John Nash, Jr, Capt John Morton, Capt Nathaniel Venable, Col {Thomas Read, James Venable, Francis N Watkins The following were subsequently added to this number· Rev David Rice, Col. Patrick Henry, Col. John Tabb, Col. William Cabell, and Col. James Madison, Jr.

The College succeeded the Academy in 1783 by Act of the General Assembly, of that date, and the following were noted as the incorporators Rev John Blair Smith, Patrick Henry, William Cabell, Sr., Paul Carrington, Robert Lawson, James Madison, John Nash, Nathaniel Venable, Francis Watkins, John Morton, Thomas Reade, William Booker, Thomas Scott, Sr., James Allen, Charles Allen, Samuel Woodson Venable, Joseph Parke, Richard Foster, Peter Johnston, Rev. Richard Sankey, Rev. John Todd, Rev David Rice, Rev. Archibald McRobert, Everard Meade, Joel Watkins, James Venable, and William Morton

By an Amendment to the Charter, secured February,

1919, the number of trustees was reduced to twenty-five, and vacancies occurring in the Board to be filled by the Synod of Virginia

The following constitute the Board of Trustees at the present time (1921).   J. B. Bittinger, D.D., Charles A. Blanton, M.D., J. E. Booker, D.D., W. C. Campbell, D.D . A. B. Carrington, A B Dickinson, Hon. Don P. Halsey, J Nat Harrison, Hon H. R Houston, Hon. F. B Hutton, Paulus A. Irving, M.D , Hon C P. Janney, Col C C. Lewis, Jr., F. T. McFaden, D.D., H. W. McLaughlin, D.D., W. W. Moore, D.D., LL.D , J Scott Parish, Col. John H. Pinner, W H T Squires, D D , Ernest Thompson, D.D , Hon. James L. Treadway, Hon E. Lee Trinkle, A L' Tynes, M.D., Hon A. D. Watkins, B F. Wison, D.D.

The literary degrees conferred under the Charter, were first bestowed, September 22nd, 1786, at which time the degree of A. B. was awarded Kemp Plummer, David Meade, James Watt, Ebenezer McRoberts, Thomas McRoberts, Nash LeGrand, and John W. Eppes, seven in all. The last two distinguished themselves in after life, the one as an Evangelist, the other as a member of Congress.

The following compose the Faculty of the institution at the present time:

Joseph DuPuy Eggleston, A.M , LL.D., President. (See, "Who's Who in Prince Edward.")

A. W. McWhorter, A.M., Ph.D. Dean

Henry Clay Brock, B Lit., Professor Emeritus of Greek.

J. H. C. Bagby, M A , M E , Ph.D., Professor of Physics and Astronomy.

J. H. C. Winston, A.B., B.S., PhD , Professor of Chemistry and Geology.

William H. Whiting, Jr., A B , A.M., Professor of Latin and Spanish.

STATE FEMALE NORMAL SCHOOL, FARMVILLE—Main Entrance—Spring Time

See Page 301.

Ashton W. McWhorter, A M , Ph D., Professor of Greek

John A Clarke, A B., M.A., Professoı of French and German.

Asa D. Watkıns, A.B., B D , Professor of Englısh.

James S. Mıller, B.S., C E., Sc D , Professor of Mathematıcs.

J B Massey, A B., B D , D.D , Professor of Bıble, Phılosophy, and Psychology.

Thomas Cary Johnson, Jr , B.A., M.A., Professor of Hıstory and Economıcs

Thomas Smyth, B.S., Professor of Biology.

Benjamın D. Paınter, A B , B S , Assıstant ın Mathematıcs and Modern Languages

F. T. McFaden, Instructor ın Mathematıcs.

Despıte the fact that repeated efforts have been made to secure an adequate endowment, ıt ıs a fact that Hampden-Sidney has today the smallest endowment of any standard College ın the whole Southland.

Founded ın faıth and prayer, it makes a confident appeal to the aıd and loyalty of ıts constıtuency; the whole of the Unıted States of America!

The usual Socıeties and Fraternıties flourish among the students

Athletics also flourish, a fine athletıc field of some five or six acres—Venable Fıeld—immediately adjoıns the college buıldıngs.

A fine lıbrary of some 15,000 volumes ıs avaılable to the student

The present enrollment of the College is one hundred and eıghty

Some four hundred former students of Hampden-Sidney saw service during the Great World War, eleven of whom made the Supreme Sacrıfice

UNION THEOLOGICAL SEMINARY

This institution originated in the efforts of the Hanover Presbytery and the Synod of Virginia, to give the candidates for their ministry a more complete theological training than was then available. Such efforts were put forth as early as 1812, but it did not get into regular operation until 1824. It was located in the immediate vicinity of Hampden-Sidney It had a very successful history but was moved to Richmond in 1898 Many of the most successful ministers of the Presbyterian Church look back with fond recollections to the years spent at the Union Theolgical Seminary while it was located in Prince Edward County.

To the Rev John Holt Rice, D.D , born November 28, 1777, and who died in Prince Edward County, September 2, 1831, belongs the credit for the founding of this institution. He was then an instructor at Hampden-Sidney It was at the head of the Seminary that he passed his last years. He was famous as an orator of unusual powers and as a writer of ease, fertility and force.

STATE FEMALE NORMAL SCHOOL

On March 5th, 1839, the Legislature of Virginia incorporated "The Farmville Female Seminary Association." Messrs. W. C. Flournoy; James E. Venable; Thomas Flournoy; William Wilson; George Daniel; Willis Blanton; and James Ely were the incorporators. The capital stock was $30,000, to be divided into 300 shares each, of the par value of $100: (*Acts of* 1839, *page* 120).

By deed dated May 26th, 1842, George Whitfield Read and Charlotte his wife, in consideration of $1,400, conveyed to "The Farmville Female Seminary Association," lots Nos. 105 and 107 containing one acre of land. These lots were the same which James Madison, trustee for Josiah Chambers, had, in consideration of $1,250, conveyed to George W. Read by a deed dated April 3rd, 1836. For these deeds see Deed Book 22, page 56, and Deed Book 23, page 384.

While excavating for the foundation of a new building that was erected for the State Female Normal School, in 1897, the Corner Stone in the old building of the Farmville Female Seminary, above referred to, was dug up and opened. There was no box in the stone, but a hole about 4 by 5 inches, and 3 inches deep. Across the top of this hole was a silver plate, bearing the following inscription:

Farmville Female
Academy
Built by Joint Stock
Company, A. D. 1839.

Inside of the hole was a copy of the New Testament, a newspaper, three silver coins—5, 10, and 25 cent pieces—and a Masonic emblem or badge. The back was all that remained of the New Testament, and the letters on that faded away a few minutes after being exposed to the air. A piece of the newspaper about an inch square could be read

This original building was completed in 1842 and was at once occupied and used for the purposes for which it was erected   It was at this time that the final payment of the purchase price of the property was made.

Solomon Lee, Esq., was first in charge as Principal.   He was followed after a few years by his brother, Rev. Lorenzo Lee.   A northern man named Coburn, and remembered mainly as the possessor of a very long nose, succeeded him.   Then in 1850 Mr John B Tinsley succeeded to the office of Principal, and was succeeded in rather rapid succession by two men named Gould and Lamont, respectively.   About 1860 Mr A Preot, Esq, assumed the reins and remained some nine or ten years, which included the difficult years of the war and the more difficult years of the Re-Construction Period that succeeded.   A Rev Mr. Crawley conducted a school there for one year during 1871 or 1872.   He was succeeded by the Rev Paul Whitehead, who was followed for a short term by a Miss Carter.

By an Act of the Legislature, passed May 24th, 1860, the charter of the company was amended, and the name changed to "The Farmville Female College."   This corporation held the property until Janaury 15th, 1873, when it was conveyed by deed to Mr. G M Bickers, pursuant to a resolution adopted by the stockholders in a meeting held July 1st, 1870, when they determined to sell and, after paying its debts, distribute the proceeds amongst the stockholders   By deed dated May 29th, 1882, Mr Bickers conveyed the property to the Rev. Paul Whitehead and others, Mr. Whitehead being the Principal of the College at that time.

By deed dated April 7th, 1884, "The Farmville College," a corporation of which the aforementioned Rev Paul Whitehead was President, conveyed it to the town of Farmville, and, by a deed of the same date, the town of Farmville conveyed it to the State of Virginia, in consideration that the State would establish on it a Female Normal School.

"A system of free schools for Virginia was established, July 11, 1870, by the first Legislature to assemble after the War between the States As these schools struggled year after year for a stable footing, it became more and more evident that they must be supplied with specially trained teachers before they could reach the desired efficiency To make provision for this pressing need, the Legislature at its regular session in March, 1884, passed the following Act establishing the Normal School.

"Be it enacted by the General Assembly of Virginia:

1.   That there shall be established, as hereinafter provided, a normal school expressly for the training and education of white female teachers for public schools.

2.   The school shall be under the supervision, management and government of W H Ruffner, J. L. M Curry, John B. Minor, R M Manly, L R Holland, John L Buchanan, L. A Michie, F N Watkins, S C. Armstrong, W B Taliaferro, George O Conrad, W E Gaines, and W. W Herbert, as a board of trustees. In case of any vacancy, caused by death, resignation, or otherwise, the successor shall be appointed by the Governor. The Superintendent of Public Instruction shall be *ex-officio* a member of the board of trustees.

3.   Said trustees shall, from time to time, make all needful rules and regulations for the good government and management of the school, to fix the number and compensation of the teachers and others to be employed in the school, and to prescribe the preliminary examination and conditions on which students shall be received and instructed therein. They may appoint an executive committee, of whom the Superintendent shall be one, for the care, management and government of said school, under the rules and regulations prescribed

as aforesaid. The trustees shall annually transmit to the Governor a full account of their proceedings under this act, together with a report of the progress, condition and prospects of the school.

4   The trustees shall establish said school at Farmville, in the County of Prince Edward; provided said town shall cause to be conveyed to the State of Virginia, by proper deed, the property in said town known as the Farmville Female College; and if the said property is not so conveyed, then the said trustees shall establish said school in such other place as shall convey to the State suitable grounds and buildings for the purpose of said school

5.   Each city of five hundred inhabitants, and each county in the States shall be entitled to one pupil, and for each additional representative in the House of Delegates above one, who shall receive gratuitous instruction.   The trustees shall provide rules for the selection of such pupils and for their examination, and shall require such pupil selected, to give satisfactory evidence of an intention to teach in the public schools of the State for at least two years after leaving the said normal school

6.   The sum of five thousand dollars is hereby appropriated to defray the expenses of establishing and continuing said school.   The money shall be expended for that purpose under the direction of the trustees, upon whose requisition the Governor is hereby authorized to draw his warrant on the treasury.

7   There shall be appropriated annually, out of the treasury of the State the sum of ten thousand dollars to pay incidental expenses, the salaries of officers and teachers, and to maintain the efficiency of the school, said sum to be paid out of the public free school fund; provided, however, that the Commonwealth will not in any instance be responsible for

any debt contracted, or expenditure made by the institution
in excess of the appropriation herein made.

8 The Superintendent of Public Instruction shall render to the Second Auditor an annual account of the expendi-
tures under this act "

It was not until 1886, however, that the institution was
incorporated by the Legislature, under the name of the State
Female Normal School.

That Farmville secured the school was owning to the
fact that the town offered to give to the State a building
formerly used as a girls' school, and this offer was warmly
supported by such influential men as Dr. W. H Ruffner, Dr.
James Nelson, then pastor of the Baptist Church at Farmville, and Dr. W. H. H Thackston, at that time mayor of
Farmville and most anxious to promote its interests

The first meeting of the Board of Trustees was held in
Richmond, April 9, 1884, and organized by the election of
Dr. J. L. M. Curry, president, Dr. J. L. Buchanan, vice-
president, and Judge F. N. Watkins secretary and treasurer.

The Board was confronted by a serious difficulty at the
outset in the shape of the seventh section of the law establishing the school This provided that the money set apart for
the support of the school should be taken from the public
free school funds. The question was at once raised as to its
constitutionality. It was the opinion of the Attorney-Gen-
eral, and, later, of the Court of Appeals, that the seventh
section was "unconstitutional and void" in so far as it attempted to divert the public school funds

The Board of Trustees thus found itself without funds for
the proposed work, until an extra session of the Legislature
amended the section, August 23, 1884, by passing a law requiring that the ten thousand dollars be paid out of the treas-

ury of the State, "which was just what should have been done at first "

At the first meeting of the Board, Dr W H. Ruffner was unanimously chosen president At the same meeting a committee composed of Dr Ruffner, Dr. Curry, and Dr Buchanan, was appointed to formulate a plan of organization of the school. The committee made its report June 10, 1884, but, because of the delay in getting the funds to run the school, the report was not adopted until September 17, 1884 The school was then ordered to be opened October 30th, following, although, to quote Dr. Ruffner's words, all they had was "a principal, an appropriation, a rough scheme, and an old academy building,—not a teacher, nor a book, nor a piece of apparatus or furniture."

The school was opened promptly at the appointed time, however, with Dr Ruffner as president; Miss Celeste E Bush, of Connecticut, as vice-president; Miss Clara M Brimblecom, of Boston, for vocal music; and Miss Lillian A Lee, of Connecticut, for drawing and mathematics To this number were later added Miss Pauline Gash, of North Carolina, teacher of English; and Mrs. Clara Bartkowska, of Richmond, Va , to have charge of the preparatory school These six persons formed the first Faculty of the school During the first year Mr Beverly H Robertson was added to this faculty as teacher of science, Latin, and algebra; and Miss Belle Johnson, as teacher of piano music In this first session there were enrolled one hundred and ten students, of whom forty-four were accommodated in the building. There were three graduates, viz: Annie Lydia Blanton; Lulu M Duncan; and Lulu O Philips.

To Dr W H Ruffner, and to Dr J L. M Curry, undoubtedly belongs the credit for the Normal School idea in Virginia, and the State was fortunate indeed in securing the services of two such able men to launch and guide the new undertaking By this means the new venture set out on correct Normal School lines and the vexations, due to constant experimentations, were thus avoided. Thus the pioneer school of its kind in the Southland was assured a proper foundation, and Farmville Female Normal School was a success from the very start.

A more extended note respecting these two remarkable men will be found in chapter thirteen, on biography

The school had in turn, the following to serve in the office of President. Dr. William Henry Ruffner, 1884-1887. James Atkinson Cunningham, LL.D , 1887-1896. Robert Fraser, LL.D., 1898-1902 Joseph L Jarman, A.B., LL.D , 1902, to the present time. (See further, Chapters on Biography and Who's Who)

When Dr. Jarman assumed the presidency of the institution, the entire plant; grounds, buildings, etc , were valued at only $90,000; the present valuation exceeds $500,-000. During Dr. Jarman's regime, twenty-eight separate pieces of property have been purchased, so that the school grounds now comprise some twelve acres all told.

For thirty-seven years Mr Benjamin M. Cox has served the institution as Business Manager. His daughter, Miss Mary White Cox, is the efficient Head of the Home Department.

Mrs. Bessie G. Jamison is the housekeeper

Miss Lillian V. Nunn is the supervisor of the laundry department.

Mr. William Marshall Atkinson is the college constable.

STATISTICS OF GROWTH

Students

1884-1885 _ _ 121	1899-1900 _ _ .351
1889-1890 ___ .._ 248	1909-1910 _ ___ 616
	1921-1922 _ __ _637

Faculty

1884-1885 _ _ _ 8	1899-1900 ___ _ ____ 13
1889-1890 _ 9	1909-1910___ __ __ ___ 32
	1921-1922 _ __ _ 42

Home Department

1884-1885 ___ _ 1*	1899-1900 ___ __. 3
1889-1890 _ __ _ 2	1909-1910 _ _ _ 12
	1921-1922 _ _ _ 13

Lady Prmcipal

COLORED SCHOOLS

This sketch of the colored schools of the county, like the sketch of the colored churches, was furnished by the Rev. P. W. Price, a most excellent colored preacher, who, in addition to his pastoral duties (he serves a group of colored Baptist churches) is also the principal of the splendid colored school at Farmville, with an enrollment of about 400 children under his care. The sketch is given almost verbatim. The attention of the careful reader will be arrested by the statement of the exceedingly short and inadequate school term, and by the beggarly salary paid the teachers of these schools.

A few years after the Civil War, when the days of the re-construction were well over, the doors of a few public schools were opened to colored people. These schools, about six to begin with, were taught by white people for some years, until some of the colored students became qualified to assume the task of teaching.

The real thirst for an education on the part of the colored community has added very greatly to the school advantages presented to colored students and, at the same time, created a deep sympathy in the hearts of many white friends.

Hundreds of those who attended these colored schools of the county, have finished higher schools, returned to their homes, and through strenuous effort, and with the co-operation of the school authorities, have increased the number of colored schools in the county to thirty-three, with a teaching force of fifty-one.

The average length of the school term is from five to six months, and the average monthly salary of the teachers, between $35 and $40.

Chapter Thirteen

Prince Edward County Biography

1. Henry Watkins Allen.
2. J. L. M. Curry.
3. John Atkinson Cunningham.
4. Asa D. Dickinson.
5. Walter Gray Dunnington.
6. Robert Fraser.
7. Patrick Henry
8 Joseph Eggleston Johnson
9. John Peter Mettauer.
10. James Nelson.
11. William Henry Ruffner.
12. Francis N. Watkins.
13. Peter Winston.
14. Daniel Witt.

PRINCE EDWARD COUNTY BIOGRAPHY

HENRY WATKINS ALLEN: *Brigadier-General, Confederate States Army, and Ex-Governor of Louisana.*

Henry Watkins Allen was born in the county of Prince Edward, near Farmville on the 29th day of April, 1820.

His father, Dr. Thomas Allen, a graduate of Hampden-Sidney College, was of Scotch extraction. His mother, Ann Watkins, was descended from a Welsh family

The first mention of a "Watkins" in the history of Virginia, was of one "James Watkins," a companion of "Captain John Smith," in his expeditions of 1607-8. The Watkins are related to many of the best Virginia families; the Finchards, Carringtons, Venables, etc. In the Revolutionary War a troop of horse, known as "Watkins Troop," raised in Prince Edward county, fought with conspicuous bravery; their leader. Thomas Watkins, grandson of Thomas Watkins of Chickahominy, at the battle of Guilford Court House, March, 1781, was distinguished for his gallantry; winning laurels in single combat.

Henry W , the subject of this sketch, was the fourth son of Dr. Allen. A biographer (Sarah A. Dorsey) describes him as "rash, but true; quick, but not malignant; flashing with sudden ire, but sweet and sound in temper; with nothing hidden, nothing mean, heartfelt warmth, earnest affection, constancy, generosity. no revenge, with a softness and tenderness of soul almost feminine."

In 1833, Mrs Allen having previously died, Dr. Allen, with his motherless children, moved into Kay county, Missouri, leaving the remains of the gentle wife and mother to rest beneath the green sod of "Old Virginia."

With the subsequent history of Allen we may not deal in detail in so short a sketch, save to note the fact that in 1861 he re-visited Virginia, and spent a short time with his relatives in Prince Edward county. Whilst there he went to the family cemetery to see his mother's grave. "Never," says his cousin, the late Honorable Francis N. Watkins, father of Judge Asa D Watkins, present Commonwealth's Attorney, a sketch of whose life appears elsewhere in this work, "did I witness such uncontrollable emotion as seized him as he approached that hallowed spot "

Henry Watkins Allen died in exile, in the city of Mexico, on Sunday, April 22nd, 1866, at 11 o'clock in the morning.

WALTER GRAY DUNNINGTON
See Page 320.

DR. J. L. M CURRY *Born in Georgia,* 1825. *Died in Asheville, N. C., February* 12, 1903.

His father was a prominent landholder and slaveowner of Georgia, but the subject of this sketch spent his early life on a plantation in Alabama. He graduated from the University of Georgia at the early age of eighteen, then studied law at Harvard University, graduating when twenty years of age. At the age of twenty-one he became a member of the United States Congress from 1857 to 1861, when his fine gifts of oratory attracted much favorable attention.

In 1866-67 Dr. Curry served as President of Howard College, Alabama. For thirteen years he was Professor in Richmond College and also President of the Board of Trustees of that institution. He often occupied the pulpit as preacher, although he had no regular charge. He was at one time President of the Foreign Mission Board of the Southern Baptist Convention.

For twenty-two years as agent of the Peabody Fund, and for twelve years of the Slater Fund (which was used exclusively for the education of the negro) he had more to do with the organization of the common school system of the south than any other man. While agent for these two funds, Dr. Curry was twice sent to represent his country at a foreign court; first as Minister Plenipotentiary to Spain by appointment of President Cleveland, and afterwards as representative at the Coronation of the Spanish king. ,

It was under Dr. Curry's leadership that the establishment of State Normal Schools was inaugurated in the South. It was he who originally drafted the bill for the Virginia School at Farmville. He was elected the first President of its Board of Trustees.

Before coming to his work in Farmville, he was already distinguished as a statesman, diplomat, educator, and author.

He died at seventy-eight years of age, at Asheville, N. C., on February 12, 1903.

DR. JOHN ATKINSON CUNNINGHAM   *Born, June 24, 1846. Died, October 9, 1898.*

The subject of this sketch, the second President of the State Female Normal School of Farmville, Va , was born in Richmond, Virginia, June 24, 1846   His paternal grandfather, Edward Cunningham, came from Ireland, to Virginia in 1770, and made a large fortune through establishing iron works that were situated near the present site of the Tredegar mills in Richmond, and, through a chain of country stores which extended from Virginia nearly to Ohio   The father of the subject of this sketch, bearing the same name, received his schooling at William and Mary, at Harvard, and at the University of Pennsylvania, from which latter institution he graduated in medicine in 1825.   He married Miss Mary Johnston, a granddaughter of Peter Johnston of Longwood, near Farmville, and donor of the land on which now stands Hampden-Sidney College.

John Atkinson Cunningham, Junior, was the only child of this union   He was very delicate in health and received most of his early education from a French governess.   Afterwards he attended private schools, but immediately before the breaking out of the War between the States, he was a pupil at New London Academy, Bedford County.

At the age of seventeen he entered the Confederate Army and served as a private to the end of that struggle   After the war he pursued his studies at the University of Virginia, where he graduated in chemistry, Latin, moral philosophy, natural philosophy, pure mathematics, and French. He afterwards receive his Master's degree from the University of Nashville, and in 1896 Hampden-Sidney College gave him the honorary degree of LL.D.

In 1874 Mr. Cunningham married Miss Florence Boyd, of Nashville, Tenn., who lived for not more than a year afterwards. In 1887 he married Miss **Martha Eggleston**, daughter of Mr. Stephen Eggleston, of Cumberland county, Virginia.

For a short time after leaving Nashville, Tennessee, where he had taught in the University of Nashville, Mr. Cunningham was in business as a druggist in Richmond, Virginia. In 1877 he was made Principal of Madison School in that city, where he taught with great success until he came to Farmville.

The ten years of Dr. Cunningham's Presidency of the Normal School at Farmville, were years of steady and substantial growth. In his first year ninety-three students were enrolled in the Normal School department; in his last there were two hundred and fifty.

He died, October 9, 1898, at Farmville, Va., aged 52 years.

JUDGE ASA D. DICKINSON. *Born*, 1817. *Died*, 1884.

Asa D Dickinson was born in Nottoway County, Va., in 1817, the son of Robert Dickinson and Mary Purnal Dupuy His father was a prominent farmer and citizen of Nottoway County, while his mother sprang from the Huguenot family of that name. Two brothers of his mother, Colonels Asa and Joseph Dupuy, were for many years representatives of Prince Edward County in the Virginia Legislature. Judge Dickinson's mother was a niece of General William Purnal.

The subject of this sketch received his collegiate education at Hampden-Sidney College, from which institution he graduated with high honors, in 1836. He afterwards studied law at William and Mary College, and commenced the practice of his profession in 1840.

He was twice married. His first wife was a Miss Michaux of Prince Edward county His second wife was a Miss Irvine of Campbell county. His family consisted of five sons; two, R. M., and Purnal, by the first marriage; and four daughters.

In 1857, Judge Dickinson was elected to represent the county of Prince Edward in the State Legislature and again in 1859. He subsequently served two terms in the State Senate. He also was a member of the Confederate Congress from the district composed in part of the county of Prince Edward. He was disfranchised by reason of this connection with the Confederacy, but his disability was removed by the Congress of 1870, at which time he was elected Judge of the Third Judicial Circuit, in which position he continued for fourteen years; until his death, which occurred, July 22, 1884, as a result of an apoplectic seizure which attacked him while bathing in the Rapidan River.

During the strenuous days of the War between the States,

Judge Dickinson won, and retained, the favor and the confidence of President Jefferson Davis.

For thirty-seven years, Judge Dickinson was a member and a ruling Elder in the Presbyterian Church. He was also a Trustee of Hampden-Sidney College. He lived most of his long life near Worsham, where he commenced the practice of law.

He was buried in the College Church Cemetery at Hampden-Sidney, the burial service being conducted by his pastor, the Rev. Charles White, D. D.

Mr. Blair M. Dickinson, a grandson of Judge Dickinson, is the honored Principal of the Farmville Public School Another grandson is Mr. A. B. Dickinson, a prominent lawyer of the City of Richmond, Va.

WALTER GRAY DUNNINGTON

Born, Farmville, February 12, 1849

Died, Farmville, August 2, 1922.

Walter Gray Dunnington was, for many years, one of the most prominent tobacco merchants of the entire South.

He was born in Farmville, February 12, 1859, and died in the county in which he was born, August 2, 1922. He was the son of James W. Dunnington and Sallie Madison. He was, on his mother's side, the grand-son of Col. James Madison. The Dunningtons, were originally Maryland people. On both sides of the house, Mr. Dunnington came of English ancestry. The habitat of which was the county of Berkshire, in England.

Soon after growing up Mr Dunnington went West, and for some time lived in the vicinity of Kansas City, Mo. After about two years he returned to his old home in Farmville and went into the tobacco business, in which business his father also had been engaged.

His operations in tobacco were of such magnitude that they extended into Norway, Sweden, Germany, France, England and Holland. While he conducted his business chiefly from Farmville, he had very large interests in Louisville, Ky., and spent a considerable part of his time there He also conducted many of his business operations in New York City. In his own line of business, he was one of the "big men" of the State, and, for that matter, of the nation as well. He was the means of making Farmville one of the leading export tobacco markets of the State.

Mr. Dunnington never held political position of any kind, having no inclination in that direction At one period, however, he had been a member of the Town Council of Farmville. For many years he served as a member of the board of trustees of Hampden-Sidney College, at which institution his three sons were educated. He was a man of simple tastes, modest and unassuming, yet, at the same time, aggressive and full of energy, alert in speech and bearing, and possessed of remarkable business acumen.

Mr. Dunnington was married, October 12, 1876, to India W. Knight. daughter of Capt. John H. Knight, a gallant soldier of the Confederate Army, who survives him. Their family consisted of six children, five or whom survive him. They are Walter Gray Dunnington, Jr., a prominent lawyer of New York City; Dr. J. H. Dunnington, an eye specialist of New York City; Mrs. A. G. Clapham, of Washington, D. C., Mrs. E. Southall Shields, of Farmville, Va.; and J. W. Dunnington of Farmville, for many years associated with his father in the tobacco business in that place. His youngest child, named for his Norwegian friend, Conrad Langaard, died in infancy.

Mr. Dunnington was devoted to his family. He was a most loyal friend and, while he consistently shrank from publicity. his deeds of kindness to those in distress were multitudinous. His death brought a remarkable career to a a close. His remains were laid to rest in the cemetery at Farmville.

DR. ROBERT FRAZER.

Robert Frazer was the third President of the State Female Normal School at Farmville. He became President in February, 1898. He was intended by his father for law. His academic course at the University of Virginia was interrupted by the War between the States. Disabled from wounds, he returned to the University in the fall of 1863, and took up the study of law with Professor Minor. He was never satisfied with that step, preferring the profession of teaching to that of the law. Later he took up teaching and the law was abandoned

In 1871 he bought the Fauquier Institute, a good boarding school for girls, at Warrenton Here he remained until 1882, when, under the urging of Dr. J. L. M. Curry, he accepted the Presidency of Judson Institute, at Marion, where he remained five years, and had a phenomenal success Overwork at Marion, broke his health, so that he had to devote three years thereafter to recuperation.

In 1891 he was called to the Industrial Institute and College of Mississippi, at Columbus, to serve as its President Here he remained for seven sessions, and made the school the pride of the State.

He came to Farmville with a mind richly stored with knowledge, a broad vision of life, and a varied and extensive experience in schools of many types. His four years' work in Farmville was characterized by the same zeal and earnestness that he had displayed in other places. He was extremely conscientious in his convictions of duty.

When Dr. Frazer resigned the Presidency of the State Normal School in 1902 in order to enter upon the duties of Feld Agent of the Southern Educational Board, he left behind him many grateful memories of a courteous, cultured, sympathetic, Christian gentleman of earnest purpose and unbending principle, staunchly loyal to his lofty ideals of duty.

PATRICK HENRY.

After his final incumbency of the Governorship of the State (1784), the celebrated Patrick Henry made his residence for a time in Prince Edward County, dwelling upon the banks of the Appomattox from the latter part of 1786. until 1794.

Entries in the Registry Office at Farmville on page 187, book 9, under date of, October 13, 1792, show that he. on that day, conveyed to Augustus Watson of Nottoway, and holding of 936 acres, on the Appomattox River, for 936 pounds "current money of Virginia." The property was described as follows. "Beginning at Tarlton Woodson's line on the Sandy Ford road, thence along his line, north seven and one-half degrees west two hundred and twenty poles to pointers Thence north, eighty-one degrees east twenty poles on Venable's line, to a branch. Thence down the said branch as it meanders to Appomattox river. Thence down the said river one hundred and fourteen poles, to a corner on the banks of the said river. Thence south five degrees, west one hundred and fifty poles to pointers. Thence south twenty-four degrees east eighteen poles, to a poplar fell down. Thence south sixty-four and a half degrees east three hundred and fifty poles to pointers. hence south sixty-three degrees west one hundred and twenty-four poles, to a white oak. Thence thirty-three degrees west, to the road. Thence up the said road as it meanders, to the beginning, with all houses, woods and under woods, ways, waterance, water courses, etc."

Signed, Patrick Henry,
Dorothea Henry, (his wife)

And witnessed by. Tarlton Woodson,
John Miller,
Woodson Allen,
John Watson.

A second deed to the same property, by the same persons, is recorded in book 9, on page 327, as being given shortly after the first one.

In connection with the same transaction, a commission to privately examine Dorothea Patrick, who was then at Charlotte Court House, was appointed, as recorded in book 10, on page 442, in the same registry office.

A further instrument, constituting "James Fontain, of Kentucky" his attorney, to close a certain estate, is recorded in the same registry office, in book 8, page 212, in 1790.

The exact location of the house in which Henry lived in Prince Edward county has been a matter of considerable dispute, but, after exhaustive research, Mr Roy Mathewson, realtor, of Farmville, writes as follows: "Mr Henry's first purchase of land in Prince Edward was twenty acres, conveyed to him by his friend Venable, who was known as Abraham Venable, T , and T distinguishing him from several others of the same name. * * * * * * * * The recorded deed does not so state, but, by a comparison of the metes and bounds of the 20 acres first conveyed, with other descriptions, it is probable that the house in which Patrick Henry lived was built by the father of Abraham Venable T, who was also Abraham Venable, but known as Abraham of Prince Edward. * * * * * * * The house in which Mr. Henry lived was burned in the seventies There are a few people living today who have seen it. Their descriptions agree that it was a large two story frame dwelling with a high brick basement. A two story portico running along half of the front, was supported by high columns. There was a double row of large locust trees from the house to the road, a distance of several hundred feet, and the usual office building at the road end of the row of locusts. * * * * * * * * * Its location is near the Farmville-Lynchburg Highway, about five miles west of Farmville and about half a mile north of

Appomattox Church. It is also about four miles from Hampden-Sidney.

The farm was known as "Cliffside," but that name seems to have gone out of use about fifty years ago and does not serve to identify the property now."

The above description means that the place was about one mile N. W. from the present Tuggles station on the Norfolk and Western R. R. The present owner is L. H. Williamson.

Patrick Henry was, soon after taking up his residence in the county, elected as one of its delegates in the Assembly, where he reassumed his old position as leader. He continued to serve in every session of the Assembly until the end of 1790, at which time, because of increasing physical disability, he finally withdrew from all further official connection with public life. He however, continued to practice law within the county.

Writing concerning him in connection with this law work, Dr. Archibald Alexander, then of Hampden-Sidney College, says:

"In executing a mission from the Synod of Virginia, in the year 1794, I had to pass through the County of Prince Edward, where Mr. Henry then resided. Understanding that he was to appear before the Circuit Court, which met in that county, in defense of three men charged with murder, I determined to seize the opportunity of observing for myself the eloquence of this extraordinary orator. It was with some difficulty that I obtained a seat in front of the bar, where I could have a full view of the speaker, as well as hear him distinctly. But I had to submit to a severe penance in gratifying my curiosity; for the whole day was occupied with the examination of witnesses, in which Mr Henry was aided by two other lawyers. In person, Mr. Henry was lean rather

than fleshy. He was rather above than below the common
height, but had a stoop to his shoulders which prevented him
from appearing as tall as he really was   In moments of animation, he had the habit of straightening his frame, and
adding to his apparent stature. He wore a brown wig, which
exhibited no indication of any great care in the dressing.
Over his shoulders he wore a brown camlet cloak. Under
this his clothing was black, something the worse for wear
The expression of his countenance was that of solemnity and
deep earnestness   His mind appeared to be always absorbed
in what, for the time, occupied his attention   His forehead
was high and spacious, and the skin of his face more than
usually wrinkled for a man of fifty. His eyes were small
and deeply set in his head, but were of a bright blue color,
and twinkled much in their sockets. In short, Mr. Henry's
appearance has nothing very remarkable, as he sat at rest.
You might readily have taken him for a common planter,
who cared very little for his personal appearance. In his
manners, he was uniformly respectful and courteous. Candles
were brought into the Court House, when the examination of
the witnesses closed; and the Judges put it to the option of
the bar whether they would go on with the argument that
night or adjourn until the next day. Paul Carrington, Junior, the attorney for the State, a man of large size, and un-
common dignity of person and manner, and also an accomplished lawyer, professed his willingness to proceed immediately, while the testimony was fresh in the minds of all.
Now for the first time I heard Mr. Henry make anything of
a speech; and, though it was short, it satisfied me of one
thing, which I had particularly desired to have decided:
namely, whether like a player he merely assumed the appearance of feeling. His manner of addressing the Court
was profoundly respectful. He would be willing to proceed
with the trial, "but," said he, "my heart is so oppressed with
the weight of responsibility which rests upon me, having the

lives of three fellow-citizens depending, probably, on the exertions which I may be able to make in their behalf (here he turned to prisoners behind him), that I do not feel able to proceed tonight. I hope the Court will indulge me, and postpone the trial till the morning." The impression made by these few words was such as I assure myself no one can ever conceive by seeing then in print. In the countenance, action, and intonation of the speaker, there was expressed such an intensity of feeling, that all my doubts were dispelled; never again did I question whether Henry felt, or only acted, a feeling   Indeed I experienced an instantaneous sympathy with him in the emotions which he expressed; and I have no doubt that the same sympathy was felt by every hearer   As a matter of course, the proceedings were deferred till the next morning. I was early at my post; the Judges were soon on the bench, and the prisoners at the bar. Mr. Carrington——opened with a clear and dignified speech, and presented the evidence to the jury. Everything seemed perfectly plain   Two brothers and a brother-in-law met two other persons in pursuit of a slave, supposed to be harbored by the brothers. After some altercation and mutual abuse, one of the brothers, whose name was John Ford, raised a loaded gun which he was carrying, and presenting it at the breast of one of the other pair, shot him dead, in open day. There was no doubt about the fact. Indeed, it was not denied. There had been no other provocation than opprobrious words. It is presumed that the opinion of every juror was made up from merely hearing the testimony, as Tom Harvey, the principal witness, who was acting as constable on the occasion, appeared to be a respectable man.

"For a clearer understanding of what follows, it must be observed that the said constable, in order to distinguish him from another of the same name, was commonly called Butterwood Harvey, as he lived on Butterwood Creek. Mr Henry, it is believed, understanding that the people were on their guard against his faculty of moving the passions and through them influencing the judgment, did not resort to the pathetic as much as was his practice in criminal cases. His main object appeared to be, throughout, to cast discredit on the testimony of Tom Harvey This he attempted by causing the law respecting riots to be read by one of his assistants. It appeared in evidence that Tom Harvey had taken upon him to act as constable, without being in commission; and that, with a posse of men, he had entered the house of one of the Ford's in search of the negro, and had put Mrs Ford, in her husband's absence, into a great terror, while she was in a very delicate condition, near the time of her confinement. As he descanted on the evidence, he would often turn to Tom Harvey—a large, bold-looking man—and with the most sarcastic look, would call him by some name of contempt; "this Butterwood Tom Harvey," "this would-be constable," etc. By such expressions, his contempt for the man was communicated to the hearers I own I felt it gaining on me, in spite of my better judgment; so that before he was done, the impression was strong on my mind that Butterwood Harvey was undeserving of the smallest credit. This impression, however, I found I could counteract the moment I had time for reflection. The only part of the speech in which he manifested his power of touching the feelings strongly, was where he dwelt on the eruption of the company into Ford's house, in circumstances so perilous to the solitary wife. This appeal to the sensibility of husbands—and he knew all the jury stood in this relation—was overwhelming If the verdict could have been rendered immediately after this burst of the pathetic, every man, at least every husband, in the house, would have been for rejecting Harvey's testimony, if not for hanging him forthwith "—J W. Alexander, "Life of Archibald Alexander," 183-187.

In the year 1794, being then fifty-eight years of age, and possessing a reasonable competence, Patrick Henry decided to withdraw from his profession and resolved to spend his remaining days in retirement. He therefore, removed from Prince Edward county, to Long Island in Campbell county, and there, in 1795, he finally established himself on an estate in the County of Charlotte, called Red Hill, where he continued to reside for the rest of his life; which gave him his burial place; and which remains in the possession of his descendants. This considerable description of his residence within the county of Prince Edward is given because the people of the county are naturally proud of the fact that they were honored by the residence amongst them of so great and so good a man. He was born at Studley, in the county of Hanover on May 29, 1736, and died at Red Hill in the county of Charlotte on June 6, 1799.

GENERAL JOSEPH EGGLESTON JOHNSTON.

Joseph Eggleston Johnston was the eighth son of Peter Johnston and Mary Wood, who was the daughter of Colonel Valentine Wood, of Goochland County, whose wife was Lucy Henry, sister to Patrick Henry. He was born at Cherry Grove, Prince Edward county, February 3, 1807. He was named after Joseph Eggleston, a military associate of his father, and the Captain of the company of Lee's Legion of which his father, Peter Johnston, was Lieutenant.

In 1811, Peter Johnston, with his family, removed to a place which he named "Panecillo," on the edge of Abingdon. This removal was consequent upon Johnston's appointment as a judge of the General Court of Virginia

His education was begun by his parents, both of whom were distinctly competent to give it. This was the custom in those days, amongst the "gentry." This work was carried on by the parents until the lad was old enough to enter the Academy at Abingdon; a fairly good classical school. Young Johnston was a good student, and made the most of the opportunities afforded him, both at home and at school. He ever maintained a fondness for the classics. Homer was his favorite.

In 1825, when he was eighteen, he secured, through the influence of James Barbour, United States Senator from Virginia, and Secretary of War under President John Q Adams, the appointment to the Military Academy at West Point as a cadet He thus obtained an entrance into the field of his cherished ambition, for he had long desired to be a soldier. He was descended from a long line of Scottish Clansmen

In the above year, having successfully passed the necessary examinations, Joseph E. Johnston was admitted as a cadet at West Point. He was one of the one hundred and five who were so fortunate as to enter in that year. Robert E. Lee, slightly older than himself, and the son of the commander of Peter Johnston, young Joseph's father, in the War of the Revolution, was one of his fellow students. Their tastes and habits being of the same character, they soon became fast friends, which friendship continued throughout their lives. Seven other young Virginians were fellow students of the two friends, all of whom dropped out, leaving young Johnston and Lee to pursue their studies together as the sole representatives of their beloved State. They graduated together, the only remaining representatives of the Old Dominion, in 1829, Lee standing second to Charles Mason, of New York, in the class of forty-six. Johnston, hindered in his studies by a serious affection of the eyes that precluded his studying at night, stood thirteen.

Young Johnston's first military service was as second Lieutenant in the Fourth Artillery; the next, in garrison at New York; which was followed by similar duty at Fortress Monroe. This period extended from 1829 to 1832, when his actual active campaigning began in the Black Hawk expedition of 1832, under General Scott.

In so brief a sketch as this must of necessity be, it is manifestly impossible to follow, in any detail, the stirring military career of this favorite son of old Prince Edward county, and no effort will be made to do so.

On July 10, 1845, when he was 38 years of age, Johnston, having attained the brevet rank of Captain, was married to Miss Lydia McLane, a young woman of remarkable beauty, and great personal accomplishments. The family to which Mrs. Johnston belonged is one greatly distinguished in the annals of Delaware and Maryland. The union was a singularly happy one, and the fact of the absence of offspring seemed but to draw them the closer together.

During the progress of his military career it was the

misfortune of General Johnston, that a serious estrangement subsisted between himself and President Jefferson Davis, of the Confederate States, which caused him to be often superseded, so that he was ever preparing campaigns from which others reaped much of the glory and most of the reward. He possessed a singular ability to subordinate himself for the good of his beloved Southland, and a patience that finally reaped its just reward in the esteem of his contemporaries, so that, scarcely second to the immortal Lee, he is entrenched in the affectionate regard of the peoples of the South, and respected by the erstwhile enemies of his people, as one of the great Generals of all time.

At the conclusion of the hostilities, that marked the defeat of the South in the War between the States, General Johnston took service with a railroad, and later with an express company. Later still he engaged in the insurance business in Savannah, where he remained for nearly a decade

In 1877 he returned to his native State, taking up his residence in Richmond. In 1878 he received the nomination of the Democratic party and was triumphantly elected to Congress where he served for one term as a member of the House of Representatives. He seldom spoke in the House, but was an honored and influential member throughout his term, at the close of which he was appointed as Commissioner of Railroads under President Grover Cleveland, retaining his residence in Washington.

On February 22, 1887, his beloved wife died at their residence in Washington This was a crushing blow, so that he could never afterward trust himself to speak her name, and his house remained from the time of her death exactly as she had left it A union of singular happiness was thus brought to a pathetic close. Mrs. Johnston had, for a long time, been a martyr to suffering, during which her husband's attentions were as unremitting as those of a youthful lover.

From the time of the death of Mrs. Johnston, the old General gradually became weaker, though he still maintained his upright posture and steady gait. On the night of March 21, 1891, he peacefully passed away at his residence, 1023 Connecticut Avenue, in the city of Washington. The immediate cause of his death was heart failure. He was in his eighty-fourth year when he died. He was buried in the Greenmount Cemetery, Baltimore, beside the wife he loved so dearly.

Nothing marks his resting place save the simple inscription, selected by himself:

JOSEPH E. JOHNSTON,
Son of
Judge Peter & Mary Johnston of Va.,
Born at
Longwood, Prince Edward C., Va.,
February 3, 1807.
Died March 21, 1891.
Brigadier General, U. S. A.
General, C. S. A.

DR. JOHN PETER METTAUER. *Born* 1787, *Died* 1875.

The father of John Peter Mattauer, was a surgeon, who, with a brother, followed the fortunes of Lafayette. After the battle of Yorktown, the French army was quartered at various points in Virginia With one regiment, sent to Prince Edward county, were the two brother surgeons. Francis Joseph Mettauer, one of these brothers, obtained permission to remain in Prince Edward county, rather than return to France. Later on he married Eliza Gaulding and to them was born in 1787, John Peter Mettauer.

Comparatively little is known of his early childhood or of his youth, save that he was raised in an atmosphere of surgery. He very early imbibed a love for surgery and resolved to make that work his profession

The embryo surgeon was sent to the neighboring college of Hampden-Sidney for his literary training; from which institution he graduated with the degree of A.B. in 1806. He then went to the University of Pennsylvania for the study of medicine and graduated with the degree of M. D in 1809. Young Mettauer was exceedingly fortunate in selecting this University, for medical work was then being conducted under the most favorable auspices at Pennsylvania. The ablest instructors then obtainable were on the staff of that institution. He also was so fortunate as to enjoy a very extended practice in the Philadelphia Dispensary during his stay in that city.

Returning to Prince Edward county, the young doctor at once entered upon the practice of general medicine. Soon, however, his preference for surgery and his marvelous skill in that branch of his work, attracted wide attention and patients from great distances began to seek him out. From all parts of the United States they came, some even from abroad Into Prince Edward Court House (Worsham), a representative village of "ye olde time," came pouring an ever increasing stream of the sick and the ailing, in quest of the skillful aid of the young surgeon. These were sufficient, with their varied retinue of personal attendants, to tax to the utmost the modest accommodations afforded by the private hospital operated by Dr. Mettauer, and by the two houses of entertainment at Kingsville and Worsham, referred to in the terms of that day, as commodious "taverns."

In 1837 Dr. Mettauer organized his Medical Institute, which later on, became a part of Randolph-Macon College. Most of these young students were from points in Virginia and numbered amongst them, many who in later life attained eminence in the practice of medicine This Institute was kept up until 1848, when it became the Medical Department of Randolph-Macon College, located in Mechlenburg county.

Dr. Mettauer was a voluminous writer, though many of his most valuable works were never published. He was a daring inventor of surgical instruments, making many of them at old Peter Porter's shop in Farmville with his own hands.

He was a man of striking appearance, being tall, well-formed, and robust. Unlike most of the young physicians of those days who rode horseback in making their rounds, young Mettauer used a carriage for that purpose. His most striking pecularity was his insistence on wearing a preposterously tall "stove pipe" hat, upon any and every occasion. He never attended services in the churches, doubtless because that would necessitate the removal of his head-gear. He even objected to removing his hat when testifying in a case in court. He even left instructions that he was to be buried with his hat on, with the result that it required a special coffin of a trifle over eight feet long to contain his remains with this favorite article of head-dress and the considerable number of special instruments and the large parcel of letters from his first wife, which, by his special direction, were buried with him. He even wore this hat at meals it is said !

Piercing black eyes, were over-shadowed by an heavy over-hanging brow, above which rose a high and most intellectually shaped forehead.

Eccentric in action and commanding in appearance he was a marked man in any assemblage.

His passion for his home county of Prince Edward amounted to almost an obsession. He tried a brief settlement at Norfolk and engaged as professor of surgery at Baltimore, in Washington University, but the pull of "home" soon had him back in Prince Edward county where he stayed until he died.

In November of 1875, being then eighty-eight years of age, Dr. Mettauer was called to attend a case of morphine poisoning A short walk through wet snow made his feet wet. As a result he developed a deep cold, which soon resolved itself into pneumonia, from which, in two days, he died. Alert and erect, he laid down his work while still in the harness. A most useful life was thus crowned with an heroic death Close to the scenes of his useful endeavors for his fellows he lies buried, a strong, unselfish soul, taking a well-earned repose. Prince Edward county is justly proud of her surgeon son.

JAMES NELSON, D.D., LL.D. *Born, August* 23, 1841;
Died, November 13, 1921.

Although Doctor Nelson was not a native of Prince Edward County, so much of his labor was done in, and for, the county, that it is fitting that this notice shall be taken of him here.

He was born in Louisa county, Virginia, on August 23, 1841. The War between the States began when he was still at school. He joined the Confederate Army and was for four years Chaplain of the Forty-fourth Virginia Regiment. What was known as "the great revival" began in the brigade to which young Nelson was attached, and it is said that hundreds of Confederate soldiers were converted through his labors.

With the close of the war he entered Columbian College, Washington, and graduated at the head of his class. He then served as pastor of a church in that city, and later became general evangelist for the Baptists of Maryland. In 1875 he accepted the pastorate of the Farmville Baptist Church and began at once to establish a Normal School for women there. He repeatedly appeared before the Legislature and the Governor and finally won out in his project and the Female Normal School of Farmville, the progenitor of like schools at Radford, Fredericksburg, and Harrisonburg, came into being.

In 1881 he went to London, England, as a delegate to the World's Sunday School Convention, and while in that city, preached in the church of the famous Charles Haddon Spurgeon.

In 1885 he left Farmville to accept the pastorate of the Baptist Church at Staunton, Virginia, where he lectured before the Staunton Female Seminary and other schools in addition to his duties as pastor of the Staunton Church.

After leaving Staunton, he was for nearly thirty years President of the Woman's College of Richmond. The school, when he took charge of it, was near extinction Its long history, its old prestige, and its multitude of alumnae alike seemed unable to save it. Dr. Nelson, in a few brief years, re-established it on a sure footing, made it for many sessions a most useful agency and, at the proper time, most generously stood aside and closed the college that Westhampton College might be opened.

In choosing his teachers, Dr. Nelson was guided by a sure instinct that even he could not explain. Dr J. A. C. Chandler, now President of the College of William and Mary, was picked by Dr Nelson while still a very young man, as one of his teachers. Among other of his teachers, were Hiss Lenora Duke, later Mrs. Chandler; Dr. M A. Martin; Dr. W. A. Shepherd; Dr. F. C. Woodward; Dr. Emory Hill; Christopher Garnett; Miss Mary Carter Anderson, now Mrs Charles S. Gardner; Miss Marian Forbes; Miss Addie Garlick; and Miss Catherine Ryland, now Mrs. Garnett.

Dr. Nelson was the despair of every college executive, for it was said of him that he could do more work with less money than any college president in Virginia. He had a marked spiritual influence over the student body of the college.

Dr. Nelson died on Sunday, November 13, 1921, at 904 Grace Street West, Richmond, Virginia, and was buried at Hollywood Cemetery in that city.

DR. WILLIAM HENRY RUFFNER.

He was the son of Dr. Henry Ruffner, a distinguished Presbyterian preacher, who was, for many years President of Washington College, now Washington and Lee University. Thus, the subject of this sketch was reared in a home of culture. From the college of which his father was President he, in 1845, received the degree of M.A. He afterward studied theology at Union Theological Seminary, and at Princeton, New Jersey. He was at one time Chaplain of the University of Virginia, and later became pastor of Seventh Presbyterian Church, Philadelphia In 1853, on account of broken health, he withdrew from the ministry.

He wrote much on educational and agricultural subjects, and was at one time editor of the Virginia School Journal, and of the New England Journal of Education He was State Superintendent of Public Instruction in Virginia, from 1870 to 1882. This office had just been created and he was the first to occupy it. His difficulties were multiplied from the fact that he had to provide for two distinct races of people at a time when feelings were apt to run high; moreover the War between the States, that presented that problem, had left his constituency almost too poor to be taxed for education. In founding the new system he wrote, traveled, lectured, visited schools, held meetings, and organized teachers' institutes, until 1882, when a change in the politics of the Administration brought about his retirement. It was from this retirement and with his vast experience behind him, that he was called in 1884 to undertake a new pioneer work, and he became the first head of the State Female Normal School of Virginia, located at Farmville. He was also helpful in founding the Agricultural and Mechanical College, and Miller School, and was at one time a member of the Board of Hampton Institute (Colored).

What Horace Mann, thirty-three years before him, had done for Massachusetts, Dr. Ruffner did for Virginia.

He lived to a good old age and died November 24, 1908, beloved and honored by all.

JUDGE FRANCIS NATHANIEL WATKINS. *Born April* 14, 1813. *Died* 1885.

Judge Watkins was born in 1813, and spent his entire life in Prince Edward county. He was a member of the Virginia Legislature in 1867-1868, and Judge of the County Court of Prince Edward for fourteen years. He was Secretary and Treasurer of the Board of Union Theological Seminary for forty years, of Hampden-Sidney College fourteen years, and of the State Normal School for the first year of its existence, when his valuable and active life was brought to a close in 1885. He was an ardent friend of education, especially of the common school system.

DOCTOR PETER WINSTON. *Born in Richmond, Va., June 5, 1836 Died at Farmville, Virginia, January 30, 1920, and buried at Farmville, Virginia.*

Doctor Peter Winston was born at Richmond, Virginia, June 5, 1836. He was graduated from Hampden-Sidney College, Prince Edward county, with the degree of A.B.; attended the University of Virginia for one year, and also the University of New York, where he graduated in Medicine. Then he was for one year a student in Paris at the University of France, from whence he returned, in obedience to his country's call, in 1861, to become a surgeon in the Confederate Army, which position he held through the period of the War between the States. He afterwards located in Farmville, Virginia, where he practiced medicine to the time of his death in 1920. He was mayor of Farmville in 1873-1874, and was a Delegate to the State Legislature in 1914, 1916, 1918 from Prince Edward County.

He was Moderator of the Appomattox Association of Baptist Churches in 1873 and 1874, and again in 1914 and 1915 He was a prominent and deeply interested member of the Farmville Baptist Church for many years.

He was for twenty-four years physician to the State Female Normal School, at Farmville, Virginia, and was a trustee of Hampden-Sidney College for a great many years, as well as of the State Board of Correction.

He had reached the ripe age of eighty-four when he died.

On September 15, 1868, he married Miss Mollie Emma Rice in Farmville, Va., and she survived him at his death.

REV. DANIEL WITT, D.D. 1801-1871.

This noted divine was the son of Jesse Witt and Alice Brown, then living in Bedford county, near to what is now Bedford City, then known as Liberty. He was born, November 8, 1801. As a result of hardships endured during the Revolutionary War, his father was compelled to use crutches and found it a difficult matter to care for his large family on the small farm that he had managed to purchase. He was a man of vigorous and rather remarkable intellect Both father and mother were ardent Baptists. Under the circumstances of the family, the boy Daniel, received but limited educational advantages, his early school days extending but little over three years. Of a rather delicate physique, the outdoor life made necessary by demands of the little farm and the large family, was a most fortunate thing for him, as it gave the needed strength for the work of the after years.

Until the fourth Sunday in August, 1821, nothing particularly striking occurred in the life of the young man. On this day, however, a "section meeting"; a religious gathering much after the fashion of the "protracted meeting" of later days, but conducted by a designated section of the Baptist Association of Churches, held at Hatcher's Meeting House, and at which Elders Davis, Leftwich, Harris, and Dempsey were the preachers, was being held. The meeting lasted all day and resulted, on October 21, 1821, in his avowal of conversion. To get to this meeting he journeyed farther from his home than he had ever before done; some twenty miles.

On the second Sunday in December, 1821, with the ice on the water, the subject of our sketch, and his older brother Jesse, were baptized and received into the fellowship of the Little Otter (now Bedford City) Church Almost immediately he began to preach and met with much acceptance, although it is said that he then possessed but ONE sermon. On April 13, 1822, his Church licensed him to preach. He was soon preaching throughout the counties of Henry, Patrick, Pittsylvania, and Campbell. Upon the organization of the General Association of Baptist Churches in 1823, young Witt, with Jeremiah B Jeter, his lifelong friend, were designated its first missionaries and set apart for work in the western part of the State, included in their field being the counties of Franklin, Henry, Patrick, Montgomery, Grayson, Giles, Wythe, Monroe, Greenbrier, Pocahontas, Alleghany, Bath, Rockbridge, and Botetourt.

He was formally ordained to the ministry, in his home Church, Little Otter, on August 7-8, 1824.

In February, 1827, he preached at an Associational meeting of the Appomattox Association of Baptist Churches, held at Sandy River, Prince Edward county, in Sharon Baptist Church, and this led to his acceptance of a call to that Church. And thus began a ministry, unique in many ways, that was to extend over a term of forty-five years, to be terminated only by the death of the devoted pastor. He purchased a modest home near to his Church where he spent the rest of his years and in which he died, Novmber 15, 1871.

The honorary degree of D.D. was conferred on Mr Witt by Columbian College, Washington, D. C. He was the Moderator of the Appomattox Association of Baptist Churches for eleven of its sessions, and was President of the General Association, at its Petersburg session in 1861.

He was thrice married. In 1829 he was married to Miss Mary C Cocke, of Cumberland county, who died in 1834 In 1836 he was married to Miss Mary A Woodfin, who died in 1842. In 1849 he was married to Mrs. Mary Ellen Temple, who survived him.

His family consisted of four sons.

Upon the wish of his Church, Dr. Witt was buried near the pulpit where for so many years he had proclaimed the message of life eternal. Shortly after his death, a handsome marble shaft, suitably inscribed, was erected by Sharon Church and other friends, and there he sleeps!

JAMES A. DAVIDSON, Mayor of Farmville, Va.
See Page 352.

Chapter Fourteen

"Who's Who" in Prince Edward County

1. Robert Kincaid Brock.
2. Edward Taylor Bondurant.
3. James Augustus Davidson.
4 Joseph Dupuy Eggleston.
5. Edgar Graham Gammon.
6 George Jefferson Hundley.
7. Joseph L. Jarman.
8 Asa D. Watkins.

"WHO'S WHO" IN PRINCE EDWARD

Someone has said that "history is but the lengthened shadow of the human race" That is the reason for this, and the preceding chapter on "Biography."

The men who are cited in this chapter, though still living, have already rendered such service in their respective spheres, for the good of their fellow citizens of Prince Edward county, as to mark them out for distinction.

To the lasting discredit of humanity let is be said that we are all too prone to wait until after the obsequies, before doing justice to those who have served us

Of course it is not intended to intimate that these alone have served their fellows faithfully and well, but they stand in a representative capacity in their several callings, in that service which every robust citizen feels to be incumbent upon those who enjoy the privileges of our democratic institutions.

And that is the reason for these two chapters. These men have either made, or are making, history.

ROBERT KINCAID BROCK.

The subject of this sketch was born in Buckingham county, Virginia, May 29, 1878   His father was Henry C. Brock, for thirty-two years a professor at Hampden-Sidney College; and his mother, Mary Carter Irving, daughter of the late Robert Kincaid Irving, at one time a member of the Virginia House of Delegates; of the State Senate, and Clerk of the County of Buckingham. He is a nephew of the late Robert A. Brock of Richmond, for many years Secretary of the Virginia Historical Society, and of the Southern Historical Society.

He graduated from Hampden-Sidney College in 1897 with the degree of A B He then taught for one year in Surry County, and for one year in Halifax County. For four years he conducted a private school in Charleston, West Virginia.

He received his legal education at the University of Virginia. Is a member of the Chi Phi Fraternity. Was at one time the president of the Alumni Association of Hampden-Sidney College.

He began the practice of law in Farmville in 1904 where he soon formed a partnership with Judge A. D Watkins, which has continued to the present time

He was elected to the Senate of Virginia in 1912, where he served for four years as a member of the Committees of Finance; Schools and Colleges; Courts of Justice; and Fisheries and Game, of that body.

He was a delegate to the State Democratic Convention in 1908, 1912, 1916, and 1920, and was the alternate delegate to the National Democratic Convention in St. Louis in 1916.

He was Chairman of the Prince Edward Chapter of the Red Cross from the time that the Chapter was organized during the Great War, which office he still holds.   He was

Chairman of the Legal Advisory Board of Prince Edward County during the War.

He is Secretary of the Prince Edward Public Health Association; and of the Electoral Board of the County; Examiner of Records for the Fifth Judicial Circuit since 1918; and Secretary-Auditor of the Virginia Normal School Board since October 1919.

He volunteered for service in the Great War in the spring of 1918, making application for admission to the Third Officers' Training Camp, but was rejected. He applied again to the Fourth Officers' Training Camp, and received appointment to Camp Lee; was inducted into the service before the local Draft Board; and was ordered to report, November 13th, 1918. Through the signing of the Armistice on the 11th of that month, this appointment was cancelled.

Mr. Brock stands high in the estimation of his fellow-citizens of Prince Edward county for his splendid public spirit and devotion to duty.

EDWARD TAYLOR BONDURANT.

The subject of this sketch was born in Prince Edward county, near Rice, October 22, 1864, and has lived in the county all his life

In 1881 he professed religion and united with the Christian (Disciples of Christ) Church in April of that year.

When sixteen years of age, owing to the death of both father and mother, and being the eldest of the boys of the family, he was forced to leave school and assume the management of the home farm, which he did so successfully that all the debts against it were paid off, and in 1893, by decree of the Circuit Court, his father's farm was sold to him by the legatees.

He married Agnes Leigh Clark, October 20, 1886. Side by side they have fought the battle of life, with the hope that their children might have a good education and prove a blessing to the world.

Having been a tobacco grower practically all his life, he very early became very much interested in the promotion of an organization for securing better prices for that commodity for the growers of it. In 1905 he led in a movement to that end. Failing at that time to secure sufficient strength to accomplish the hoped-for results, that organization went into the loose warehouse business. He was made manager and continued to serve in that capacity for eight years with a marked degree of success. During all these eight years he continued to attend to the managment of his farm as well. In 1913 he was sent by the U. S. Government to Austria, to investigate the conditions under which Virginia tobacco was being bought by foreign governments. The war coming on soon afterwards, his mission proved abortive of results.

In 1920 he was sent to the Legislature in succession to

the late Dr. Peter Winston. He was re-elected in 1922 without opposition

Mr. Bondurant is deservedly popular amongst all classes of people in the county, but it is amongst the farmers that he enjoys his greatest popularity.

JAMES AUGUSTUS DAVIDSON.

The subject of this sketch, is the son of William Meade Davidson and Julia Wiltse Davidson, and was born at Farmville, Virginia, May 31st, 1877, and has lived in Farmville all his life.

He attended the public schools of his native town, finishing his course in February 1892.

On the 28th of October, 1903, he was married to Miss Birdie Waddell Cox, of Richmond, Virginia, and has a family of three Children · James A., Jr.; Paul William; and Frances Wiltse.

He served two terms as a memberof the Farmville Town Council; from September 1, 1916, to September 1, 1920, when he was elected Mayor for the term of two years; from September 1, 1920, to September 1, 1922, winning by a substantial majority over his fellow-councilor, Mr. E W. Sanford.

He is the junior member of the firm of Stokes and Davidson, wholesale and retail grocers of Farmville, which firm occupies the finest grocery premises in the town, situated on Main street; a new and handsome structure, erected in 1920

Mr. and Mrs. Davidson are prominent socially, throughout the county and are deservedly popular amongst the host of their friends, whom they frequently entertain in their beautiful home on Third street.

DR. JOSEPH DUPUY EGGLESTON, Junior, A.M., LL.D.

Dr. Eggleston began life as a country boy near Worsham, in Prince Edward county. He was graduated from Hampden-Sidney College in 1886, was prepared for college at old Prince Edward Academy at Worsham, Va., under Professor J. R. Thornton, and, at eighteen, was at work in a one-room school in Missouri, at $15 a month He was soon promoted to a two-room school in Prince Edward, his native county, and, a little later, to a three-room school in Georgia.

Teaching was then given up temporarily because of ill-health, and he went to work in a drug store. In eighteen months he had worked up from a twenty-five-dollar a week clerk, to the head of the business.

He then returned to the school-room, and for two years taught in a High School in Asheville, N. C., twice during that time declining the office of principal of it. He then succeeded Mr. Claxton as Superintendent of the Asheville schools. He filled this position most successfully for seven years, finding time also to become one of the organizers of the Asheville and Buncombe County Good Roads Association, and was an active member of the executive committee of the Asheville Business Men's Association. At the end of nine years work in Asheville he returned to Virginia in order to be near his father, who was in failing health.

He was on the editorial staff of the B. F. Johnson Publishing Company only a short while before he was asked by President Dabney, of the University of Tennessee, to help in organizing the Bureau of Publicity and Information of the Southern Educational Board.

Upon the death of Mr. T. J. Garden, shortly after, Mr. Eggleston was appointed to fill his unexpired term as County Superintendent of the schools of Prince Edward.

Then he was elected State Superintendent of Public

Instruction in Virginia, which office he filled with characteristic energy and conspicuous success for seven years.

As State Superintendent of Education, he was *ex-officio*, a member of the Board of Visitors of the State Normal School for Women, at Farmville At the request of United States Commissioner of Education, P. P. Claxton, he resigned the State Superintendency in order to become Chief Specialist in Rural Education for the United States, but in six months, was unanimously called as President of Virginia Polytechnic Institute, where he remained for six years. In that period, 1913-1919, the enrollment of V. P. I increased from 460 to 781.

Asked to take the Presidency of his Alma Mater, Hampden-Sidney College, he declined unless it should become the property of the Synod of Virginia. When the College came under the control of the Synod, he accepted the Presidency and assumed office, July 1, 1919

Dr. Eggleston has written extensively for leading papers in Virginia and North Carolina; is a member of Beta Theta Pi, and Phi Beta Kappa Clubs, and author, with R W. Bruere, of "The Work of the Rural School."

Farmville and Prince Edward county are greatly honored in the work of this distinguished son of theirs.

THE REVEREND EDGAR GRAHAM GAMMON, D.D.

The subject of this sketch is the present Pastor of College Presbyterian Church, at Hampden-Sidney, Virginia.

His father was the late Rev. James Polk Gammon. His mother's maiden name was Susan Southall Langhorne.

He first saw the light of day, September 10, 1884, at Asheville, North Carolina.

When about two years of age his parents moved to Virginia, where he was reared. He entered Hampden-Sidney College in 1902, and graduated in 1905, with his A.B. degree.

Upon his graduation he taught school for three years, and, in 1908, entered Union Theological Seminary in Richmond, from which institution he graduated in 1911 with his B.D. degree

His first ministerial labors were at Clarksburg, West Virginia, where he remained for only one year, resigning to take up mission work at Harlington, Texas, on the Mexican border. Here he did aggressive and successful Home Mission work for a period of five years.

From Harlington, in the fall of 1917, he came to his present work at Hampden-Sidney

During the war he did Y. M. C. A. work at Hampden-Sidney College, with the Student Army Training Corps, and was deservedly popular with the young men with whom he worked

He received his D.D degree from Hampden-Sidney College, which institution takes pride in the splendid work he is doing with the student body of the college, with whom he is extremely popular.

JUDGE GEORGE JEFFERSON HUNDLEY.

The subject of this sketch was born on the 22nd day of March, 1838. He is the son of Josiah Hundley and Cornelia Jefferson Hundley, both of whom were born and reared in Amelia county, Virginia. His mother died when he was three years old, and his father, when he was ten. After his mother's death George was taken to the home of his grandmother, Mrs Nancy Jefferson, the widow of John Garland Jefferson, and was raised by her. He lived in the county of Amelia till he grew to manhood. He received his education in the private schools of that day, in Amelia county. He was put out to business when quite young, but before he was full grown, managed by his own efforts and with the help of his mother's sister, Mrs. Nicholas Carrington, to continue his education at Fleetwood Academy in Nelson county, Va., and at Hampden-Sidney College, and his legal education at Judge Jno. W. Brockenbrough's Law School in Lexington, Va. He had to borrow money to enable him to complete his education, but paid it all back by his individual efforts afterwards.

He obtained his license to practice law in April 1861, being examined by Judges R C. L. Moncure, Wm J. Robertson and William Daniel, three Judges of the Court of Appeals of Virginia, said court being then in session in Richmond. Returning then to the home of his cousin, Wm. C. Carrington of Howardsville, Albemarle County, with whom he had read law before going to law school, young Hundley volunteered in the Howardsville Blues, a company then being organized to enter the War between the States, on the side of the south; was elected a Lieutenant in the company and joined our army at Manassas Junction This company formed a part of the 19th Virginia Regiment and took part in the first battle of Manassas.

In 1862, in company with his cousin, Lieutenant Carrington, he "joined the cavalry" being attached to the 5th Virginia cavalry, and served until the end of the war. He was severely wounded in 1863 and performed his last service at Appomattox Court House in 1865.

After the surrender, the courts being closed, young Hundley organized a private school at Howardsville, Va., and taught school until February 1866, when he settled at Buckingham Court House, Va., to practice law. When he went there, after purchasing some civilian clothes, he had exactly $15 left in cash, but soon got a good practice, and with the proceeds, paid off his debts then remaining unpaid He took an active part in the struggles of the best people against the oppressions and outrages of the enemies of the South, in the days of the Re-Construction Period.

Young Hundley was nominated for the Virginia Senate from Buckingham district, twice. The first time he was defeated by a small majority, in a district with an overwhelming negro majority. The second time he was nominated by the Conservatives, or Democrats, of that day, during his absence from the district, without solicitation on his part, and was elected by a good majority, and served in the Senate for four years

At the close of his term in the Senate, he declined re-election and moved to Richmond to practice his profession. He had enough of political office holding, but, whilst still in the Senate, and also subsequent to his retirement from politics, he championed the cause of white supremacy, and canvassed the State in every election for the cause of democracy and white rule. While he was still in the Senate, a bill was passed re-organizing the Militia of the State and he was appointed a Brigadier-General of Militia, by Governor Walker.   ,

While in Richmond he purchased an estate near Amelia

Court House and, having married, he moved to his home county of Amelia and practiced law there and in adjoining counties, and sometimes argued cases in other States. In 1895 an attempt was made to repeal the Walton Law, which was, at that time, the only protection the people of south-side Virginia had against negro domination, by a proper restriction of suffrage, and General Hundley, as he was then known, was appealed to by the Democrats of Nottoway and Amelia, to stand for election to the Legislature This he refused to do at first, but being assured that he would be elected without opposition, he consented and was returned. Some leading Democrats from the white sections of the State, who had been leaders in the Legislature for many sessions, championed the repeal of the Walton Law. Mr. Hundley led the defenders of that law and, after the hardest fight of his life, succeeded in defeating the repeal of the law, thereby saving white supremacy in south-side Virginia, until the new Constitution established it permanently by Constitutional restrictions of Suffrage.

In 1898 Governor Tyler appointed Mr Hundley Judge of the 3rd Judicial District of Virginia, composed at that time of nine counties: viz Amelia, Powhatan, Cumberland, Buckingham, Appomattox, Prince Edward, Charlotte, Lunenburg, and Mechlenburg. Under the new Constitution, Judge Hundley having removed to Farmville, the circuit was divided, and he became Judge of the present 5th Judicial District, composed of five counties He has been on the Bench for twenty-four years, during which time he has tried many important and celebrated cases.

Judge Hundley is descended, on his father's side, from Josiah Hundley, who emigrated from England in 1759 and settled in Williamsburg, Va., and through his mother, Cornelia Jefferson, from the Jeffersons of the Revolution. His grandfather was George Jefferson, who was the first cousin, intimate friend, and boyhood playmate, of Thomas Jefferson, President of the United States. Through his mother, he is descended also, from Elizabeth Giles, the only sister of Governor Wm. B. Giles, of Virginia. His grandfather, John Garland Jefferson, of Amelia, was a protege of President Jefferson, who took him to Monticello, to read law under his supervision, and in President Thomas Jefferson's works, Vol. 4, page 388, there is published a letter to George Jefferson. In Vol 5, of the same work, there is published a letter to John Garland Jefferson, son of George Jefferson Both of these letters are couched in the most affectionate terms.

Judge Hundley's ancestors have fought for their country in every war, Colonial or National, that this country has been engaged in. He, himself, served throughout the War between the States, during which he was severely wounded. His father Josiah Hundley the 3rd, served under General Taylor, in the Mexican war

Judge Hundley's son, Robert Garland Hundley, was trained at Fort Meyer, and commissioned as Lieutenant of Infantry when barely old enough to receive a commission, and served through the Great World War in France, during which he was severely wounded. He is now practicing law in Richmond.

JOSEPH L JARMAN, A.B , LL.D., *President State Female Normal School, Farmville, Va.*

Dr. Jarman, fourth President of the State Female Normal School, Farmville, Virginia, was born in Charlottesville, Virginia, on the 19th of November, 1867. His father, William Dabney Jarman, served in the Confederate Army, in the War between the States. His mother was Catherine Goodloe Lindsay, of the well known Lindsay family of Albemarle county.

His early education was obtained in the public schools of Charlottesville. At the early age of fourteen (having been left an orphan) he was sent to the Miller Manual Labor School, where he remained from 1881 to 1886. In competitive examination he won the Miller Scholarship at the University of Virginia, where he was a student from 1886 to 1889, devoting himself especially to the natural and physical sciences.

Upon the completion of his course at the University of Virginia, he returned to Miller School as a member of the faculty, but remained there for only one year, as, at the end of that time, he was called to the chair of natural science at Emory and Henry College. He remained at Emory and Henry for twelve years, leaving there in January 1902, to take up his present position at Farmville.

During his stay at Emory and Henry College the degree of A.B , was conferred upon him by that institution, and, since he has been in Farmville, Hampden-Sidney College has honored itself by conferring upon him the degree of LL.D.

Dr. Jarman is a member of the American Chemical Society; the American Society for the Advancement of Science; and the Virginia Historical Society. He was a member of

JUDGE GEORGE JEFFERSON HUNDLEY
Fifth Judicial District
See Page 356.

the State Board of Education for eight years, viz: from 1906 to 1914; and was Chairman for the Red Cross; the Y. M. C. A.; and the United War-Work campaigns during the World's War, securing from Farmville and Prince Edward County the splendid total of approximately $25,000, for these interests.

Notwithstanding his multitudinous duties, Dr. Jarman is very active in the work of the Methodist Episcopal Church in Farmville, of which he is a loyal and consistent member, being Chairman of the Official Board of that Church.

JUDGE ASA DICKINSON WATKINS.

Judge Watkins was born in 1856 and has lived in Prince Edward county all his life. He is one of the most influential and best esteemed citizens of Farmville, in that county, having been officially intimately acquainted with the public affairs of the county since he was twenty-one years of age.

He was Judge of the County Court from 1886 to 1891, and Attorney for the Commonwealth from 1891 to the present time.

He was a member of the Virginia House of Delegates, 1897-98, and of the State Senate from 1899 to 1904.

He succeeded his father, the late Judge F. N. Watkins, in 1885, as Secretary-Treasurer of the Board of Trustees of the State Female Normal School, at Farmville

He has also served as a member of the Board of Trustees of Hampden-Sidney College for the past twenty-nine years. He is a member of the Board of Visitors of the Negro Normal and Industrial Institute of Petersburg, Virginia, and is a member of the State Inter-Racial Commission at the present time.

He is an ardent friend and an active exponent of education for the masses

He is a member of the Presbyterian Church in Farmville where he served, first as Deacon, and later, as Elder, which latter office he still holds.

In 1886 he married Miss Nannie E. Forbes, daughter of Col W W Forbes, of Buckingham county. His family consists of four sons and four daughters.

Chapter Fifteen
The Judiciary of Prince Edward County

THE JUDICIARY OF PRINCE EDWARD

No inconsiderable part of such an historical sketch of the county as we are endeavoring to give, must rest in tradition. Tradition, properly substantiated, forms a legitimate source of history generally, because actual documentary evidence is not available in respect to many vital items of the history of the changeful conditions that have been the lot of the Southern States.

This is true in a very large measure respecting the Judiciary of Prince Edward county.

Much of the subjoined matter was furnished by Judge George J. Hundley, from a peculiarly retentive memory, but in the material facts it has been verified by such documentary evidence as is available.

Subsequent to the Revolutionary War, and prior to the War between the States, the Juduciary of the County, in the main, followed the subjoined plan:

The Court of Appeals, the highest State Court, was composed of five Judges, who were elected by the people under a restricted franchise. This system resulted in the election of men of high repute, so that this court was held in great respect It had general jurisdiction.

The District Court of Appeals, which was composed of three Circuit Court Judges, elected by the people under restricted franchise, which had appellate jurisdiction over both civil and criminal cases.

The County Courts, composed of five Magistrates, were appointed by the Governor, and had general jurisdiction in civil cases, but in criminal cases acted as an examining board only. One of their number, selected by themselves, was appointed to act as presiding magistrate. Under this system, one of their number, under the rule of seniority, was entitled to the office of Sheriff. These courts stood very high in popular esteem, being usually composed of educated men, some of whom had even studied law, as was rather customary amongst the "gentlemen" of that day and period.

We have thus seen, that prior to the Civil War, the Judges were elected under a qualified white franchise, which resulted in the election of men of substance and standing, whose decisions stood high in the esteem of the superior courts. At this time, in order to be entitled to vote, the citizen was required to be a landowner, who could vote wherever he owned land

Amongst the Judges thus selected were such men as Judge R. L. E. Moncure; Judge William Daniel; Judge William J. Robertson; of the Court of Appeals; and Judge William Leigh; Judge Lucius P. Thompson, Judge Hunter Marshall; Judge — Nash; Judge — Meredith; and Judge William Crump, of the Circuit Court

During the war the Judges thus elected continued to discharge their duties. The above named Judges were in office during this period.

After the war these officers were removed, and others; in many cases disreputable men, were appointed by the military authorities who took supervision of the courts of justice. Virginia was made into Military District Number One, for this, and other purposes.

One of these military appointees, was one, Philip A. Bowling, a native of Buckingham, who presided over nine counties which included Amelia, Buckingham, and Prince Edward counties. He belonged to one of the most prominent families of Virginia. During a debate between him and John Randolph of Roanoke, noted for the "edge" of his tongue when aroused, the latter referred to Bowling as "the degenerate son of a worthy sire." As a young man he gave every promise of a brilliant and useful career, possessing a fine mind and an imposing presence. He was elected to the Legislature while still in his early twenties, and supported a proposition to abolish slavery in Virginia, which was lost by a very narrow margin, said to be one vote His vote is said to have been influenced by the fact that one, Arthur Tappen of Massachusetts, an ardent abolitionist, came to Richmond in order to advocate abolition, bringing with him his young daughter, a most attractive young woman, between whom and young Bowling an affection sprung up that resulted in their becoming engaged to be married. About this time a great agitation was made by the advocates of slavery, so that his vote in favor of abolition made him very unpopular in certain influential quarters He made desperate efforts to regain his popularity, but was ever afterwards unable to regain his former position, and gradually became a political pariah.

His family bitterly opposed his marriage to Miss Tappen and finally induced him to marry a Miss Eppes, a most excellent young lady of North Carolina. Miss Tappen also married shortly afterwards

Disappointed both matrimonially and politically, Bowling gradually sank until he became a drunkard and a gambler His wife dying, he moved to Farmville, where he rented a small office, in which he slept and lived While here, his very bedding was sold from under him for debt

In the meantime the husband of the former Miss Tappen died, and hearing of it, Bowling wrote to her something after this fashion: "I am bankrupt in morals and in purse, I gamble and I drink whiskey; and if you will marry me I will come and see you at once;" to which she replied: "I will be glad to see you." He went to Boston and saw her and they became engaged Though her father was so bitterly opposed to the marriage that he threatened to shoot

Bowling, they were married and returned to Virginia to live.

It was this man whom General Canby, in charge of Military District No 1, appointed as Judge over the district which included Prince Edward county. In order to qualify, Bowling took the "Iron Clad Oath" declaring therein that he had never sympathized with, or aided the South in the War between the States!

His wife, for whom he entertained a genuine affection, had a very salutary influence over him, so that he became somewhat less dissipated, but still remained far from a model of sobriety. Mrs Bowling accompanied her husband on his circuit of the counties in his district and was much chagrined at his dissolute conduct, for she was a most excellent woman. They lived on a farm near to Amelia Court House. Bowling continued to serve until the civil government was rehabilitated. After he was set aside upon that occurrence, he went back to his old life of dissipation.

The military supervision ended, the Underwood Convention; better known as the "Black and Tan Convention;" a convention make up of negroes, carpetbaggers, and scalawags (these "scalawags" were southerners who had turned renegades for money, or plunder reasons) assumed control and the "Reconstruction" days proper, began. This Convention, thus composed, proceeded to change the entire judicial system. It introduced the northern system, entailing a vast increase in the number of officers and in the amount of expense for judicial purposes. They proceeded to disfranchise all the leading southerners who had participated in the war on behalf of the South, either in the Government or in the Army, so that they could neither vote nor hold office. Every man now elected to office, including the judiciary in all its branches, had to take what was known as the "Iron Clad Oath," thereby swearing that he had neither participated in, nor sympathized with, what was called "The Rebellion." The same oath was required of the voters. After this arrangement had been agreed to, a general election was ordered. Under the limited franchise thus achieved, vast numbers of the white men of the South were shut out from the polls, and every male negro of twenty-one years of age was permitted to vote. As one result of this plan many negroes were elected as Magistrates, Constables, etc., and some were sent to both Houses of Congress, and to both Houses of the State Legislature. They were also elected as County Clerks, Treasurers, Commonwealth's Attorneys, etc. Amongst those sent to represent Prince Edward county in the State Legislature and Senate appear the names of James D Bland (negro) John Robinson (negro) N. M. Griggs (negro). The Convention generally was made up of negroes, carpetbaggers, and scalawags. The representatives of the South to both Houses of Congress were generally of the same type

When the native white southerners again secured control in the Convention of 1901, the work of the Underwood Convention was set aside almost in its entirety, save that the system of County Judges in a modified form was retained, and the Magistrates Courts finally ceased to exist as formerly. During the interim of the Underwood Convention Judge F. N Watkins, Judge J M. Crute, and Judge Asa D. Watkins, served as Judges in Prince Edward county. The Convention of 1901 did away with the purely county courts, as the Underwood Convention had done away with the purely magisterial courts. Under the Underwood Constitution the Circuit of the Fourth Judicial District, which included Prince Edward county, consisted of nine counties, in which court was held but twice in the year. Under the Constitution of 1901 the number of the counties were reduced to five, in each one of which court was held much more frequently.

The Circuit Judges, sitting in Prince Edward county

under this Circuit arrangement, have been Judge Asa D. Dickinson, Judge Francis D. Irving, Judge Samuel F. Coleman, and Judge George Jefferson Hundley, the present incumbent.

As previously stated, an orderly and exhaustive review of the judicial system as affecting Prince Edward county, is practically impossible within the scope of this work, but the foregoing will perhaps serve to give a general survey of the system

The following are the present officers of the Court

Horace Adams, Clerk.

Gordon E. West, Deputy Clerk.

John A Clark, Sheriff.

Judge Asa D. Watkins, Commonwealth's Attorney.

Chapter Sixteen

Agriculture in Prince Edward County

AGRICULTURE IN PRINCE EDWARD

The soil of the county is much like that generally prevailing in this part of the State. It is generally good, though in places somewhat "run down" through over-cultivation without adequate fertilization. It is varied, sandy, red and chocolate loams, or gray loam. It is generally rather highly productive and well adapted to the production of the various farm crops of this part of State. Tobacco, wheat, and corn, are the chief farm products of the county.

All forage crops, especially the legumes, are easily grown; and the grasses,—clover, timothy, red top,—show good profits.

This is not a natural grazing section, except for sheep, in which case, however, it ranks well, but its adaptability to forage crops and grasses, has given it some prominence as a dairying section. Cattle and hogs are profitably raised.

All fruits and vegetables, common to the State, do well. Potatoes frequently yield phenomenally well.

Marl, coal, and copper ore, are found in the county, with some evidence of the presence of other minerals.

The forest products are poplar, pine, and oak for the main part. In recent years there has been some considerable cutting of this timber. At the present time two flourishing lumber concerns are in operation in Farmville, besides several temporary concerns in other parts of the county.

The major part of the county is in a state of good cultivation. The surface of the land is rolling.

The land is watered by the Appomattox River and its many branches.

Agricultural statistics for the county will be found under the head of "Statistics" in chapter seventeen.

Chapter Seventeen

Prince Edward County Statistics

1. POPULATION.
2. MARRIAGE AND DIVORCE.
3. VITAL STATISTICS.
4. AGRICULTURE.

PRINCE EDWARD COUNTY STATISTICS

POPULATION

Total, 1920	14,767.
Male	.7,410.
Female	....7,357.
White	6,584.
Negro	8,183
Negro majority	2,401.

Increase in white population over census of 1910, 772.
Decrease in negro population from census of 1910, 275.

Per cent of negro population 55.4.

Population per square mile, 41.5.

Number of dwellings in county, 2,910.
Number of families in county, 3,055.

MARRIAGE AND DIVORCE, 1920.

MARRIAGES.

White couples, 47.   Black couples, 95.

Total, 142.

DIVORCE DECREES GRANTED, 1920.

Total for the county, 20

Adultery, 3; Desertion, 15; Cruelty, 1; Imprisonment. 1.

White Male Plaintiff: Adultery, 1; Desertion, 1.

White Female Plaintiff: Adultery, 1; Desertion, 1.

Black Male Plaintiff   Adultery, 1; Desertion, 7.

Black Female Plaintiff: Desertion, 6.

It will be noted that the color of those alleging "Cruelty" and "Imprisonment" is not given

VITAL STATISTICS, 1920.

Total births	381
Illegitimate	35
Legitimate	346

DEATHS

Infants under one year	24
Typhoid	2
Whooping cough	3
Diphtheria	1
Influenza	11
Tuberculosis of lungs	31
Meningitis	1
Bronchitis	1
Pneumonia	17
Congenital debility	8
Other causes of early infancy	1
Cancer	4
Puerperal	2
Accidents	4
Burns	1
All other causes	83
Total	194
Excess of births over deaths	152

PRINCE EDWARD COUNTY VIRGINIA
DEPARTMENT OF COMMERCE
BUREAU OF THE CENSUS

PRELIMINARY ANNOUNCEMENT *AGRICULTURE
FOURTEENTH CENSUS: 1920.

Released July 14, 1921.

The director announces, subject to correction, the following preliminary figures from the Census of Agriculture, for Prince Edward county, Va.

Farms and Farm Acreage	Jan 1, 1920	Apr 15 1910		FARM VALUES	
FARMS ._..	1,843	1,682	+9.6	Value of land and buildngs.	
Operated by					
White farmers	859	758	+13 3		
Col'd farmers	984	924	+6 5	January 1, 1920 _ _	$6,650,780
Operated by Owners and					
managers . _	1,263	1,216	+3 9	April 15, 1910	3,036,432
Tenants	580	466	+24 5	Increase, 1920 over 1910	
Land in farms,					
Total, acres	177,522	180,661	—1.7	Amount _ _ ..... _	3,614,348
Improved,					
acres	71,373	66,177	+7.9	Per cent _ _ _ ._	119.0

DOMESTIC ANIMALS	Jan 1 1920	Apr 15 1910*	PRINCIPAL CROPS	Acres Harvested	Quantity Harvested
Farms reporting			Corn _1919	15,022	230,909, bu.
domestic animals	1,746	1,589	1909	13,509	218,660, bu.
Animals reported			Wheat 1919	5,879	65,049, bu.
Horses _____	2,234	2,003	1909	4,744	49,457, bu.
Mules _ _____	983	493	Hay _1919	4,152	4,769, tons
Cattle _____	4,067	4,394	1909	4,090	4,845, tons
Sheep ____ __ _	383	1,034	Tobacco _		
Swine _ __ ____	6,821	6,008	1919	7,056	3.531,579 lbs.
			1909	6,444	5,107,637, lbs.

*The figures for domestic animals in 1910 are not very closely comparable with those for 1920, since the present census was taken in January, before the breeding season had begun, while the 1910 census was taken in April, or about the middle of the breeding season, and included many spring calves, colts, etc.

Chapter Eighteen

Miscellaneous

MISCELLANEOUS

SOCIAL AND ECONOMIC CONDITIONS

In the early days of the Colony, almost as a matter of necessity, rather than of choice, the simple life was the general rule, for both the rich and the poor alike. What was true of the Colony generally was true of Prince Edward particularly.

In the modern acceptation of the term there was but very little comfort or luxury.

For the most part the houses were quite rude and generally small. Glazed windows were still somewhat of a curiosity. All the lumber was sawn by hand and the nails were wrought by the blacksmith. Practically all articles of domestic use were made at home.

On nearly every plantation there were negro smiths, carpenters, masons, shoemakers, etc., and generally speaking, all implements of agriculture, few and very primitive, were homemade. The same was true of all house furnishings.

Roads were but little better than bridle-paths so that horseback was the usual mode of travel. A "bridal tour" usually meant that the bride went to the home of the groom, riding behind him on the same horse. Books were few, but that mattered little to most of the folk because they were for the most part, very busy during the daytime and there was little light for night-reading.

The well-to-do got their clothes, and their wines, and some of their furnishings from England, but the poorer people wore home-spun. The "ladies" had their imported linens and silks, which, because they were most excellently made and because there were but few occasions for them being worn, were handed down to their daughters who were not ashamed to wear them. The planters wore broadcloth on public occasions, with short breeches, knee buckles, and silk stockings   Pewter, even amongst the well-to-do, was much commoner than china, or than silver.

The negro women were taught to card, spin, and weave, and to cut and make the clothes of the children and servants.   The negro men were taught to make the rude utensils of the farm or of the household, and to raise the farm crops.

Far more attention was paid to the morals of the people then than is given today   The Church wardens kept a sharp eye for sinners, bound out orphans, and the children of parents who did not take proper care of them, kept down immorality as well as they could, and appear to have taken their responsibilities in these respects rather seriously.   Men were taken before the Grand Jury for Sabbath-breaking; were prosecuted at law for not attending Church; were publicly whipped for cheating at cards and were severely punished for swearing.

Educational facilities in those days were few and very simple, but so far as it went, education was of a practical and very thorough character.   Ordinarily the "three R's" would constitute the curriculum, but Latin was taught to all who wished, or were required by their parents, to learn it.   Many of the rich had private tutors and both in these private schools, and in the more public institutions of learning, the birch and the ferrule were more or less generously administered.   For the most part the boys received a better education than fell to the lot of the girls.   The girls were usually taught music and the old fashioned "spinnet," a sort of primitive piano, was the instrument played.

The chief agricultural products of these early days in Prince Edward county, were cereals, hay, and tobacco, which were carried, either by ox-cart to Richmond, or by batteau down the Appomattox to Petersburg.

The earlier records are somewhat prolix in the number

of the crimes and their punishments that they contain. Many of these punishments would today be called excessive and barbarous, but they were identical with those inflicted in England itself. A crime of a servant against his master; or of a wife against her husband, when of a grave nature, was called "petty treason" with correspondingly severe punishment; most often death. Hog stealing appears to have been so persistent that special penalties were provided for it That punishment came at last to take the form of death. Then, as now, hogs seemed to have a special fascination for the negro and many of them suffered the extreme penalty.

The crime against women, though of much rarer occurrence than today, was by no means unknown as has been asserted.

One of the most unique laws, at least to us of these lax days, was that prescribed for habitual absence from Church; 50 pounds of tobacco or its equivalent in cash, defaulting which, the penalty was to be "Ten lashes on the bare back." That was the law for about forty years, 1680-1720!

Though the severity of the punishment was somewhat abated, it was still a misdemeanor for many years later, as evidenced by the fact that the Grand Jury at the May Court, 1755, amongst others, made a presentment against one "John Conneson for not going to any Place of Worship in one Month " All of which is suggestive of the close watch set by the officials over the morals of the community life of Prince Edward county in those "good old days " One can scarce refrain from wondering what would be the meas--ure of official duty if the same care were to be undertaken today!

A PATHETIC LETTER

The following most interesting letter is on file at the Court House in Farmville. It is exceedingly illuminating as showing the conditions under which our progenitors lived in those now far distant days Taken in connection with the court proceedings which are appended, it is very suggestive of the severity of our fathers.

The manuscript is as follows:

THE FOLLOWING LETTER
WAS WRITTEN BY FREDERICK BRIGGS TO HIS
WIFE, WHILE UNDER SENTENCE OF DEATH, FOR
HORSE STEALING; AND WHO WAS EXECUTED, TO-
GETHER WITH HIS COMRADE, M'ELHENEY, ON
THE 16th OCTOBER, 1789, IN THE COUNTY OF
PRINCE EDWARD   IT PRESENTS AN ARTFUL
WARNING TO THOSE WHO LIVE DISHONESTLY,
AND WHO WICEKDLY TRANSGRESS THE KNOWN
LAWS OF GOD.

"My Dear Wife—

The hand of Justice has arrested me in Virginia, at a great distance from you and my other dear friends, whom I never more expect to see; I do, therefore, write this to acquaint you with my lamentable fate, and to convey a wretched father's last request and charge to the children whom my bleeding heart cherishes with a fondness that only death can destroy.—On the 3rd of August, I was taken up, together with my companion, M'Elheney, in Nottoway County, charged with carrying off the horses of a Mr. Spencer, in Charlotte, about fifty miles from the place of our capture. From the jail of Nottoway, we were sent, on the 13th of the same month, for trial, to Charlotte county; where we were detained in prison till the 30th, and then, by the examining court, were sent down to Prince Edward, to be tried before the District Court; on the 1st of September, our trial came on, and the jury having brought us in GUILTY, on the 9th, we received the awful sentence of DEATH!

What a melancholy scene does the history of a few days present to your view! Surely I must have been infatuated to have brought myself into a situation where every day's anguish of mind would more than balance the follies and fancied pleasures of all my past days of dissipation; and, yet these distressful days are the prelude to the tremendous day of my execution, and the most tremendous day of standing at the bar of the eternal God, in judgment.

Oh! my dear, what shall I do? My soul shudders at the Catastrophe to which I am reduced, and which I am unable now to prevent. O! that I had contented myself at home in industrious labor, with you and my dear, DEAR children—then I might have enjoyed peace, with the most homely fare; whereas, now, I am torn violently from you all, forever! and have brought distressing ignominy and reproach upon myself and family. But this regret is useless now—I have no prospect of any relief, but from the God of mercy and compassion. To Him, I have been attempting to turn my distressed thoughts, and to seek His mercy and grace, ever since my confinement in Charlotte But the thought of you and my poor dear children, so overwhelms and overburdens my distressed mind, that I scarce can command one calm reflection.

My dear creature; as I never more expect to see you in this world, I beseech and charge you to take care of our poor children as well as you can—let me entreat you, by the love and affection that always subsisted between us, not to suffer any person to use them ill, if you can help it I hope that the dying words of a husband that loves you, will prevail with you to keep the children out of the way of bad company, lest the untimely wretched fate of their poor father

should be their's Let me also beseech you, to take more care
of their precious immortal souls, than we both have done;
and that you may the better succeed in this, be engaged for
your own salvation—for death may be as near you as it is
me; it may seize you, at home and in security, as well as it
has unexpectedly approached me—and I am sure, if you saw
the grim messenger, as plain as I now view him, ready to
grasp you in his dreadful arms, you would feel your need
of a change of heart, and an interest in Jesus Christ, who,
only, can save the lost. O! fly, fly from the wrath to come,
and warn our beloved children, also, to escape the terrors of
the law Bring them up in the fear of God, and keep them
from the vile practices of a sinful world; so may you look
for a blessing from that merciful God, who is the widow's
guardian and the orphan's friend. Oh; if I were a faithful servant of that God, how easily I might leave you under
His protection and fatherly care, for He hath promised, in
Jeremiah, 49 ch 11v, "Leave thy fatherless children, I will
preserve them alive, and let thy widow trust in me." Now,
my dear, let my entreaties prevail with you to seek the Lord
for yourself and for your children; and when I am dead and
forgotten, as I soon shall be, let me be considered as yet
speaking in this mournful letter. Call my dear fatherless
children around you, to hear what their miserable father has
to say to them.

Come, my fatherless, unfortunate little ones: come, listen
to your dying parent's last request and charge. I have been
too negligent of your precious perishing souls, while I was
with you—I now confess it, before God and you, and would
try to make one feeble attempt, before I die, to say something to you for your good. I beseech, I conjure, I command
you all, to seek the Lord in the days of your youth; quit the
follies of the idle and thoughtless, and try to give yourselves up to God in time, lest His wrath burn fiercely against
you forever. Don't give way to frolicking and company-

keeping; these ruin and destroy many a soul Be resolved
to seek God's mercy, let others do what they will; pray much,
avoid the wicked, and all of you carefully associate with
people of good characters. Be industrious, for idleness leads
into bad company, extravagance and wickedness of every
kind; it often leads into dishonesty and RUIN. My dear
daughter, by beloved Nancy Goodrich, I think I see you
weeping by your mama's side, while she reads; let me address you particularly, you are grown up to be a woman;
remember that virtue and religion will be your greatest orna-
ments If you behave well and shun bad company, you
may be happy and esteemed, though your unfortunate father
is not. Assist your dear distressed mother; obey her, and try
to comfort her in her afflictions—may the almighty God bless
you, my dear child, and make us meet in a better world. How
can I support under the grief that wrings my heart while
I bid you a long farewell. My poor Howell and Edward,
will you remember your poor father's words; my heart bleeds
for you, my poor dear fellows, lest you should live wickedly
and die miserably—resolve to be good boys, and obey your
poor dear mother in all things; do your best to help her, in
an honest way. If you behave well, and be industrious. you
will always be encouraged by good people. Never associate
with idle, wicked company, lest you come to the unhappy
end of your unfortunate father—my poor boys, seek and
serve the Lord, and He will bless you. Oh! that He will
pity your youth and teach you His ways—farewell, my
dear fellows, farewell! Clerimon and Dolly, little Tommy
and Queen Polly; dear babes and children, how I could press
you to my bosom, if you were here; but, oh no, my rough
irons would hurt your tender limbs. Oh, for one parting
kiss from my dear children, but that cannot be; I am to die
without seeing you; then, remember what your dear daddy
says to you—be good children, pray to God every day, do
what your mama bids you, and as you grow up, help her

with all your might to provide and maintain you all in an industrious way. My sweet little children, I am not fit to bless you, but I hope the God of Mercy will.

My blessed wife, if you have had another child since I left home, let it also know my fate when it gets old enough, and warn it thus to avoid an end like mine. Tell my poor mother, that her hapless son is just about to be hurried out of this world—I expect she will be shocked and distressed, but I hope God will support her   I hope my brothers and sisters will have compassion on my distressed family, and not grudge to do them every kindness in their power—the Lord will reward their kind hearts, if they act thus and also serve Him. I here bid them all an affectionate farewell. My dear soul; it is but justice that, with my dying hands, I record how I regard you, and declare, that I never saw a woman on whom I could better depend. May God reward your FAITHFULNESS.

Let Howell be bound apprentice, when about nineteen, to some trade; let him have his choice. If you ever marry again, bind out all the boys; but if you live a widow, you cannot do without them—keep what little there is together, for your needy rising family. And now, as it appears probable that we shall never see each other in the face again in this world, let us try to cast ourselves into the arms of God's mercy, and seek His favor, that we may be allowed to meet in a happier world hereafter   And now, my dearest love, how shall I take my last leave of you on earth! Oh, how shall I say that we must meet no more, until the Heavens and the Earth pass away—there must we meet before the JUDGMENT SEAT! How can I bear to think that I am dead to you forever! My God, support my wife—and, oh, have mercy upon her wretched, but most affectionate husband.   FREDERICK BRIGGS."

"P S. The time appointed for our execution, is the

16th October. Keep this letter to show to the children as they grow up, and take a copy of it, which I wish you, for my sake, to read often to them. Farewell, my dearest wife, farewell!   F. Briggs."

The first Order in this case stands under date of Tuesday, September 1, 1789, as follows: "William Mackelhany and Frederick Briggs, late of the Parish of Cornwall, in the County of Charlotte, labourers, who stand jointly indicted for felony, were led to the Bar in the custody of the Jailor. and thereof arraigned and severally pleaded not guilty to the indictment, and for their trial put themselves upon God and their country, whereupon an jury," etc.

They were then remanded to jail, and on the 9th, September, at the same court, the following entry occurs· "William Mackelhany and Frederick Briggs, late of the Parish of Cornwall, in the County of Charlotte, labourers, who stand jointly convicted of Horse Stealing, were again led to the Bar, and, being asked what they had to say why sentence of Death should not be pronounced against them according to law, severally answered they had nothing to say further than they had already said. Therefore it is considered by the Court that the said William Mackelhaney and Frederick Briggs, for their offense aforesaid, be severally hanged by the neck until they be dead, and command is given to the Sheriff of Prince Edward County, that he do execution of this judgment at the public gallows on Friday the Sixteenth Day of October next, between the hours of ten o'clock in the forenoon, and four o'clock in the afternoon."

And it was done accordingly.

AN OLD COURT ORDER

The following page of an old Court Order, is interesting, as illustrative of the method of doing the county business at that time in vogue·

"At a Court in the County of Prince Edward, the Twenty-ninth Day of November, 1754, for laying County levy.

PRESENT: John Nash, James Wimbish, David Flournoy, James Erwin, and Thomas Haskins, Gentlemen, Justices.

	lbs. Tobacco.
To the Clerk, for his Ex Officio	1248
To the Sheriff's for Ditto	1248
To Mr. Clement Read, King's Attorney	936
To John LeNeve, for laying off Ten acres Land, Prison bounds	350
To Honourable, the Secretary for Commission Peace and Dedimus and writ of election of Burgesses	357
	4139
To John Le Neve for two Record Books at 43s each	
To John Le Neve for one Record Book at 26s £5 12 0	
To Honourable, the Secretary for the second Commission of the Peace and Dedimus	112
	112
To John LeNeve for sending for a Commission of the Peace, etc. £1.10 0	
To Richard Washburn for one old Wolf's Head certified by George Walker	100
To Abraham Baker for one old Wolf's Head certified by James Wimbish	100

To William Searcey for one young Wolf's Head
    certified by George Walker   50

    250

To the Sheriff for Sundry Services, Gross, 300   240
To the Clerk for Sundry Services, Gross, 90   63
To Captain Anderson, for Guarding Abraham
    Womack 25 days,   750
To Captain Anderson for Guarding Timothy
    Sullivant 19 days, ...   570

    1623

To William King, 17 days Guard over Womack
To William King, 6 Days Guard over Chapman   690
To Joel Stubblefield, 29 Days a Guard   870
To Alexander LeGrand, 6 Days a Guard   .. ..   __ 180
To John Philips, 6 Days a Guard   . .. 180

    1920

To Captain Anderson, for the use of his kitchen
as a Prison, 49 Days   .   _ £4.0.0
To Captain Anderson for changing for Court
    House   300

    300

To Mr. Nash, for paid John Bentley, Sending
for Books   £2 10.0
To Richard Perryman, for Prison Chimney
    £1 .6.0
To Captain Anderson, for Labouring Diet
and Time   .   ..   £1.15.0

    £6.13.0

To Tobacco to be sold for Discharge Money Debts .22593
To Sheriff's Commission at six per cent on 33040   1982

                                                    33040

To the County Credit by 826 Tithes at 40 lbs. per
    Pole   ..   .. _ .. . 33040

Ordered that the Sheriffs of this County Collect of every tithable person in this County, 40 pounds Tobacco per Pole, and in case of non-payment, to Distrain.

And it is ordered that the Sheriff enter into Bond next Court. Mr. John Nash is appointed to receive of the Sheriff of this County 22593 lbs of Tobacco as Collected and Dispose of the Same at the Best Price he can get, and that he account with this Court for the same when required.—
Jno. Nash."

It will be observed that Tobacco served as a common medium of exchange, doubtless because of the shortage of money, in "those good old days," hence we have no monopoly of that distressing ailment.

WONDER BOOKER

WONDER BOOKER, celebrated negro character, living in the County, attained the advanced age of 126 years, dying within the County in 1819.

He was a slave and belonged to Mr. George Booker. He received the name "WONDER" "from the circumstance that his mother was in her 58th year at he time of his birth. He was of great strength of body, and his natural powers, which were far superior to those of color in general, he retained in surprising degree He was a constant laborer in his master's garden until within eight or ten years of his death."

A notable feature of the minutes of the early days of the County, contained in the Order Books of the County Court, is the large space given to cases respecting property rights in negro slaves, and many cases of felony and misdemeanors committed by negroes. That all was not an unclouded Paradise in the days of slavery, is thus made very manifest, for then, as now, a disproportionate part of the time of the Court was taken up with cases arising from the colored element of the population.

CROWN DEED FROM GEORGE THE SECOND

Doubtless there are very few families in Prince Edward County in position to boast of continuous residence upon land devised directly from the British Crown in the days of the Georges, Second and Third. There are fewer still who have retained, and can produce, the original Sheepskin Deed.

Numbered amongst these few are the Elams of the western section of the county. Mr William Carter Elam holds title to a part of such a grant, with possession of the original Crown Deed, written on genuine "sheep-skin." He is a direct descendant of the Lodwick Elam to whom the grant was made and the property so devised has never wanted one of that descent and bearing that honorable name, to own and reside upon the land. He owns, lives upon, and works. a part of the original grant which has never been out of the family. Mr Elam's post office address is Prospect, Virginia. A married sister, Mrs. Robert H. Reynolds, also resides upon another section of the original grant

Two parcels of land were devised to Lodwick Elam; the first, containing four hundred acres, under date of March 20, 1745, in the nineteenth year of the reign of the Second George; the second, for three hundred and ninety-five acres, bearing date of May 23, 1763, in the third year of the reign of the Third George; the king of the Revolutionary period

Believing that the student of history will be interested in these rare documents, we have ventured to re-produce the earlier one of the two deeds.

"GEORGE THE SECOND, by the Grace of God, of Great Britain, France, and Ireland, King, Defender of the Faith, &c.,

TO ALL TO WHOM THESE PRESENTS MAY COME, Greetings:

KNOW YE, that for divers good causes and considerations, but more especially for and in consideration of the sum of FORTY SHILLINGS, of good and lawful money for our use Paid to our Receiver General of our Revenues in this our Colony and Dominion of Virginia.

WE HAVE Given, Granted, and Confirmed, and by these Presents, for us, our heirs and successors, Do Give, Grant, and Confirm unto Lodwick Elam, one certain Tract or Parcel of Land containing Four Hundred Acres, lying and being in the County of Amelia on the Head Branches of the North Fork of Falling Creek and bounded as follows, to wit

BEGINNING at a corner white oak on the north side of the said fork; thence South eight Degrees, West one hundred and sixty-nine Poles, crossing the fork to a corner red oak. Thence West eight Degrees, North three hundred and eighty Poles to a corner large white oak in a Branch of Vaughans Creek, Thence North eight Degrees East one hundred and sixty-nine Poles to a Corner white oak, Thence East eight Degrees south three hundred and eighty Poles to the beginning

WITH ALL Woods, Underwoods, Swamps, Marshes, Low Grounds, Meadows, Feedings, and his due share of all Veins, Mines and Quarries, as well discovered as not discovered, within the bounds aforesaid and being Part of the said Quantity of four hundred Acres of Land, and the Rivers, Waters and Water Courses therein contained, together with the Privileges of Hunting, Hawking, Fishing, Fowling, and all other Profits, Commodities, Hereditaments whatsoever to the Same or any Part thereof, belonging, or in any wise appertaining.

TO HAVE, HOLD, Possess and Enjoy the said Tract or Parcel of Land and all other, the before-granted Premises and every Part thereof with their and every of their Appurtenances unto the said Lodwick Elam, and to his Heirs and Assigns forever, To the only use and behalf of his, the said Lodwick Elam, his Heirs and Assigns forever,

TO BE HELD of us, our Heirs and Successors as of our Mannor of East Greenwich in the County of Kent, in free and common Soccage and not in Capite or by Knights Service.

YIELDING AND PAYING unto us, our Heirs and Successors for every fifty Acres of Land and so proportionately for a lesser or greater Quantity than fifty Acres, the Fee Rent of one Shilling Yearly, to be paid upon the Feast of Saint Michael the Arch Angel and also Cultivating and Improving three Acres Part of every fifty of the Tract above-mentioned within three Years after the Date of these Presents.

PROVIDED always that if three Years of the said Fee Rent shall at any time be in Arrears and Unpaid, or if the said Lodwick Elam, his Heirs or Assigns do not within the Space of Three Years next coming after the Date of these Presents, Cultivate and Improve three Acres Part of every fifty of the Tract above-mentioned, Then the Estate hereby Granted shall Cease and be Utterly Determined and thereafter it shall and may be Lawful to and for us, our Heirs and Successors to Grant the same Lands and Premises with the Appurtenances unto such other Person or Persons as we, our Heirs, and Successors shall think fit,

IN WITNESS whereof we have Caused these our Letters Patent to be WITNESS our Trusty and well-beloved William Gooch, Esquire, our Lieutenant Governor and Commander-in-Chief of our said Colony and Dominion at Williamsburgh, Under the Seal of our said Colony, the twentieth Day of March, one thousand seven hundred and forty-five, In the nineteenth Year of our Reign.—

—— William Gooch."

(Endorsed on the back, "Lodwick Elam's Patent for 400 acres, Amelia")

The reader will, of course, bear in mind the fact that Prince Edward County was not yet divided from Amelia county; that was done by act of 1753; the property above-described was, however, situated in that part of Amelia County afterwards cut off to constitute Prince Edward County.

But little punctuation was done in this original document, laboriously transcribed by hand, most of what appears has been done by the author where thought necessary to make clearer the intent of the patent.

The writing was done in splendid penmanship style and remains in a condition of remarkable legibility despite the many intervening years.

Chapter Nineteen

Bibliography

BIBLIOGRAPHY

The following books, papers, and magazines have been called into requisition in preparation of this work:

Howes' "Historical Collections of Virginia."

Chandler and Thames' "Colonial Virginia."

McDonald's "Life in Old Virginia."

Ridpath's History of the United States.

Henning's "Acts of the Legislature."

State Library Papers on the House of Burgesses and Delegates.

State Library List of Revolutionary Soldiers of Virginia, 1912.

Virginia State Library, Ninth Annual Report of the Library Board and State Librarian, 1911, 1912.

McAllister's "Virginia Militia of the Revolutionary War."

Virginia Historical Magazine.

Captain John Smith's History of Virginia. Two volumes.

Meade's "Old Churches and old Families of Virginia."

Foote's "Sketches of Virginia."

John Randolph's Address. The war of 1812.

McGuire and Christian, "The Confederate Cause and Conduct in the War Between the States."

"The Rebellion: Official Records of the Union and Confederate Armies"

"William and Mary College."

Adams' "Thomas Jefferson and the University of Virginia."

"The Virginian" Normal School, Farmville, 1909.

Sarah Dorsey's, "Recollections of Henry Watkins Allen."

Tyler's "Life of Patrick Henry"

"The Life of General Joseph E Johnston."—

"A Sketch of Dr. John Peter Mettauer of Virginia." Dr. G B. Johnson

Jeter's "Life of Daniel Witt, D. D."

Bennett's "History of Methodism."

Semple's "Baptists in Virginia"

Unitel State Census reports; Department of Agriculture "Handbook of Virginia": Files of the "Farmville Herald"; "Manual of West Hanover Presbytery," etc. etc.

And, in addition, I am gratefully indebted to generous help received from Dr. H. R McIlwaine, State Librarian of Virginia; Dr. W. A. Harris of Richmond University; Judge G J. Hundley, Farmville; Judge J. M. Crute, Farmville; Mrs. Roberta H Large; Senator Robert K. Brock; Dr. J. D. Eggleston, President of Hampden-Sidney College; Mrs. George Ben Johnson, Richmond; Dr J. L. Jarman, State Female Normal School, Farmville; to the State Officers, and to a kindly host of friends, who in various ways have assisted in the compilation of this work.

The County Records and Deed Books, which were found to be in a remarkably good state of preservation, have been most diligently searched, in which arduous labor most cheerful and timely assistance was rendered by Mr. Horace Adams, County Clerk, and Mr. Gordon E. West, Deputy County Clerk.

FINIS

CPSIA information can be obtained
at www.ICGtesting.com
Printed in the USA
LVHW010725140622
721221LV00004B/81